COMMUNIST V

D

Communist Women in Scotland

Red Clydeside from the Russian Revolution to the End of the Soviet Union

Neil C. Rafeek

I.B. TAURIS
LONDON · NEW YORK

Paperback edition first published in 2016
by I.B.Tauris & Co. Ltd
London • New York
www.ibtauris.com

First published in hardback in 2008 by
Tauris Academic Studies, an imprint of
I.B.Tauris & Co. Ltd

ISBN: 978 1 78076 041 4

A full CIP record for this book is available from the British Library
A full CIP record is available from the Library of Congress

Library of Congress Catalog Card Number: available

Printed and bound by CPI Group (UK) Ltd, Croydon, CR0 4YY
From camera-ready copy edited and supplied by Oxford Publishing Services, Oxford

MIX
Paper from responsible sources
FSC www.fsc.org FSC® C013604

Contents

List of Illustrations

Acronyms and Abbreviations

AEU	Amalgamated Engineering Union
AGM	annual general meeting
AJA	Andrew Jackson Archive
ARP	Air Raid Precautions
BHC	Bob Horne Collection
BRS	*British Road to Socialism*
BSP	British Socialist Party
BUF	British Union of Fascists
CCP	Czechoslovakian Communist Party
CIA	Central Intelligence Agency
CLP	Communist Labour Party
CND	Campaign for Nuclear Disarmament
COMECON	Council of Mutual Economic Assistance
CP	Communist Party
CPB	Communist Party of Britain
CPGB	Communist Party of Great Britain
CPL	Clydebank Public Library
CPSU	Communist Party of the Soviet Union
CSM	Ceskoslovenský Svaz Mládeze (Czechoslovak Union of Youth)
CSS	Catholic Socialist Society
DLSA	Democratic Left Scotland Archive
EC	executive committee
EPC	elections preparation committee
FPC	Frieda Park Collection
FSL	Fife Socialist League
GCA	Glasgow City Archive
GDR	German Democratic Republic
GDSSSU	Glasgow and District Socialist Sunday School Union
ICI	Investment Company Institute

ILP	Independent Labour Party
IPD	inner party democracy
IRIS	Industrial Research and Information Service
IWW	International Workers of the World
MHC	Marion Henery Collection
MLGR	Mitchell Library Glasgow Room
NAC	National Abortion Campaign
NCBSSS	National Council of British Socialist Sunday Schools
NCP	New Communist Party
NATO	North Atlantic Treaty Organization
NEC	national executive committee
NLF	National Liberation Front
NLR	*New Left Review*
NMM	National Maritime Museum
NUM	National Union of Mineworkers
NUSS	National Union of School Students
NUWM	National Unemployed Workers' Movement
NWAC	National Women's Advisory Committee
PCI	Partito Comunista Italiano
PPPS	People's Press Printing Society
SDP	Social Democratic Party
SLP	Socialist Labour Party
SRA	Strathclyde Regional Archive
STUC	Scottish Trades Union Congress
SWAC	Scottish Women's Advisory Committee
TGWU	Transport and General Workers' Union
TUC	Trades Union Congress
UCS	Upper Clyde Shipbuilders
WGML	William Gallacher Memorial Library
USSR	Union of Soviet Socialist Republics
WAC	women's advisory council
WIDF	Women's International Democratic Federation
WLM	Women's Liberation Movement
WTC	Willie Thompson Collection
YCL	Young Communist League

Preface and Acknowledgements

In April 2007 Neil Rafeek passed away after a lifelong struggle with poor health. Anyone who knew him knew of his single-minded and often stubborn nature. It may be that the ongoing struggle he had with his health added to his determination. He was self sacrificing in his service to his ideals. The organizing and collecting of oral testimonies can be demanding and arduous work. Yet, against the impact on his own health, he would simply cite the hardships that those he was interviewing had often had to endure.

Neil was the first person to achieve an oral history Ph.D. in the history department of the University of Strathclyde. This book is the product of that work and reflects his passions as a social historian, demonstrating how history is not only made by 'ordinary' people, but just how extraordinary their lives really are.

Privately he was proud that the indispensable contribution of women to the Communist Party in Scotland and their experiences had been recorded. As well as being an enormously important record it is also (we feel) an illuminating analysis of the party throughout its history and its changing composition.

Maybe it is always the case with very driven people that they are their own harshest critic and often dismissive of what they ought to pride themselves on. Neil would have been the last to congratulate himself on his insight or his decency – those qualities that made him such an ideal oral historian. Nevertheless, it is for this – his deep rooted humanism – that we will remember him. Below we have included the original preface and acknowledgements he wrote before his death.

***

There are many more people who have been of great help and encouragement, principally my supervisors Arthur McIvor (especially for his stamina and support) and Jim McMillan, both of whose tolerance and understanding were essential. Thanks also to members of the History Department at the University of Strathclyde for their help, contacts and inspiration, Graham Smith from Dundee who gave essential advice on the practicalities of an oral history (though all faults with technique are my own) and to Catriona Burness at St Andrews University for interview and publication information.

The writing of this study took four years. Since starting it I have got to know many former members of the Communist Party of Great Britain very well. I must thank all those who agreed to be interviewed and whose contributions were essential. For knowledge of communist politics I must thank foremost Audrey Canning at the William Gallacher Memorial Library/Democratic Left Archive for continuous help in finding material, Bob Horne a former CP industrial organizer, party official and a founder of the Communist Party of Scotland, Willie Thompson at Glasgow Caledonian University and Douglas Chalmers Scottish Secretary of the Democratic Left and John Foster Scottish Secretary of the Communist Party of Britain.

I must express my deep appreciation to all the women interviewed for access to their lives and personal material, such as books, pamphlets, papers, documents and information, including a wide range of photographs. I would especially like to thank Ouaine Bain, Janey Buchan, Katy Campbell, Kathryn Chalmers, Mary Docherty, Marion Easedale, Ella Egan, Marion Henery, Susan Galloway, Effie O'Hare, Pat Milligan, Isa Porte, Jenny Richardson, Marion Robertson, Christine Sloan, Irene Swan and Mary, Eric and Frieda Park, as well as Billy Quinn for material when starting out.

Special thanks to my mother, brothers Richard and Bruce, Ruth Lewis, Eddie Cable, and all postgraduates at Strathclyde University and elsewhere whom I got to know, especially David Forsyth, Tommy Gardiner, Billy Kenefick, Catriona McDonald, Martin Mitchell and Sandy Renfrew who were there from the start. Also Moira Alexander, Ruth Donald and Maggie Erickson for help with the first ten transcripts.

Finally a special mention for Rose, May, Mabs, Katherine, Effie, Mary and Marion H., whose contribution to socialism is now over and all those Party women not mentioned in history.

Chapter 1

Introduction: Where are Women in Communist Party History?

> It is possible for historians with a bad conscience about mentioning women (and in Scotland the bad conscience is understandable) to fall into the trap of representing women only as oppressed victims – burying them with full honours so to speak. It is surely more accurate (though it means a lot more work), to try to see relations between the sexes as more complex than a simple oppressor/ victim model.[1]

In this study I address the neglect of women in the historiography of the Communist Party of Great Britain. I seek through oral evidence to show to what extent women were involved in the CPGB in Scotland, what their political influences were and their level of involvement in the party structure. Most of all I redress the imbalance in CP history by relating the experiences of ordinary members, their political activities and their developing political outlook. In this way I seek to reveal branch and party life over the seven decades of its existence through the experiences of women in the party. Specifically, I aim to trace the practical and ideological development of women members in Scotland from their earliest experiences in the party, often in the Young Communist League, up to their departure from the CPGB or indeed up until its demise in 1991. I aim to give a comprehensive account of lives in the CP; how typical they are will be discussed later in the chapter.

It is necessary to look at the CPGB, which, despite having a smaller impact than many on the continent, played a noticeable and arguably a critical role in the British labour movement.[2] We also have to address the nature of the CP and the place it occupied in the political spectrum and the implications this has had for the resulting material.

By challenging capitalism and questioning social values at all levels, the CP attracted fierce loyalties from members and supporters, or conversely hatred and scepticism from its opponents. The political line always determined the CP's actions. This was effectively disseminated through the rigours of democratic centralism whereby once an issue had been debated and a decision made, all would abide by and argue for it on a unified basis. Because of its continual exclusion from, and dominance by, the Labour Party, the party became an effective political machine, though its attempt to become a mass party failed. This is not to dismiss the CP as irrelevant. In labour and industrial activity it has had an important influence, often limited to certain areas or to distinct unions but still enough to affect the policies of organizations, especially where communists gained a foothold. This included local-level activity in housing schemes, voluntary organizations and specific-issue groups. As Hinton states: 'The essence of communism as it developed in Britain was the focusing of socialist political life outside the "legitimate" arena of electoral politics, in the politics of the street, the housing estate and, above all, the factory.'[3]

Hence, if the CPGB was not a major political force, it was an active political pressure group capable of propagating its views in the areas within which it operated. This needs to be stressed because although the party failed electorally, it is wrong to presume that this was reflected socially and that its members were isolated and marginalized. On the contrary, in this study I shall show how communist women worked in their communities, were often respected and *still effected* changes, however small, in the political activities they pursued. It is to the credit of the CP's organizing skills that it has always been taken seriously and was treated as a threat by Conservative governments, which arrested CP activists during the period leading up to the General Strike[4] and, under a national coalition, banned the *Daily Worker*[5] in 1941. The cold war, which started in the late 1940s, saw increased discrimination against communists in trade unions, most notably in the Transport and General Workers Union.[6]

Few CP histories are impartial. Because the authors are often politically aligned, CP history in Britain is divided not just between right and left but among the left as well. Many authors outside the party are unsympathetic, while party historians are inevitably biased, first because they have sought to redress the balance against the party as given by the establishment and often the media, and second because they have sought to explain, usually in a narrative, the party's history in a positive light. It is inconceivable that the party would have sanctioned a critical history when it faced hostility from so many sections politically. This does not excuse any neglect of criticism: 'It is one of life's ironies that an organization that has produced so many brilliant historians has, until very recently, had the greatest difficulty in coming to terms with its own history'.[7]

This explains why communist historians tended to concentrate on Marxist theory, as popularized by Burns and Cornforth,[8] interpretations of history, notably by Jackson, Morton and Hutt,[9] and autobiographies and biographies. Klugmann's[10] 'standard' work was the first major attempt at a party history and it filled a historical gap the party felt was still missing after 46 years of existence. While fascinating, it consisted of rather uncritical narrative, whereas Branson,[11] who carried on the task, was more critical of *certain* past policies. His most recent volume,[12] however, seems to be in danger of undervaluing the post-1945 history of the party and this could be a mistake. In this study I rely heavily on material from 1945 onwards, which reveals, at least in Scotland, the extent to which the party was still active and in some areas very relevant.

The lack of a history of the experiences of party members must be associated with party discipline. Disillusioned members had always criticized the party's internal methods, though these were often too subjective to be reliable.[13] In 1964 Newton[14] attempted a detailed sociological study of the party and of the diversity of its membership. It was highly original and partially successful, yet cooperation was withdrawn and the amount of respondents he intended to interview, originally to be 100, was in the end severely limited.[15] Also, the suspicions of party members and their complete anonymity casts doubt on the authenticity of the participants and on their answers. The study, which sought to obtain the respondents' political views on a wide range of subjects as well as an introspective analysis of their background, social occupation and views of themselves in society, produced some worthwhile testimony. There are some interesting views on Hungary, the attitude of people generally towards communists and the high level of white-collar and professional workers in the party.

Newton felt that the participants he managed to interview were completely honest, but because party officials chose them he could not say they were representative. Despite the restrictions, the work was original in its use of oral testimony. Newton estimated that 'only about 15 per cent of British Communists are women',[16] which was a drop from 26 per cent in 1944.[17] 'More than half of all British Communists in 1932 lived in the Scottish and South Wales coal fields'[18] and Newton also states that 'Glasgow can be regarded as the most important city in the British Communist Party's history.'[19] Yet, accepting the centrality of the mass theory developed by Cole, Newton states 'as a rule women are not as politically radical as men' though he accepts that the textile industry 'does not form a clear exception to the mass theory of radicalism'[20] and points to the lack of radicalism in mining communities in the northeast of England. The 1950s saw more open criticism in the party, with many leaving over Hungary and the lack of internal democracy, yet loyalty and *belief* in the leadership continued: 'Those in the British Party who are not submissive to the *elite* tend to defect sooner or later, and in the main the rest believe that the Party is democratic ... and that even if there were an *elite* they would not submit to it.'[21]

One can see the problems of a study like Newton's because, especially before the 1990s, many members would speak with caution rather than enthusiasm. This is a vital point when attempting to understand the loyalty of ordinary members. Newton's study was original because, as a sociologist, he naturally tried to understand the motivating factors of ordinary members; he had no interest in policy formulation or the inner workings of the leadership. It is unlikely that a broad representative group would have been willing to speak out about all aspects of their lives in the CP. The formal change of the party's name in 1991 and the events in the Eastern Bloc changed the whole nature of access to former party members. The historical link from 1920[22] and the loyalty to the party that existed was far less important, if not redundant; what had been living socialism for many was now gone. Although ex-members still often react with caution, they are more 'open' and less suspicious. I felt that some were even proud and positive that their participation in events was now being recognized. Sadly, many former activists have passed away having never been recorded – a loss of which CP historians are all too aware.

The memoirs of communist activists naturally describe their personal history and their route to political involvement. The classic non-theoretical party works by Pollitt,[23] Gallacher,[24] Hannington,[25] Stewart,[26] and Piratin[27] are propagandist and deliberately rousing. Their purpose was twofold: to describe individual development and to show the historical perspective of the CPGB over two to three decades. In this respect, these biographies and numerous others serve a worthwhile purpose. They relate the experiences of those whom even the labour establishment distrusted and are good descriptive works of *activists'* experiences in the party since 1920. They are also inspirational socialist classics written both for contemporary activists and for encouraging new members. Yet, although the authors were often from the shop floor and their activities involved continuous work at grassroots level, these works are 'leadership' histories and this can present problems. The party and organizations they supported are taken as a cohesive body and there is little analysis of the actual organization *per se*. So, despite the main communist leaders *leading* from below, there is inevitably a structure that leads to a hierarchy that relates party experience broadly. Therefore, one has to go deeper to find the involvement of women in the CP and fellow organizations. The authors were still better-known male activists who had usually served an apprenticeship or worked in industry. Even if many party members had industrial experience, were they all labour 'aristocrats' in industry as their leaders were? Therefore, these works often reflect an activist's history from the view of skilled male workers who came to form the leadership of the CPGB or its satellites.

Croucher[28] has shown the level of women's involvement in the National Unemployed Workers' Movement (NUWM), the distinct part they played and, mentioning Maud Brown and Lillian Thring (who were not in the CPGB), the type of women who took a leadership role. They were 'confident, assertive women … able to make their mark in a milieu which women of more proletarian origins seem to have found more difficult'.[29] Also, Brown, 'since her appointment as national women's organizer, made the NUWM the principal focus of Communist women's agitational activity'.[30] These details and revelations of women's contribution counter the *perceived limited* view of events through autobiographies, recollections and the *actual* events as uncovered by historians. Croucher, especially in his conclusion, does great justice to the NUWM and sees its role as vital in changing government policy.[31] By showing the precise involvement of women and their role in hunger marches,[32] their organizing skills and militant activity, he adds weight to this argument. By revealing the gender role in working-class history and specifically communist history we may add to the true level of involvement and influence on working-class people, institutions and communities. It may show a wider political consciousness among women rather than their isolation from and neglect of political movements. In this study I try to show how political consciousness can develop through practical political activity.

We may define an 'ordinary' member as one who did not hold a full-time or paid job in the party and who was not on the district or executive committees. One would categorize those on such bodies as the leadership, at least in their area. Yet, a long-term member may briefly have served or worked in this capacity and then continued being an ordinary member. It is precisely this experience that has been missing from CP history, the ordinary views of those active in their local branches and implementing policies that came from the district and area committees. Women have been neglected in both areas. As early as 1921, Helen Crawfurd Anderson, who wrote an as yet unpublished autobiography, was 'appointed onto the executive committee and she held this position for many years',[33] as well as editing a 'page for women' in the *Communist*.[34] There is, however, a lack of published material on the experiences of women party members active since 1945, a period covering 45 years of party history compared with only 25 years preceding it. In *A Miner's Lass*[35] Mary Docherty relates the formative experiences of a young communist woman in Fife up to 1945. She recounts her practical experiences and everyday incidences of party life more than the developing ideology of a party member. More revelatory material might have been brought to the surface had it been a collaborative work with a historian who may have contributed a structured thematic discipline, as McShane succeeded in doing with Smith.[36]

Helen Crawfurd Anderson's memoirs[37] sadly lack detail of her communist work and more importantly her views on the party's development from its beginnings. Although written in the late 1940s, there is much narrative on her formative years and, importantly, mention of the suffragettes, but no real depth to her later political beliefs despite mentioning her visit to the Soviet Union and impressions of Trotskyism.[38] While Crawfurd was the most renowned Scottish communist woman in the party, achieving national status and a place on the EC, she failed to develop her experiences beyond a broad chronological history. A more intense and deep political work would have revealed the nature of communist politics from a unique point of view, namely a Scottish woman at British level in the party who had been politically active for women's enfranchisement, active in the anti-war movement and in the period on Clydeside prior to the formation of the party in 1920. It is also coloured by its moral tone and the discipline of religion, in this instance her Presbyterian upbringing.

Polemical works against the CP came mainly from its opponents on the ultra left. These works, theoretically and analytically approached from a strong Trotskyist angle, attack the CPGB for its loyalty to the Soviet Union and hence, in their terminology, its defence of Stalinism and all that this entails. Dewar, Woodhouse and Pearce,[39] and Bornstein and Richardson[40] are typical in that they come from three different Trotskyist sects but agree on their overall criticism of the CP. These histories justify the Trotskyite line yet fail to acknowledge the CPGB's achievements, most notably why it still managed to attract politically conscious workers in noticeable numbers compared with the comparative (even absolute) failure of other left-wing parties that espoused revolutionary politics. Calling such works 'monodimensional', Kevin Morgan is rightly critical:

> Trotskyist historians give little idea of the 'motivations' of those who joined the Party, of the nature and complexity of their allegiances or of the practical and political pressures to which they were subjected. All we get is a critique of the Party line, and usually a very poor one.[41]

Until Willie Thompson[42] covered the whole of the party's history from 1920 to 1991, little had been written about the party internally from the 1950s onwards. With a lot of inside information and personal experience, he dismantles the monolithic structure and shows the conflicts and personalities behind the party's demise.[43] It is weighted towards the effects of party policy on members and, importantly, we see how the party organization operated and the central importance of the power structures when used to circumvent or squash dissent and attacks on the leadership.

Thankfully, CP women have not been totally neglected. Sue Bruley[44] balances a political history with women's history. The level of commitment to women members was limited and links with the Communist International in its early days are shown. Bruley concentrates on giving a pre-CPGB history of the suffrage movement and its splits and then includes an industrial case study towards the end. This is as much an investigation of the importance of women's issues as it is of the political experience and ideological development of women in the party. Therefore, unlike this study, it fails to relate the political experiences and consciousness of women; it is more concerned about the party's approach to women members and is informative on important policy developments affecting them. This is done from a feminist angle with fundamental criticisms of the party's lack of commitment to women and for failing properly to address these faults; 'the revolutionary party needed a subordinate sex to service its male revolutionaries so that they could fight capitalism.'[45] Bruley shows the level of female members, 16 per cent at its high point (2500 women members),[46] and the limited influence of women's sections. In the period studied, women were never more than one-fifth of the membership and usually only one-tenth. Gender divisions in society are therefore mirrored in the party.[47] There was a limited amount of oral testimony in the text and this could be because the thesis was written at a period of major differences in the party and so details may have been less forthcoming.

C. M. Gabbidon's 'Party Life'[48] is another important work for CP scholars. Having interviewed 55 people, of whom the testimonies of 33 were used, branch life between the wars in Brighton, north London and Glasgow are covered. Crucially, Gabbidon comments on how documentary evidence can conflict with oral evidence[49] and this is an important point in dispelling the myth of a compliant and permanently obedient membership. There is brief mention of the Socialist Sunday School[50] and the importance of Irish immigration in the make-up of the Glasgow branches. There are good quotations of Glasgow members' criticisms of the Labour Party and how there was little or no consideration of joining that party in preference to the CP.[51] National and cultural differences within the CP that gave the party in Scotland a distinctly strong working-class base are discussed: 'Glasgow Party branches appear to have had more contact with each other with the leadership on Glasgow District being more familiar and accessible than those intellectuals on the London District.' This is a remarkable quote when one compares it with the experience of Irene Swan in Chapter 7 of this book. Once again there is criticism that women in the party were not treated as equals and the party 'failed to institute a departure from established norms in society and the Party itself'.[52] Gabbidon sees sexual division condoned in the party and epitomized by women running the *Daily Worker* bazaars. Covering many areas of branch life such as education and including oral testimony on Hungary and Czechoslovakia, the work is seminal in addressing branch life and the view from below. The only criticism is that the three geographical examples show diversity but also make for uneven reading and comparison, no doubt unavoidable as the party was uneven in its spread.

Some works have rightly concentrated on activity in communist strongholds and the reasons for their dominance in certain areas. This has resulted in more revealing material: 'And in fact, the most enlightening works on British Communism have been studies, not of the party "line", but of specific areas of Communist politics or particular industries and communities in which its members were firmly embedded.'[53]

To explain the dominant political ideology and its birth, development and continuing effect on workers' political consciousness, Nujam[54] concentrates on one industry, mining, and one area, Fife. She is critical of aspects of Marxism[55] and of Foster's[56] case study of workers' ideological evolution to a vanguard body. She rightly states that studies on labour movements and trade unions tell us nothing about the participants. There is a chapter on the CP in Fife and its crucial role in the pit communities and miners' union. Here there is much use of oral testimony from 40 'formal, semi-structured'[57] interviews. The oral content describes work in the industry and the role of the CP. The dialect of the participants is retained in the quotes, which are of a good length and introduce much vitality to the study. It is also contemporary with much information on the background and events during the miners' strike of 1984–85. Nujam states that: 'Communists express their beliefs within a more coherent politicized framework which provides them with a structural body of theory within which to place their ideas and arguments.'[58]

Macintyre[59] shows how the two Scottish 'Little Moscows' (two of the three were in Scotland), where the CP gained strong enough influence to elect members onto the district and county councils, were exceptions and unrepresentative of working-class communities in British society. In Maerdy in South Wales, women and children were involved and 'in some cases the wife was more committed than the man'.[60] The two mining villages, Maerdy and Lumphinnans in Fife, suffered discrimination from the labour establishment in the miners' union and this strengthened the party.[61] It would be apposite to discuss the importance of the labour process in determining ideology, for here we have both the ingredients – poor social conditions and factories or pits with production lines – that led Price[62] and Savage[63] to emphasize different areas of importance of working-class life in determining political commitment.

Price emphasizes the centrality of the work process in determining the *lack of ideology* in the British working class compared with Europe. 'Whereas French workers could be seen to possess a radical, even revolutionary, ideology and orientated their class action towards politics, British workers were more militant at work but supine when it came to politics.'[64] Price rightly sees the dominance of economism as retarding the growth of more radical politics than that of 'labourism'. But the postwar period from 1945 saw an entrenchment of 'traditional structures' in British society. Price shows the increasing strength of the trade unions in organizing effectively in the workplace, and increasing the number of shop stewards and local bargaining power, especially in engineering.[65] This led to less effective interventions from full-time union officials and centred the debate on the strength of unions in society and the possibilities of an industrial democracy.[66] Also, controversially, it limited the unofficial strikes that had become regular items in the national press and at the main party conferences. Strong unions and local bargaining power, if it led to standard agreements, had more economic pull at the shop-floor level. 'What was peculiar about the 1950s and 1960s was the way it shifted beyond the local workshop level to become associated with national militancy.'[67]

Industrial militancy benefited the CP because it could organize effectively at the workplaces in industries where unions were strong. The party could influence the national policy of unions through CP members who were often branch officials, shop stewards and convenors. The intentions of purely industrial struggles can also be exaggerated, as Price, who is not guilty of this, points out. 'The encroachment of the informal system of industrial relations were localized, transient, and received no institutional representation in politics or wider culture, presented no generalized challenge to conventional power and authority relationships.'[68] This obviously shows the *limitations* of industrial militancy in radicalizing people unless it is tied to an overall understanding of the role of labour in society.

Savage goes further and seems intent on proving that at least in Preston, which is the focus of his study, political activity for the Labour Party increased for reasons *other than* industrial activity. Tapping female and neighbourhood 'bases of support' 'also generated unprecedented levels of electoral support'.[69] This is not the place to discuss the intricacies of Labour politics, but Savage attributes a growth in women's organizations to neighbourhood activity. The industrial worker is *de-*

emphasized in importance and the social environment is promoted to being a primary cause of electoral growth. One feminist group (the Women's Citizens Association) links electoral support for the Conservatives to the Labour Party's reluctance to develop policies for women. The Labour Party gained more support when it emphasized statist policies. Savage, coming from the opposite direction of Price, states: 'We must recognize the disconnectedness of various social practices: because militancy exists in one arena we must not infer it in another. Industrial conflict is not a primordial experience which necessarily affects wider political allegiances.'[70] The latter part is true but 'which necessarily' does not mean 'does not' or 'cannot'.

Savage argues unconvincingly against the radicalizing effects of the labour process. He sees the growth of the Labour vote when there was a halving of trade union membership in the 1920s as proof of a non-connection. Might it not show the shift from industrial to political spheres *precisely because of those connections*? Perhaps the loss of economic muscle left the Labour Party as the only avenue to political change. One might also argue that the period Savage covered coincided with the Labour Party's ascendancy and that much of its growth was due to the national alternative it presented to local or industrial considerations. It seems a giant leap from the isolation of women from the Labour Party because of its lukewarm policies towards them, to then say that the 'ability of the local Labour Party to join in struggles over public services, often related to the mobilization of women, was a critical factor behind the Party's fortunes [in Preston]'.[71] Price and Savage are mutually exclusive in their theories and one has to point to the commonality of the industrial and social struggle. The industrial struggle is neglected to explain Labour's rise in Preston. Yet in these communities some women will have been married to men working in industry or vice-versa and so, though not directly involved in the labour process, women were acutely aware of it because they serviced the family. This also goes for workers and their relatives who were active in the community at large.

Knox,[72] who is sympathetic to Savage, emphasizes the low level of trade union membership in Scotland compared with England and Wales in 1892 and the role that sectionalism played industrially on Clydeside, there being 100 unions in Scotland in 1900.[73] He points to the long dominance of the Scottish Liberal Party and social and political factors such as housing and Irish Home Rule being of more importance in determining political allegiances: 'experience of exploitation may define membership of the working class, but consciousness is the outcome of a much more complicated web of experiences and relationships.'[74]

We now have to see the relevance of these two theories to our specific interest, namely women in the CP. Price's emphasis on the effect of the labour process is tempered by awareness that it did not *revolutionize* the working class politically. It was defensive. We should remember that the CP leadership is not the proletariat, which is the essential and vital body to win socialism, but the elite of full-time revolutionaries who lead the workers' party that develops and nurtures the political consciousness of the masses. This was the classic input of Leninism,[75] which shaped CPs internationally. Industrial workers are in direct conflict with capital at the major source of its wealth and so the actions of organized labour in the production process are more direct and can effect immediate change unlike any other. But work in other spheres was also important. No matter where communists were involved, by having a strong political ideology either from youth or through being involved in social or economic struggle before joining the party, they were committed to the same struggle no matter where they concentrated their work. Reminiscences of industrial workers like Arthur Exell of Coventry[76] may show the centrality of struggle in the factory but also that this is only one area of struggle.

The employment of women could influence their political involvement, though they were still excluded from much public life. Women were involved in local battles and, in the Vale of Leven, 'at critical junctures the ties of class and politics overrode the divisions of gender.'[77] In two Scottish communities (Vale of Leven and Fife) CP members served as magistrates and on committees making it 'possible to implant the radical consciousness within the official order'.[78] This meant a socialist interpretation of statutory duties. Women were involved in the party's activities and 'The communists certainly had views on the position of women that were well in advance of general attitudes, but they were by no means immune themselves from assumptions of masculine supremacy.'[79]

Macintyre shows the CP putting over its views successfully. The three villages are an exception yet so was the CP as a party, distinct from any other. It is here that we must question the absorbing of revolutionary politics. In another work Macintyre attributes great importance to the Russian Revolution and the 'real theoretical need'[80] this fuelled, and the scientific nature of British Marxism until the early 1930s. The level of communist education in the CPGB was criticized internationally,[81] which suggests that the advances the party made could have been even greater. Contrasting 'labour socialism' with 'Marxism', he shows that the communists had a theoretical advantage and its vital ingredient was the success of Bolshevism. Was this process dependent on the right circumstances and geographical area or the level of ideological awareness needed for such views to take root and produce an active CP member? Or was it both?

McKibbin reveals the contradictions in Britain that stifled the growth of a CP. There was a mass working class, the majority of whom worked in industry and were manual workers. The structure of the British economy and industry narrowed 'the base of political collectivism'[82] among the working class. Much of this was attributable to small-scale workshops. McKibbin concurs with Stedman Jones that political activity took up only a small part of working-class life. 'For some men politics was their hobby but for most it was not.'[83] Contractual as opposed to coercive politics, ideological dominance and the lack of an intelligentsia are essential points and McKibbin attributes much to the predominating character of British society in limiting communist influence and the development of Marxism.[84]

It is hard to compromise on any of the two theses and one feels certain that the most important element increasing socialist activity and drawing people into communist politics from the 1920s onwards was the presence of a genuine CP in Britain from 1920. Had MacLean or Pankhurst's alternatives taken root, it is questionable to what extent they would have stalled the CP's influence, but the party gathered momentum by attracting those sympathetic to its formation and retaining them through continuous education and activity. Macintyre seems to suggest that, notwithstanding the distinct characteristics of the towns and villages cited, it was political organization and ideology that produced success. This would then confirm the role of the vanguard party in attracting the most politically developed workers. The latter were both consciously active in the labour movement and those wrestling with the theoretical concepts that led to a distinct Marxist–Leninist party in Britain linked to the Soviet Union.

Pamela Graves's *Labour Women*[85] is a comprehensive and detailed study of the period from 1918 to 1939. She increases our knowledge of women in the Labour Party in the same way as Bruley did of women in the CP. It is strong in several areas. She clearly depicts the development of women's aspirations and then their disappointments and disproves any suggestion that they were passively involved in Labour politics through sectionalism and by not pushing for major changes. Graves shows how determined some women were to fight for equal rights with men and for legislation legalizing abortion. She is also very critical of the reaction of the Labour hierarchy, including women such as Marion Phillips,[86] in their attempts to circumvent radical policies. The evolution of policy decisions in women's sections and at British conference level is well accounted.

Graves sees the women who joined the CP expecting to play a more equal role with men and not expecting to be siphoned off into women's sections[87] and much of the oral testimony in this study bears this out. Such expectations arose from the early influence of parents, especially fathers, from the Socialist Sunday School and later a natural affinity they felt with the Women's Cooperative Guild. Concurring with the above-mentioned works, the work process definitely seems less of an influence in leading women into Labour politics during this period.[88] Ironically, in this study one might also see similarities with Labour women, though more evidently after 1945, which might lead to criticism of the CP for designating a stereotypically domestic role to female members in the Scottish district of the party. The role of the Scottish Women's Advisory Committee (SWAC) can be seen as either perpetuating sexual division or nurturing and educating women members.

In the CP women were not confined to women's sections or the SWAC, so they were not ghettoized, but, however ironic this may be, it would be remiss not to mention the strong (indeed damning) criticisms that a feminist historian could raise when studying communist politics in Britain. Graves's claims to having a representative sample need to be qualified; 100 respondents took part, 50 women and 50 men, either through oral or written testimony. This included some people in the ILP and CP. The oral testimony is more anecdotal and is not really quantified or even contextualized. It is used mostly in Chapter 2 to good effect and relates what specific people thought without claiming them to be 'typical'. The 1930s raised concerns that were central to women's struggles such as fighting against the means test and the wider issues of fascism and Spain.[89] Here there were some sympathies with the CP's stance, though the leadership discouraged or purposefully severed any links.[90]

Finally, a criticism of Graves's work must be recorded. Although claiming to be about women in Britain, this has to be qualified. The reports of women's conferences and policy decisions throughout the country justify the claim but none of the respondents was from Scotland or Wales. Therefore, while stating that 'geographical distribution matched the pattern of the movement's regional strength in the interwar period',[91] admitting that no examples from Scotland and Wales are a 'significant omission'[92] is an understatement. This is an important point for two reasons. First, it is important because of the crucial role the labour movement in Scotland played in the development of the Labour Party and specifically the ILP, of which some of Graves's respondents were members. Second, it is important because of the fundamental and continuing development of Scottish history from the late 1960s, which shows that it cannot be omitted from any British history through presumptions of automatic similarity or marginal importance to the English experience. The exclusion of regions in England might be acceptable in such a study due to marginality; the omission of one country with distinct national institutions negates a claim to any study being British.

I include testimony from women involved from the 1920s and 1930s to get some idea of their political development and early impressions of left-wing activity and life in the CP in its first 20 years. Originally, I only intended to involve women active from 1945, but it soon became apparent that this would exclude a number who were active in the 1920s who had not been properly recognized in any party history. It seems that the importance of children's organizations may previously have been *greatly underestimated* in relation to women's political development.

I begin with some of the participants' childhood experiences that led to political involvement. Some women were influenced by events prior to the existence of the CPGB. In Chapter 2 I reveal how a religious, agnostic or atheistic upbringing may have been influential or even critical in shaping a participant's communist life. Although there was not much oral testimony in this sphere, it quickly became apparent that the Socialist Sunday School and cooperative movement had influenced some children strongly, especially in Scotland, in the first three decades of the century. Much archive material suggested that its influence continued into the 1950s and even as late as the 1960s, though by this time it was nearly defunct. In the 1920s and 1930s women were very conscious of the leap they were making when they joined the CP and what effect it would have on their family and friends. Party membership put such activities into perspective and enabled women to embrace a whole philosophy that met or came nearest to their ideals. It also allowed them to work closely and collectively with other members. To opponents it seemed that anything the leadership moved was accepted, yet this had serious effects in 1956[93] and had clearly broken down by the 1980s.[94] After bitter argument, the loyalty to democratic centralism was seen as an essential element of party membership and crucial to the CP's survival as *the* revolutionary party.

Recent communist histories covering the 1930s and events up to the Second World War by Morgan,[95] and by Attfield and Williams,[96] and especially transcripts of central committee meetings published by King and Matthews,[97] have been crucial. Far from showing a dictatorial party bowing to the needs of the Soviet Union, they confirm clear disagreements over tactics and changing the party line during the 1930s and up to the Second World War. Women involved in the party at the time remembered discussing these issues at branch and aggregate meetings; and some members definitely knew about the depth of the disagreements on the central committee and whom they supported during this period.

In Chapter 3 I provide original material, despite the political themes being over familiar. We know a lot about the CP's line in the 1930s on the unemployed and issues such as Spain. From this formative period, no views of women's early impressions on entering and working in a highly disciplined and centrally structured party appear to have been published. New to this study are women's views on the importance and effectiveness of the party structure from branch level through to area and Scottish committee level. The initial impressions of women who came into the party and had to get to grips with democratic centralism and a Marxist syllabus of education are conveyed.

These two aspects of party life seem to have taken some adapting to, for their central importance was unique to the CP. Party activity in the 1930s has often been described from a British perspective. In this study I present the views of an under-represented section, women, who entered communist politics mainly via routes other than industry. Thus, because we trace their party lives from the beginnings of the CPGB and not from the post-1945 period, as first intended, we get a complete picture of the party in Scotland from its birth to its death. The early years of party life related here lay the basis for understanding the development of women in the postwar period.

The Soviet Union had an enormous influence in the CPGB. Most of the women I interviewed had been there at least once and their impressions of the socialist countries are described in Chapter 5. They had seen the development of Soviet society first hand and, despite reservations, still stood behind the Eastern Bloc in the perceived advances that had been made. Few saw the collapse coming and many were genuinely shocked when it did. The criticisms of the socialist countries are more open now and yet many of the women who went to these countries admit that they were inspired. The experience of a living socialism compensated for the lack of a mass CP at home. This was not universally the view of the respondents as there were distinct criticisms of Soviet society that were not expected but were felt at the time.

A commitment to peace and international issues was a strong aspect of women's involvement and there is evidence that this often preceded their entry into the party. The view that CP members became involved in the Campaign for Nuclear Disarmament blindly to aid Soviet peace initiatives should be laid to rest, for there is ample evidence that they saw peace as much a moral demand as a uniquely socialist one. They supported the Soviet Union because they saw it as the promoter of peace initiatives and also because it had lost so many people during the war. However, it quickly became the enemy in the cold war.

Although there is evidence that the CP stood above others on the left for its pioneering view on women, its effectiveness here also sparked off strong party conflict. From the end of the 1960s feminist politics started to gain a foothold in the CPGB.[98] The split was not so much between men and women, young and old (though most of its advocates were young), or even geographical; it was a theoretical divide between those committed to the traditional communist politics of class struggle and those who now placed gender, sexual and social issues above the classic economic and political struggle. This new aspect is discussed in Chapters 6 and 7.

More recent CP histories show a great breadth of party activity and numerous aspects of its work still to be uncovered. *Opening the Books*,[99] a compendium of new areas of research with a chapter by Bruley on communist women in Lancashire,[100] maps out many exciting dimensions of research that are in their infancy. Some chapters are by authors who have produced larger works on the party. Taking a specific time period and subject area, Srebrnik, in *London Jews and British Communism 1935–45*,[101] shows how extensive and important Jewish activists were to the

CP in the East End. His 84 pages of references and primary and secondary sources are impressive and intimidating to any new scholar of CP history. Likewise, Fishman[102] has produced an in-depth and concise study of the CP's work among unions and this thematic method will no doubt be repeated. Among the welter of research material, she has an impressive array of interviews for her study. The time spent in preparation and travel for what are only some of her sources should not be underestimated. Increasingly, there are more articles,[103] periodicals[104] and conferences covering the CPGB and more people seem willing to talk about their experiences. The amount of material available and the angles of CP history yet to be unearthed should convince most people of the level of commitment of the party membership in day-to-day political, economic, social and cultural activity over the 71 years of its existence.

MacDougall's[105] interviews with activists in the NUWM and veterans from the Spanish Civil War are extensive. They include CP members (some of whom are women) who were involved in the hunger marches and who joined the CP in the late 1920s or early 1930s. These interviews tell us more about women in the party in Scotland than any other source since McCrindle and Rowbotham's *Dutiful Daughters*,[106] a work of the late 1970s, in which six of the fourteen women interviewed were active in Labour and CP politics in Scotland. More recently, Phil Cohen[107] has picked a specific period, the cold war, in which to collect reminiscences of a communist childhood. Jackie Kay recounts her communist upbringing in Scotland;[108] her adopted father was John Kay a Scottish organizer in Glasgow. Again, the importance of the Scottish party can be seen through other respondents. However, no attempt has been made to make a serious evaluation of events through opposing or variously diverse perspectives.

Oral testimony in this study

Oral testimony is central to this study. The testimony contains opinions on the CP in Scotland that are revealed for the first time. It would have been impossible to obtain such extensive interviews and revealing testimonies had the time not been right. This was due to the demise of the CP and a decisive change in international events that had shaped respondents' lives.

While meeting and interviewing former CP women I was made very aware that the questions I asked would not have been answered previously, not because of any vindictiveness or necessarily through distrust, but because of party loyalty. When these interviews were conducted, mostly between 1994 and 1997, one was painfully aware of the traumatic experiences for many of the women of two major events. One was the collapse of the Soviet Union and allied socialist countries, most symbolically through the physical destruction of the Berlin Wall in 1989, and so the end of socialism for many CP members. The other was the decline, amid bitter recriminations, of the CPGB itself.

Many respondents felt despondent, not least because the Conservative Party was in its fifteenth year of government. Yet, once party lives were recounted and events recalled there emerged a fascinating and important history of women's activity, which I admit to having seriously underestimated at the start of my research. There was no indication in any of the literature of the true value of women party members in Scotland. The oral testimony illuminates areas of activity that publications and reports inevitably fail to reveal. I found a level of commitment and a variety of issues for which my reading of the party had barely prepared me.

As mentioned earlier, as children's organizations, the Socialist Sunday School and Woodcraft Folk had strongly influenced the political direction of many party members. Having been unaware of these organizations I became convinced that the Socialist Sunday School especially played a pivotal role in steering many women towards communist politics. There is much archive material on this organization and its roots were deep in the west of Scotland, yet it was small, indeed tiny compared with the religious organizations it sought to counter. If there was little written about women CP members in Scotland, there was even less on their formative influences. An emphasis on equality between girls and boys in the Socialist Sunday School, apparent from minutes and the *Young Socialist* newspaper, seems to have been vital in influencing some women towards expecting a more militant socialism than that of the Labour Party and ILP.

Finding women participants to interview was not difficult. I approached the three main groupings that had been part of the CPGB in Scotland – the Democratic Left, which had evolved from the CPGB, the Communist Party of Britain, formed in 1988 from splits in the CPGB, and the CP of Scotland, formed in 1992 just after the CPGB became the Democratic Left. All three organizations forwarded me names of people who might be interested in being interviewed. The women, of various ages and differing political experiences, had been active at all levels of the CPGB. Most responded initially and I soon had more than enough respondents in the west of Scotland. Even though the party was stronger in the west, and that is reflected here, it was still crucial to show the experiences of communist women throughout Scotland. Some women were contacted through recommendations, through reading party literature and enquiries about people's whereabouts, a most important angle.

Since the majority of respondents interviewed supported the new draft of *The British Road to Socialism* in 1977 and the party EC's stand on the *Morning Star* dispute in the 1980s, there is no imbalance towards the CPB. I have tried to show the balance of ideas as they were in the party and what the majority of members decided in Scotland. I would state that these major policy issues are not a concern until Chapter 7.

I interviewed a total of 41 people and amassed over 800,000 words of transcription. Of these interviewees 34 were with women and 7 with men in the CP (the one exception being a woman involved in organizing the Socialist Sunday School as was her mother before her). Only the testimony of party women is used in the main text. Undoubtedly, many of the CP histories mentioned have relied on a greater number of interviewees or respondents. However, they are often on a British wide basis and so as a percentage or as in-depth interviews they may still be deficient. Prioritized are detailed interviews that cover women's lives and different aspects of their activities in the party. Scotland was covered because it is both a country with its own identity, culture and history and was, as a 'district', part of the CPGB and essential in its contribution to the party's strength in supplying members, industrial influence and political leadership.

By covering many geographical areas in Scotland and specific branches, I intend to show the diversity of women's activity in Scotland. Had the sample of women mirrored exactly the social and geographical composition of the majority of women members, then arguably I would have concentrated almost exclusively on the west of Scotland or, at most, the central industrial belt. Admittedly, the problem arises of an unrepresentative sample being overly reflected in this study. Through party literature, specifically Scottish CP circulars and minutes, there is an attempt to show how the views expressed by the interviewees were representative and reflect how women felt about certain issues. Here an important area was the way the party handled women's issues and how much women thought should have been done in this area. (Let us not forget that they reveal the opposite at times – what was not revealed in the written word.)

Also, there were areas of disagreements that crossed gender lines and came to a head over national and international issues. Again, the danger arose of the predominant party line on policy decisions being ignored and a bias developing from myself towards any one view or group of respondents; certainly, I would not do this intentionally, but there is undoubtedly a danger here. Thus, the decisions of the Scottish committee and what were minority and majority views within the party over important debates are an essential part of the text. Of course, I am not suggesting that minutes and circulars reflect accurately what was going on in the party; they are also used here to show how differently women members might perceive events. As the party leadership usually wanted to portray the party as united, the oral evidence shows how much division there was and how it continued or was resolved. One might feel that there was more debate and dissension than originally expected given the united front, with the exception of 1956, often displayed to the public until the late 1970s. Again, this is an important aspect that arguably would not have been revealed before 1991. Despite potential problems, oral testimony is crucial here because it not only supplements the archive material used, much of it previously inaccessible, but it also greatly supplants it.

I have attempted to cover as many age groups and experiences in the party as possible. Therefore, ordinary branch activists, those who stayed within the confines of local activity, are included. Other variants are present. This included two women who had left in 1956, a mother and daughter both active in the party, women committed to the work of the SWAC, those strongly involved in the YCL, especially noticeable from the mid-1940s to mid-1970s, those who visited socialist countries and those who identified with the new feminist politics. Poignantly, some of the respondents have since died, which only confirms the value of oral testimony and the need to record the lives of communists for posterity. It also reminds one of how unique the experiences of political activists are in any epoch.

On the practicality of the interviews, a brief questionnaire was sent to women who had agreed to participate. Telephone calls were then made to explain the research needs of the thesis before the interview was set up. Often this meant staying several hours with the respondent and taping them (only a couple of women were not interviewed at home). A set questionnaire was followed, which I modified after a trial run as the responses were often poor. As the questions were pruned, answers appeared more forthcoming. However, the first ten interviews proved experimental and many of the early respondents were reinterviewed. All interviews were transcribed and sent to the respondent for spelling and accuracy as well as to exclude any material they did not wish published. In the text, where respondents are quoted, they appear in inverted commas for excerpts of fewer than 50 words. In longer quotes the excerpts are indented.

Some questions were initially far too long and received the appropriate short reply. One specific question on *The British Road to Socialism* was wrong and there was also a need to avoid a 'leading' question. Since this is a political history respondents were asked their views about opposing theories and why they may have taken a certain stance. This was done openly and in some cases questions were asked about the opposing sides and how women argued against political opponents, what support or objections there were to certain theories. Here it was sometimes hard not to get into a polemical discussion.

It is important to remember the difference between the party members interviewed. All seemed selfless in their dedication to the party but not all were expressive; in some instances activity did not extend much beyond the branch. Yet it is important that their voices were recorded, for this is not a history that seeks the most articulate women in the CP in Scotland, but the representation of a broad base.

Unforeseen sources of information were the numerous publications, letters, notes and photographs from people's personal collections that allowed me to build up a complete picture of individuals and their involvement. Specifically, much information about the SWAC came from continuous discussions with Marion Henery, a former secretary of the advisory committee, in whose home I found a number of files with original source material from the 1950s and 1960s. This has been invaluable in helping to recount the activity of the advisory committee from its base in the women's groups and party branches.

Although activity in Glasgow and the west of Scotland is depicted heavily here, the experiences of women in other major cities and towns throughout Scotland are represented. Also included is information from additional party sources, including those in important full-time party positions – an industrial organizer and two Scottish secretaries. The

1. Clarion Club outing. Marion Henery (second on left standing) with Cathie Moore, Bill Ferrie and Alex McCrindle (far right) father of Jean McCrindle.

male partner of one-time Scottish party official and later national women's organizer for the party, Margaret Hunter, spoke of her work and the circumstances of her early death. Their information helped me get a broader picture of the Scottish party and the distribution and gender balance of its membership. As full-time officials, these sources were well placed to evaluate the overall strengths and weaknesses of the party at certain times. People involved in specific groups or campaigns in the party were also interviewed. I have not sought to downgrade, denigrate or perpetuate any specific theory or to show sympathy with any one view in the party. The conflicting sides that developed in the latter years are shown and there is more analysis in this area. Preconceptions can easily be confirmed if taken out of context.

Initially, it had seemed as if the demise of the party occurred with the arrival of new theories and the increasing predominance of gender politics. What gave cause for fundamental revision of this, now admitted, bias were not only the well developed views of those who became feminists but the observations of many others who would disagree with prioritizing gender politics, but recognized their importance and why they had taken root. Also, the effect of being in paid work had a major effect on many party women and a separate study is needed on this area.

Many critical views stated here can be found in *all* political parties – disillusionment, anger, frustration, indecision. The crucial content of this study is that of a group of women committed to socialism and specifically revolutionary socialism that had its foundation in the Bolshevik revolution of 1917 and the formation of the Communist International. The women interviewed were individuals with a common political goal, consciously aware of numerous issues that demanded decisions and action. This led them to the CP and, until they left, convinced them of their continuing role in that party. And it is the role of women in the CPGB in Scotland that this work aims to reveal: their political development, changing perspectives and progression through the 70 years of CP association. This study does not have a theoretical structure or basis from which to judge the CP or to point, as could easily be done from a feminist angle following on from Bruley's study, to many of its deficiencies. It reveals the role of women in the CP in Scotland considering whether they were a marginalized group within or an integral part of the party and its work over the years. It reveals to what extent women's involvement has been underestimated or omitted from our perceptions of the CP in Scotland and indeed Britain.

Chapter 2

Becoming Militant: Socialist Politicization from Childhood, 1914–44

> Look forward to the day when all men and women will be free citizens of one fatherland, and live together as brothers and sisters in peace and righteousness.[1]
>
> *The Tenth Socialist Precept of the Socialist Sunday School*

Many different factors had led the women who joined the CP at its inception in Scotland in January 1921 into radical or revolutionary politics. Influences such as family, religion and socialism were decisive in their decision to become communists and were more pivotal than their work relations.

In this chapter we see how community-based groups, family influences and left-wing organizations helped young women develop politically. Many of the women in this study were introduced to socialist politics in childhood through the working-class children's and youth organizations that were established at the turn of the century. The Socialist Sunday School played a large part in developing a militant and well-educated cadre of young people from which the CP benefited. Other small groups promoted revolutionary politics and became prominent in the conflict between workers and the government during the First World War. 'Red Clydeside' came to symbolize not only opposition to the war regulations imposed on the workforce but also a tradition that those on the left, including the CP, could proudly point to when tracing their socialist roots.

As many respondents were active prior to the 1930s, the oral testimony is useful because it highlights the importance of certain institutions in the politicizing process. We witness life in the YCL and

CP up to and including the Second World War and see how leading communist women influenced a new generation of activists. We also look at how the Socialist Sunday School continued to benefit the CP after the 1940s.

Socialist Sunday School and other influences

A minority of children were taught socialist politics from an early age in the Socialist Sunday School, which was well established by the turn of the century. Although Labour churches and Cinderella clubs had existed in England, it was the impetus of ILP members in Glasgow that set up the Socialist Sunday School on 2 February 1896.[2] Alex Gossip, the Glasgow and district secretary of the United Operative Cabinet and Chair Makers' Society of Scotland, who associated strongly with, but never joined, the CP, and Caroline Martin a lecturer at Glasgow University, who had learnt her social theories from the New Testament,[3] were its founders.[4]

Tom Anderson, an independent maverick left-winger, was also associated with the movement. Born in Pollokshaws in Glasgow in 1863, his father – a handloom weaver, Presbyterian and radical – taught his children that they were equal to anyone.[5] Apprenticed at the age of ten, Tom Anderson became a joiner at 14 and returned to Glasgow when he was 20. He joined the ILP in 1894 and later went over to the Social Democratic Federation. He claimed to have started the first school in 1894,[6] which is doubtful, though his role in the schools was decisive. At a meeting on 13 January 1907 he was responsible for moving that women be included in the tenth socialist precept and so encouraged the equality of children in schools.[7] Anderson's small amendment meant that girls and young women would be treated as equals. Considering how often the precepts were used, one must see how fundamentally important this inclusion was in determining a less stereotypical role for young women in the schools.

Although one may point to a reactionary gender bias in lectures at the start of the century – in a lecture on 'Socialism and sex equality' Alfred Russell described women as the 'weaker vessel' and thought of sex equality as an impossible aim[8] – these views did not last long into the century. In fact, boys were free to and were encouraged to attend 'the new needlework classes'.[9] Although traditionally an exclusively female pursuit, the school emphasized the benefits of needlework for all. Girls and boys engaged in the same activities, shared classes, went on picnics together and were given equal responsibilities in the school and its education classes.

The Socialist Sunday School operated throughout Scotland and was most prominent in Glasgow where there were branches in many areas of the city. It became a part of the National Council of British Socialist Sunday School Unions in 1909, there being five unions – called districts – of which two were in Scotland – Glasgow and Edinburgh, which included Fife in its district.[10] Through regular meetings, with classes for the very young who were organized as the 'Sunbeams',[11] its aim was to educate children in the ideas of socialism[12] and to combat the influence of the churches, which in Scotland was considerable. It held that 'as the orthodox Sunday Schools serve as a recruiting ground for the churches of all creeds, so will the Socialist Sunday Schools become the chief recruiting ground for the adult Socialist organizations in the future.'[13] And so they were. Meetings were weekly and involved a comprehensive curriculum of activity: 'The Socialist Sunday School taught us not to … just accept things but to try and analyse them and try to see what was right and whether the truth was being told or whether things were being hushed up.'[14] The Socialist Sunday School aimed to encourage children to embrace a different way of life and to reject existing standards. Its approach was socialist, but more utopian than scientific. For instance, a miner would bring along a lump of coal and talk about its extraction and uses, or a baker would bring a cake and illustrate the inequality of the class system by the equal or unequal division of the cake.[15] Children were given practical lessons and logical arguments that seemed convincing and hard to refute: 'I think it was very influential, very influential.'[16]

There were branches throughout the west of Scotland and in Edinburgh and Fife. The Socialist Sunday School did not have its own premises until the 1920s, so the local cooperative society or Independent Labour Party would provide the meeting halls.[17] The ILP was affiliated to the Labour Party and was the most politically dominant organization on the left. It encouraged its members to use the Socialist Sunday School and the two organizations were seen as synonymous until the 1930s.[18]

The Proletarian Sunday School, a small offshoot that Tom Anderson, a dissident from the Socialist Sunday Schools, founded in Glasgow had little impact and did not survive long. It espoused an outright class war approach, similar to the syndicalism of the Socialist Labour Party (SLP), and was aimed at the youth.[19] Anderson's publication stressed the importance of equality and was farsighted in economic demands for women. The war had 'levelled some of our notions, and women now demand the same rate; and we say "Hear hear!", we even go further and

2. Cambuslang Socialist Sunday School picnic at the Cathkin Braes, *c.*1917.

claim a uniform rate for all workers.'[20]. In later years Anderson reminded people of the role John Maclean had played in opening his classes to women even before they had political rights: 'The Women Guilds of the Cooperative Society found in Comrade John a teacher and a friend, and I have heard many a woman speak of his class and his teaching in very moving terms.' [21]

In Fife, certain differences made the Proletarian Sunday School more acceptable to some children; it was smaller, less formal and there was no minute taking.[22] It used the songbook of the syndicalist organization, the International Workers of the World (IWW).[23] The daughter of a French émigré whose father, Lawrence Storione, had already set up the Anarchist Communist League, organized the school.[24]

> The Proletarian Sunday School was run by Lawrence Storione's daughter, Annie. Lawrence Storione had to flee from France and he came across from France dressed as a woman and he worked in the pits and it was him that used to come to the hoose to collect the dues and he'd [have] discussions with my father … [he] asked me to come to the Proletarian Sunday School.[25]

The purpose of the Socialist Sunday Schools was not merely to espouse socialist doctrine but to make young people aware of their environment and to cover as many pertinent topics as possible. It was not only an alternative to religious education and the imposed standards and morals handed down by authority. The schools also sought to educate children by discussing and coming to understand the subjects presented and not just by rote. Also 'the Sunday school formed a choir, the Cambuslang Labour Choir and that was a great experience.'[26]

Children in the schools were organized as a small minority from an early age. As young socialists they did not face overt hostility but they *were* different, not least because they were taught to be independent and 'to respect but not to bow down to others'. Their organization was openly democratic and, unlike the religious Sunday schools or state schooling, did not have a hierarchical structure. They learnt the socialist Ten Commandments by heart and put them into practice through the activities of the Socialist Sunday Schools. Speakers learnt to fear and respect the institution when addressing its scrutinizing members.[27] The schools organized rambles in the nearby countryside, socials and outdoor meetings.

While the Socialist Sunday School movement was stronger in Scotland than elsewhere in Britain, it was even stronger in Glasgow and the west of Scotland. Within this small milieu, a tradition of socialist values was well established by the outbreak of the First World War. For children at their most formative stage, events were organized to reinforce the optimistic beliefs and theories they were taught. The schools inversely reflected the indomitable strength of organized religion and the strength of the state and, like socialist activists in the dilution battles, they were a minority even in their own communities and class.

Few could doubt how far away socialism was in Britain, especially having faced the jingoism of the First World War. Yet, being part of a small cohesive group of socialists who could organize effectively, made it seem possible one day. The Socialist Sunday School taught its pupils science, geography and politics, but for some it also did a lot more. It was set up in opposition to the huge influence of religious Sunday schools[28] and reflected the numerical weakness of those who opposed organized religion. This was especially pertinent to Scotland where Protestantism and its historical influence was strong and where the influx of immigrants from Ireland, mostly Catholics, brought a new dimension to Scottish social and political life. The opposition to British colonialism from Irish Catholics who still faced some religious discrimination also benefited the left.

The discipline and tradition of Calvinism was rife, which was a point Kendall made,[29] and the strong tradition of broad-based education had its roots in the Reformation in Scotland. Regular learning and quoting from the Bible developed a child's ability to justify and develop arguments that extended beyond religion.[30] Scotland had a philosophical tradition that could enlighten people beyond the restrictions of an advanced theology. It opened minds to the logic of dialectical materialism, which the CP introduced wholesale with its Marxist syllabuses. Instead of dictatorial instruction, children were encouraged to question the speaker who addressed them. Trade unions were the strongest working-class organizations and from them the pupils at the Socialist Sunday School would learn how to conduct meetings, elect officers and take minutes. The intrinsic teaching of both bodies was for a world socialism based on peace, friendship and love and was often put over, ironically but not surprisingly, in a religious manner. It was visionary and not too fervent.

The First World War, 'Red Clydeside' and the Russian Revolution

Because the school's strength lay in its conviction, the war did not affect its activity but strengthened the resolve of members to stand by its teachings. There were signs of growth in Scotland with Glasgow accounting for over a quarter of all sales of *The Young Socialist* monthly magazine at the beginning of 1914;[31] by 1915 it could report of Glasgow, where the magazine was printed, that 'All the schools in this District are in a very healthy condition, despite the adverse circumstances which presently prevail.'[32] Notwithstanding the ubiquitous jingoism, some schools went on the offensive with authorities like the Rutherglen School, which passed a resolution to the town council protesting 'against the arbitrary treatment meted out by the Rutherglen Local Tribunal to young men who … claim exemption from military service on conscientious grounds.'[33]

Throughout the organization there were members who became victims of the military authorities because they opposed war, just as they had been taught to do. In the pages of *The Young Socialist* members would learn of the persecution of fellow comrades throughout Britain for their socialist principles, with those who practised anti-militarism and internationalism punished for being conscientious objectors.[34] As new schools sprouted in Blantyre, Govan, Ayr, Greenock and Johnstone the magazine proclaimed 'we know that nothing will shake our comrades' steadfastness in the cause of international friendship.'[35] The traditional singing of *The Red Flag* at some schools and the organization's pride in objecting to the war reflected their proud emotional internationalism at this time.[36]

During the war women became politicized in the factories to which they were sent and where government restrictions were forcibly imposed on the workforce. Socially, they were further politicized by taking a leading role in opposing rent increases. They actively campaigned in close-knit tenements and overcrowded communities, and eventually received support from protesting shipyard workers. The agitation culminated in the success of the Rent Restriction Act in 1915. Active in this agitation was young Rose Klasko (later Kerrigan).

> Now I found out about it in the shop one day when I was going up to the classes and the [Socialist] Sunday School, I learned about this and I came home and I told my mother that we'd agreed not to pay the increase in our rents. She, on the other hand, said: 'Oh, we're the first people they'll put out Rose.' She said, 'I could never do that on my own', so I went up our close, we had 14 tenants, it was a four-storey building, and explained it to all the women and they agreed to join the strike ... these women were all housewives between 25 and 60 or thereabouts and I was only 12, but I convinced my group and we never paid the extra and we never fell into debt either, we just paid the ordinary rent and that went on and Lloyd George was so upset about this, he was so anxious to keep the munitions coming from our area that he capitulated ... so that's one of the victories of British history.[37]

The ILP, which dominated Scottish Labour politics for the first two decades of the century[38] and 'until the 1930s ... was effectively the Labour Party on the ground in Clydeside',[39] had experienced the fudging and compliance of the Labour Party leadership towards the war effort. Few had come out in total opposition. The number of activists involved in the British Socialist Party or the Socialist Labour Party was far smaller in comparison, but on Clydeside they were strongly active in opposing the war. The success of their tactics depended on actions among a militant working-class population. However much the Red Clydeside period has been mythologized and though it did not necessarily suggest a possible socialist revolution, no greater anti-war episode took place in Britain.

There were limits to the industrial conflict and, despite early success, in the end it failed, but its *political effects* were permanent and undoubtedly beneficial to the coming CP. Red Clydeside educated and inspired socialists fighting against the war effort and what they saw as needless slaughter. Conflict with the establishment continued after the war. With an increase in unemployment and a world depression, skilled workers organized with army veterans against the government's austerity measures. In Scotland one of the last major conflicts before the miners' strikes, which culminated in the General Strike, took place in Glasgow over the 40-hour week. This resulted in a riot in George Square in the city centre:

> Yeah, Manny Shinwell was arrested. They read the Riot Act from the Town Hall steps, the square was packed with people and I was at the other end, you know, the station end, near Queen Street station, and I was selling *The [Strike] Bulletin* and I knew if I was caught with *The [Strike] Bulletin* in my hands I would be in trouble. But just as I was making up my mind to make myself scarce, the police, after they'd read the Riot Act started to [attack] the people and there was a lorry going up towards High Street with empty lemonade bottles I think and the chaps just grabbed these and fought back and it was a real battle, I got out of the way knowing that I was going to be in trouble once they started on people around that edge of the crowd and I don't know what happened after that, that was 1919, which was the fight for the 40-hour week.[40]

Militant socialists welcomed the Russian Revolution because it seemed to confirm the Marxist theory of workers inevitably overthrowing capitalism. Lenin's small but disciplined Bolshevik Party seemed to offer a new organization that could introduce socialism through revolution. Inevitably, people were increasingly attracted to this success against the ruling class as it became obvious by 1920 that the purely economic struggle had been decisively defeated on the Clyde.

Women pioneers in the Communist Party

For women who joined the CP in this period the road appeared logical from ILP, BSP or SLP politics to the more decisive and advanced theories of Leninism, which were the basis for the founding of the Communist International. Alexandra Kollantai outlined the importance of women to this movement:

> The new, Third, Communist International needs only to set itself the task of utilizing the female proletariat, of developing the entire breadth of its initiative in order to draw the women workers into the cause of struggling for and building a new way of life and developing a new ethic, a new relationship between the sexes.[41]

Women active on the left who had thought that the Labour Party could deliver socialism had put their hopes in the mission of the Clydeside MPs who left Glasgow for London in 1922. By this time women such as Helen Crawfurd, Jenny Hyslop and a teenage Rose Klasko had already decided to join the CP despite the odds against building a mass party because of the ILP's supremacy. Their ages also represent different generations of Scottish women who came into the CP at about the same time.

Born in 1877, Crawfurd was from a strongly religious background. Her father was a Calvinist and her mother a Methodist. She married a Presbyterian minister who was an ardent anti-militarist. Having been an active and militant suffragette in the Women's Social and Political Union, suffering arrest and staging hunger strikes, and then opposing the war, she was made secretary of the Glasgow Women's Housing Association and became active in rent battles.[42] She became honorary secretary of the Women's Peace Crusade in 1917. An occasional lecturer from the ILP at the Socialist Sunday School,[43] she served on the ILP Scottish divisional council, was part of the left-wing organization of the ILP and in 1920 she visited the Soviet Union and arrived just as the Communist International's second congress ended,[44] though she managed to meet Lenin. She joined the CPGB in 1920 and in 1921 was appointed onto its executive committee;[45] she edited a women's page in the weekly paper *Communist* and helped set up the *Sunday Worker*.[46] In the 1930s Crawfurd campaigned on Spain and various other international issues. Her influence on women members in the party was enormous and she was often seen gliding through the streets of Glasgow. As Marion Robertson remembers, 'I used to see her coming down Renfield Street with these lovely grey capes and she wore the suffragette colour … and a wee bit fluttery thing in her coat.'[47] Crawfurd made a big impression on party women who saw how she could chair public meetings. Effie O'Hare remembers when she attended a meeting for the Meerut prisoners:[48]

> I was taken into the meeting to sit there and listen and there was this lady, very nice looking, elegant lady, in the chair. Beautiful

> golden hair, everything, and she managed that conference with all the men and all the things *absolutely beautifully* and I thought 'Oh I would like to be able to do that.'[49]

After the war, in 1946, Crawfurd was appointed the first woman councillor in Dunoon. She retired in 1948, a few years before her death in 1954.

Jenny Hyslop, born in 1898, also joined the CP in the early 1920s. In 1921 she and her husband moved to Clydebank when the Rent Strike, in opposition to the Rent and Mortgages Interest (Restrictions) Act, which had nullified the 1915 Rent Restrictions Act, was underway.[50] Neighbours asked them to support the strike by paying only the standard rent and not the increase. The women were central to organizing opposition to the increases and played a cat and mouse game with the bailiffs – changing nameplates on doors or getting other people to answer the knock of the authorities. Armed with a big bell Jenny Hyslop would go down the streets announcing the arrival of an eviction squad. The people in the neighbourhood would huddle round *en masse* to stop evictions taking place,[51] sometimes with Jenny and a group of women resisting entry to the flat by barricading the doors. The strike lasted longer in Clydebank than in Glasgow and initially the strikers were successful in certain cases in getting the 'notice of increase' invalidated. The House of Lords upheld a test case, but by 1926 the law supported the factors and by 1928 the strike was finished. In 1938, co-opted by Finlay Hart,[52] Hyslop became a councillor and served for eight years. During the Second World War she was a senior officer in the warden's service and the first woman sectional head of the ARP in the west of Scotland. She commanded a post in Clydebank and was active during the two nights of the blitz on 13 and 14 March 1941 in which the town suffered hundreds of fatalities. As well as managing the horrors of bereavement and identification, along with thousands of others she lost her home.[53] However, the people's defiance to the courts over the rents started a tradition that produced later battles over the same issue in the late 1950s and early 1970s in Clydebank.

Rose Klasko was a young teenager when political opposition to the First World War developed in Glasgow. Strongly influenced by her father's radicalism and aware of the subordinate role of women, Rose became an active member of the Socialist Sunday School. Having helped the SLP in its offices and on the street, Rose noticed the differences between the parties of the left as well as the dominance of the ILP, and during the war worked against jingoism in the movement.[54] She attended numerous education classes, some of which, on economics, were given by John Maclean.[55] She helped send famine relief to Russia and at the age of 18 was a foundation member of the CP in Scotland. Prior to joining the CPGB she had been involved with the Communist Labour Party. At the second unity conference at Leeds in January 1921, the CLP took many of its members into the CPGB. Socially, she fought for better provision of contraception for women by using the Marie Stopes clinic in Glasgow, even though these enlightened institutions were for women needing to prevent further pregnancy rather than those who wished to have no children. Rose married Peter Kerrigan in 1926 and in 1935 they travelled to the Soviet Union where they stayed for a few months, for Peter was British organizer for the seventh congress of the Communist International.[56] Rose moved to London in 1939 when Peter became the party's national industrial organizer and she remained a member of the CPGB for 70 years.

Women in the party from outside the Scottish district who made an impact included Isabel Brown, who was one of five women delegates who attended the first CP congress in 1921. Born on Tyneside in 1894, her husband, Ernest Brown, was district organizer for the CP on Tyneside where she was the chairperson.[57] Ernest became Scottish organizer and Isabel stood at a by-election in Kilmarnock in 1928 where she was arrested and assaulted by the police.[58] She stayed in Scotland for 18 months and was women's editor of *The Mineworker*.[59] It was on international issues that she made her mark,[60] helping defend those accused of burning down the Reichstag. She also campaigned nationwide for the Spanish republic, which led Finlay Hart, a communist councillor in Clydebank, to comment: 'Isabel Brown bled audiences white when she appealed at public meetings on behalf of Spain.' She later became women's organizer of the CP during the war[61] and in 1948 again stood as a candidate in Kilmarnock:[62]

> Oh she stayed with me when she came here, Isabel, a grand old war-horse. I remember one meeting during the war in the public hall and it was packed and there was supposed to be a Russian film come first and it didn't turn up and Isabel kept that meeting going right through with questions on that platform in front of the screen there for the *whole* hour of the meeting. I can tell you

> something, a man that was a Tory but he'd been at the meeting because it was well advertised and he said 'Can you tell me who was that woman that took the meeting last night?' I said 'Isabel Brown, she was a schoolteacher at one time' he said 'A marvellous women and she held that meeting' he said 'And all those questions, I never heard anything like it'. That was an outsider, not any of our crowd.[63]

For women who joined before the Second World War the Socialist Sunday School had been an important pre-YCL body, which may explain the failure of the communist children's organization to take hold in Britain, as it did in some other countries. Despite the *Young Worker* eventually becoming a weekly,[64] the Pioneer movement never really took hold despite being active in the General Strike in some areas,[65] especially the coal districts, and close work with the ILP youth guild. Indeed, its membership never exceeded 1000 in Britain and its highest point was in 1927.[66] The cooperative movement was very strong in Scotland and it would prove to be an important area of work in the future for women in the CP. Many of them joined the Cooperative Women's Guild for life, despite later discrimination. The Woodcraft Folk was an independent organization for children, which, like the cooperatives, was not overtly socialist but taught equality and friendship to its members:

> I suppose my first sort of relationship with anything political was when I was very young and I joined the Woodcraft Folk. My eldest brother was involved in setting it up in the Vale [of Leven] and another brother of mine took over the job as headman. ... I joined the Woodcraft Folk and it was a Cooperative youth organization, boys and girls, it was sort of political in as much as it was associated with the cooperative movement, so between that and the fact that in my family, I'm one of nine, my elder brothers were political.[67]

Formed as an alternative to the militarist Boy Scouts, the Woodcraft Folk was for both sexes and had branches in Glasgow and the west of Scotland. Its structure and the names of its members resembled those of the organization of the Native American Indians and its open approach. The cooperative movement decided to sponsor the Woodcraft Folk because it did not have its own organization for children.[68] There were different groups for different ages, Elfins for the young and Hardihoods for the older ones. One of the areas where it met regularly was Shettleston in the east end of Glasgow:

> I was a member of the Strathclyde Fellowship it was called, the Woodcraft Folk sort of organization that I was associated with and it was in the Woodcraft Folk that I met my husband Eric, and from there I joined the Young Communist League but I would say that was mainly because of political interest within my own family that I came and not as a member of the Woodcraft Folk.[69]

Although the Woodcraft Folk was neither overtly socialist nor political, it did have a strong international dimension.[70] Meetings were held weekly and children learnt about outdoor activities by sitting around a campfire and going on outings where they met other groups. Practising the ideals of cooperation became second nature.[71] The international affiliates of the Woodcraft Folk could at times appear much stronger and more institutionalized than in Britain where there was limited support:

> When we went to Holland after the war in an exchange, this isn't the Socialist Sunday School but an exchange with the Woodcraft Folk, the trade unions in Holland all put money into the youth organization and something like that was really required in this country because we worked on a shoestring and couldn't provide halls and things although we used the Cooperative halls … it was very difficult because people who were active in the movement were trying to do the work with the children, the socialist education, the recreational work, etc. But they were also having to spend time and energy raising funds to carry out this kind of work as well, and I think this is one of the reasons for the demise because the uniformed organizations could offer so much more by way of recreational activities for the children.[72]

The Labour Party failed to develop its adult membership either educationally or ideologically in the way the Socialist Sunday School had done.[73] When leaving the schools youngsters may have expected to join an equally militant organization. The importance of the ILP in developing potential young socialists was that it was the dominant section of the Labour Party in Scotland and was the radical section of the established labour movement. In Scotland, among the left, there was already a culture of dissent and a socialist opposition against the British right-wing Labour establishment and against the conservatism of the church.

There was thus already a socialist and democratic culture when the CP was formed in Scotland and arguably the curricula and discipline expected of the party membership would be more appealing to those who had attended the schools, of which a significant number were girls. Rose Kerrigan had experienced such politicization with her formative influences coming from her father, a Jewish refugee from eastern Europe who had come to Glasgow from Dublin:

> My father, I would call him a socialist, was a radical but he wasn't a member of any party as you understood and the reason was because he never got naturalized, cost too much money then. ... He supported the Suffragettes which, when I was eight years old and they were active, I thought was wonderful ... they were very good and early on in my life I realized that it wasn't their fault that boys had things easier than us girls who were always in drudges.[74]

In many instances there was a special bond with one or both parents. If it were the father this could come from his trade union work or by young women not being limited to the domestic sphere as so many were. Having been to various left-wing meetings with her brother, Rose learnt to argue against established views in support of the First World War:

> I was 11 when the war broke out, my father was anti-war and we went to war to save 'Little Belgium', which had been invaded by the Germans. My Dad said that wasn't true; the war was imminent because Germany needed to expand markets and she had no outlet like we had; we had colonies and all that, specifically India, so they started the war. Well, when I told my mates at school this, Oh!, they called me pro-German and God knows what and I was really hounded.[75]

Influences in different environments

Not all female recruits to the CP came from working-class backgrounds with direct experience of class struggle. And, unlike those from working-class backgrounds, the middle and upper classes had more time to ponder, study and debate theoretical, philosophical and moral arguments:

> My father was an MP for West Edinburgh … John Gordon Jamieson, but I think he was a pretty incompetent MP really. … He belonged to an old and sort of paternalistic school of thought among the Tories, you don't get that sort *anymore* now. I mean he was a lover of human beings; he was a real Scotsman; he had a strong egalitarian tendency you know; he was a liberal-minded man but he believed in the hierarchy of society and the people who were privileged had been bred for centuries as masters; it was their duty to look after the poor and be kind to them and so on and so on. It was a real sort of paternalistic attitude. Well, I was very fond of him, we loved each other dearly and he used to confide in me the problems of politics. So I was brought up with politics. I was also brought up with *lots* of religion. … Well, he was in the United Free Church in fact but he was very undenominational; he was a very close student of Christ and Jesus's teaching. And when I got to the age of about 14, 15, 16, a young teenager, I found I *could not* equate Christianity, the way he had been teaching it, with his politics, and this was very disturbing.[76]

Among the upper middle-class, the experience of empire, sometimes through relatives in its administration, could lead to greater understanding of the plight of people under colonial rule. Indeed, not every civil servant was blindly obedient to the British government's policies.

> I had a cousin … Thomas Hodgkin, who was Secretary to Sir Arthur Wauchope in Palestine at the time, when I was 22 I went to stay with him in Palestine with my aunt and uncle, his parents, and we used to sit up till the dawn talking about imperialism and that was the beginning of my conversion. I found there was a whole school of thought into which I could move and develop from my own internal protest and my Christianity into this, and this was communism. … Thomas was told to leave because he had published articles in the Arab press that said 'the British Empire is cheating you of your land' and so this wouldn't do you see. He said 'the British Empire is like a rich man who is promising one sovereign to two blind beggars', that was the pungent illustration that he produced in the Arab press. So of course this wouldn't do and he was told he was given three weeks to get out, so he lost his job didn't he?[77]

The attitude of parents to religion was important because religion could be all pervasive. This constituted an entrenched part of people's culture either geographically or ethnically. Criticism of the establishment from its centre did not necessarily mean embracing left-wing politics, but questioning actions and not remaining subservient to officialdom did make one different. This is an example of a socialist consciousness being developed against the mainstream thought of people in the same class. Women came into the CP believing in the socialist politics they had learnt through different experiences. They had all rejected conventional thought and had openly become involved in socialist politics from an early age. They were now ready to make a commitment to a unique political organization that was active in several key areas in Scotland.

Communist Party life: 1920s–1930s

From its formation the CP needed to make an impact and win new members, especially in working-class organizations. It tried to influence youth groups and approached those in the Socialist Sunday School by selling papers like the *Sunday Worker*.

The increasing number of local activists the party produced could have a lasting effect on the young people who came into contact with them. The disposition of a friend's parents or person who was well-known in the community could shape the outlook of young people. Party members seemed to dedicate their lives to high profile campaigns on political and social issues like Cambuslang, where the party had taken root:

> The old man, Andy Mackie, wasn't an intellectual. He was an old miner who had worked hard all his life and [was] a really down-to-earth man who did all the knocking [at] doors, chalking [on] the pavement, speaking. He did everything, he was a one man Communist Party ... he was totally honest, respected by everyone who knew him, even his *enemies* ... that had a big effect on me.[78]

This aspect of party work may have been more impressive to female members. Community work was a more identifiable environment for women, for they were less likely to be involved in industrial organization and struggle, especially in Scotland where there was limited scope for women's employment.[79] For the first generation of communist women, the neighbourhood was their base. If the class war was obvious in a traditional industrial environment with workers pitched against management then these divisions were equally clear to communists dealing with housing problems or fighting for amenities in their locality where poverty was often widespread. All the women interviewed who came into the party before the Second World War were active in the social sphere and it is important to recognize how much of their socialist activity was applied in this area. It was also a logical step for those who wanted a radical and actively committed party not confined to parliamentary politics but based in the community as the ILP in Scotland had been at its strongest.

The CP in Fife

In the 1920s the party cultivated a strong membership base in mining towns in Fife. This developed into a considerable political force, as in other industrial areas in Scotland, for example Lanarkshire, where mining was also dominant and where communists were elected to the parish and town councils despite opposition from the Catholic Church and Orange and Masonic organizations.[80] Inevitably, Fife remained a stronghold during the 1926 General Strike. It was in this year that Mary Docherty, much influenced by her father's political activity, joined the YCL. The miners' brutal defeat made a lasting impression on her:

> Well, I hadn't much activity during the General Strike, it was just the end of the General Strike that I joined the party and I wasn't actively involved until later on. This place, it was like a death because there werenae pit horns or nothing and everything was silent and you were wondering what was wrong with it. And nae transport [was] allowed in or out of Cowdenbeath; there was pickets put on every entrance and outway, and it was only medical and foodstuff that was actually allowed in. Every organization in the town and union and trades council formed themselves into councils of action and they met every day to discuss what their next step was going to be and there was big meetings held both in the public park and marches held all the time. After the General Strike was finished the miners still stayed out on strike and the Fife miners didnae go back for a month after the other miners went back in other places; they were that disgusted at having to go back, the way they had to go back that they … to be rebellious, a month longer than the other areas.[81]

In Fife the party organized children at an early age. In Lumphinnans, the

YCL organized young people, and party members like Bob Selkirk, a miner who later served on the town council in Cowdenbeath, encouraged them. There was a lot of activity in this area with several youth groups and the growing influence of the party, which supported children who decided to challenge the traditional Victoria Day holiday and who organized a school strike to win May Day instead.

> The YCLers were supposed to be responsible for children you see, so they helped us with meetings and chalking up the slogans. The night before the school strike, on the Monday night, May Day was on the Tuesday and on the Monday night some of our bairns from Cowdenbeath went with me, and we went to Lochgelly and we chalked up from Lochgelly right doon through Lumphinnans to Cowdenbeath 'School strike, May Day for a schools strike', 'School strike for a holiday' you ken 'Children's holiday, May Day, School strike' we done that. We went to the school gates on the May Day to see how many children were off the school and asking them not to go into school, some of the YCLers went in the morning and that. Anyway the schools strike you couldnae say was 100 per cent because you couldn't expect all the bairns to come out because we couldn't get in touch. But anyway it was 50 per cent, you would say, successful because the next year when the Fife education authority were discussing the school holidays for the next year, May Day was put down for all these areas where we had been on strike, they all got May Day for a holiday, and they've had it ever since.[82]

Once communists won seats on Lochgelly town council and members on the Fife education authority, the use of the strap was restricted, better school meals were provided and May Day was recognized as a permanent holiday.[83]

In Scotland the YCL was primarily a social organization to bring young people together through various outings and collective campaigning. Isa Porte, who lost her father in the First World War when she was seven and her mother in a flu epidemic soon after, found the camaraderie she craved in its political activities.

> My friend Jessie that worked in the work I was in, in upholstery work, invited the girls to a ramble in Calderwood Glen near East Kilbride before it was a town and four of us went to the ramble

3. Glasgow May Day, 3 May 1933. CP platform. From left to right: Aitken Ferguson (back to camera), Marion Henery, Rose Kerrigan, unknown, Nell Kelly, Evans (Blantyre) and Hugh McDiarmid.

and I liked the company and I joined the Young Communist League from then. The others didn't but I did. ... Well, we had education classes, which I found very difficult. We had maybe a party member who was a bit of an educationalist, talking about money value and these sort of things and about politics generally. And we went on rambles; we enjoyed ourselves as well as being studious; we chalked pavements and were always in the anti-war sort of thing. That was it really. We had this club – the British Workers Sports Federation, which we all joined and a swimming club, had a camp at East Kilbride and rambles. Things that young people like.[84]

The CP in the Vale of Leven

In the early 1930s, the CP won elections to the county council, a continuation of its strength from the district council where it had six councillors.[85] There was a strong concentration of women workers in the Vale and no predominant skilled male working-class culture in the community. Thus, family ties were stronger, resulting in a greater social identity and awareness that politicized people.

The CP in the Vale of Leven mobilized people to fight for improved housing and sanitary provisions. There was a close working relationship, most of the time, at local level with the ILP and Labour Party and this was maintained between the wars with the three parties gaining a majority of seats on the council. Dan O'Hare, an engineer whose parents came from County Armagh in Northern Ireland, was a communist county councillor who served first on the Cardross parish council and then on the Dumbarton county council. Continually active and holding regular meetings with other councillors at the fountain on a Friday night, he went around the area with his horse and fruit cart dealing with people's problems. One of the council's successes was to build a long overdue sewerage system for the area, which was a cause for celebration in the CP and other left-wing parties that controlled the council.[86]

It was only natural that in the Vale of Leven there was a high level of activity in working-class organizations and that those born in the 1930s would be readily influenced by family members who were involved in social or political groups including the CP, which had become established along with older organizations such as the cooperative movement. A rich culture of labour movement groups offered different levels of involvement in social or political activity.[87] Yet, there still had to be a reason to choose the YCL and CP over the other parties that were active on the left, especially where there *was* a choice, as in the Vale of Leven:

> We never seemed to have very much and you could see the difference between the haves and have nots. I just felt we had to change society and thought the Communist Party was the most likely. When I was a wee lassie and there were elections going on, you were shouting for the Labour Party, 'Vote! Vote! Vote! for Davy Kirkwood' or whoever was the person but I was never ever attracted to the Labour Party … never. I joined the YCL probably when I was about 19 and from then on it was just a natural progression to joining the Communist Party, I was quite convinced that the Communist Party was the party that could change society.[88]

By the 1930s the party had made an impact on the left and had stabilized its membership, but the Labour establishment still shunned it. Apart from the Labour Party in some areas, the CP seemed the only party of the left campaigning among communities, especially since the ILP's disaffiliation from the Labour Party in 1931 had hastened its demise. This was when the CP developed its work on national and international issues.

The fight against fascism

As fascism spread in Europe the British Union of Fascists tried to recruit more people through public rallies and public meetings. In Scotland they had limited success. They concentrated their efforts in Aberdeen where they met regular anti-fascist opposition. CP members faced fines and imprisonment for disrupting fascist meetings, which they regularly did.[89] From 1936 to 1939 the local leader of the BUF, Chambers-Hunter,[90] tried unsuccessfully to expand membership in Aberdeen. The CP had already established a base in the city and women like Jean Lennox, Nora Williamson and Nan Cooney were involved soon after its formation. The YCL used social events to attract youth. Here young people could sing, dance and get cheap refreshments:

> I went along to a social of the YCL and of course [they] were very poor and they rented a room at the top of a building in 17 St Nicholas Street at that time, which is now demolished I think, and they had socials there and you used to get tea and what they called sinkers, a sinker was a great big ginger cake with raisins in it, and we used to sing and dance and things like that. But the thing that attracted me to the YCL was I thought how brave they were and it seemed so romantic to me and this drew me to the YCL, it wasnae any political consciousness or any formed idea, it wasn't Marxism or anything like that, it was really I thought this was so romantic to be fighting for working people in this way.[91]

As with all active YCL branches, *Challenge* was sold on the streets and there was a tradition of open-air agitation that was carried on by the party and could inspire people to join:

> and there were meetings in the Market Stance on a Sunday night and you would go along there and listen to all the different orators and there was a sort of cleavage in the party I think at that time even and there was a very famous family called the Shepherds and there was quite a few of them in the party and some of them used to speak in the Market Stance and Bob Cooney used to speak in the Market Stance and I think that Bob Cooney's oratory was one of the

> things that drew me to the party because he could explain everything so well and relate political events to the international scene.[92]

The Market Stance was the centre of the party's public activity and from where it regularly opposed fascists who tried to arrange meetings there. It was the meeting point for distributing anti-fascist literature and finding out from sympathizers how to oppose the fascists' public appearances.[93]

The Spanish Civil War became the major issue for communist parties throughout Europe, with campaigns to aid the republic from 1935.[94] The impression that the defeat of the republican government in Spain left was great. It was the first major international issue of which many CP members were deeply aware because regular reports came back via party speakers or publications. There was also the knowledge that some party members from Scotland had gone over to fight for the republic.

Women were directed towards collecting money and knitting for Spain. The need to support the fight against fascism was seen as urgent and as obvious as supporting peace in Vietnam would be 30 years later. Through Scottish CP members who had volunteered to fight, communists were involved in direct conflict with fascism in Spain. Such solidarity was reminiscent of aid to the young Soviet republic. It was the first of many actions of internationalism allied to supporting the foreign policy of the Soviet Union, which had changed dramatically in 1935 at the Comintern's seventh congress in Moscow, where some Scottish members were present. The new policy elicited a cold response from the Labour Party with the exception of the dissident Labour League of Youth,[95] some of whose members were so disillusioned at the end of this period that in 1939 they jumped over to the YCL in Scotland.[96] It was not just a question of there being a difference between the two parties; the CP was seemingly the only party that *cared* about the immediate prospects if the fascists advanced in Spain and Europe. The International Brigade brought together people from all countries who were often from their respective communist parties and who knew that defeat could only mean deeper conflict ahead. May Halfpenny (later Annan) joined the party as the war was ending:

> At that time, they were bringing Spanish refugees, children, over from Spain and there was quite a movement in Clydebank but the YCL … we knew a war was coming and we were against the

> war and we circularized all the organizations to hear a speaker from the YCL, the women's guilds – and the women's guilds in those days were big, big meetings, there were a lot of women at it and I didnae really have any training, or anything. The party is great for just telling you to do a thing and you go and do it and I addressed quite a number of meetings at that time. ... I remember Harry Pollitt, we had a meeting in the Clydebank town hall, again it was a huge meeting, and Harry Pollit said 'if you don't stop the bombs falling on Madrid they will fall on Clydebank' – which *what prophetic words, you can nae believe it, that it could be said.*[97]

The pertinence of Pollitt's words would become evident to the people of Clydebank within a few years.[98] Of events in the 1930s it would be the enduring sacrifice of young men who had gone to Spain to fight, many of whom had died, that would especially move future generations of party women. At the time women were active in raising funds for Spain and children in the aforementioned organizations were obviously influenced by the emphasis on this campaign.[99] The sacrifice in this harsh and brutal conflict left no room for romantic notions, but endless respect for selfless courage. The Scottish contingent accounted for 20 per cent of the total volunteers from Britain and in composition the communist contribution from Scotland was proportionately large with 60 per cent of the 476 volunteers being in the CP.[100]

In 1937 women accounted for only 16 per cent of the membership in the CP, 364 out of 2318 members in Scotland.[101] Women's sections were just being developed and Jenny Hyslop was put in charge of women's work. Of the 70 party branches 49 were in Glasgow, Lanarkshire and Fife, the latter having a membership of 305[102] – about 13 per cent of the total Scottish party membership. There were 41 factory branches, 19 of which were in Glasgow and only one each in Edinburgh and Perth, though they increased in later years.[103] The percentage of women in the CP in Scotland never rose above one-third, a level achieved in the postwar period. One wonders whether it would have been lower without the socialist politics and community activity in the labour movement that developed young women's political awareness in the absence of being industrial workers. Importantly, secular organizations, especially the Socialist Sunday School, laid a distinct path to the CP for women in the interwar period. It was in these organizations, as we shall see from women's subsequent experience of the party structures and the pressure of social norms, that for the first and last time they *were* equal.

The legacy of the Socialist Sunday School

Young women who joined the YCL in the 1940s during the Second World War were influenced by a generation that had been involved in struggles during the First World War and the pioneering years of the party. There was regular campaigning by the party, particularly in the west and in Fife. Street meetings and weekend rallies were put on to encourage the membership and win over potential recruits:

> There was a big rally in the Regal cinema in 1944, I can't remember whether it was March or April, and Bob Horne was one of the main speakers. ... There were probably all kinds of other people there but it was a *massive* meeting, that cinema in Sauchiehall Street, probably about 3000 seats it could take and it was mobbed. And I was so inspired by listening to the speeches and all that they were coming down the aisles with the membership forms and I took one and signed up and that was me, and that was me joining and I was only 15. So that was me a member of the Young Communist League – branch Maryhill.[104]

Despite YCL growth, the influence and activity of the schools was still crucial to many people destined for the CP.[105] Having always been pacifist, the Socialist Sunday School now had to decide whether to support the Soviet Union in the war. It decided against participation in the Anglo–Russian demonstration in October 1941 'as doing so would commit the union to a pro-war attitude'.[106] However, this decision was soon reversed.[107] Messages of support were also sent to the people of the Soviet Union and £5 was sent from Maryhill branch to the Soviet embassy with 'fraternal greetings to the children of the USSR'.[108] The aggregate meeting of adults decided not to take a decision on the nature of the war and, though agreeing that Russia was a socialist state, it was stated that 'war could not be justified even in defence of a socialist state'.[109] It is interesting to note that the heart of the issue was the war and there was no wholesale opposition to the nature of the Soviet state and a film show at Maryhill of Soviet films confirms a natural sympathy.[110]

Even as the numbers of schools and children attending declined there was still a strong political link with the ILP[111] and a natural link with the CP. It was this link with the CP that no doubt encouraged the Catholic Church in Pollokshaws to forbid its child members to attend the school.[112] In the postwar period and at the height of the cold war there is evidence of stronger links with organizations with views not hostile to the CP. The YCL choir[113] and some party branches were still involved with the schools. Having suffered losses there seemed to be a stabilizing of membership in remaining schools[114] and in the Gorbals the school received support from the CP women's section there.[115] The management committee decided to urge the national executive committee to support the National Peace Council campaign to ban the atom bomb[116] while there was a resolution sent condemning Labour MP Woodrow Wyatt for advocating the use of the atom bomb in the event of war with Russia.[117]

Children were encouraged to adopt pen pals through the Scottish–USSR Society[118] and the Women's International Democratic Federation urged support for a conference on children and peace in Berlin in September 1951. Later that year there was a speaker on a 'visit to Poland' and in the new year on the Berlin Peace Festival.[119]

In 1952 a move to support International Women's Day in London was defeated,[120] though an amendment was carried that it go to the schools for a decision with the result that five were in favour and three against,[121] this perhaps showing that the management committee was only out of touch when it was slightly conservative! They decided not to take part in the British Youth Festival but instead asked for a report.[122] In May the Socialist Sunday Schools marched with the disaffiliated Glasgow Trades Council, which was seen to have been too dominated by the CP and so was reconstituted.[123] May Day greetings were sent to the Labour Party, Trades Council, ILP and CP and there was correspondence from the World Federation of Democratic Youth, a body the CP supported, forwarding its constitution.[124] There were regular meetings with the British–Polish Friendship Society, which showed the film *Young Chopin*[125] and a delegate meeting agreed that a party of children from the schools in Nitshill and Pollok could attend a CP social.[126]

Later in the 1950s there was still cultural activity and socialist politics directly pertinent to the day, such as a talk on the Suez Canal; delegates from the Labour Party, CP, Trades Council, the YCL, the Woodcraft

4. Springburn Socialist Sunday School group, 1959.

Folk and the Labour Youth section attended the schools' anniversary in 1957.[127] The YCL Choir still did the rounds[128] and even ex-CP members contributed, with Harry McShane agreeing to take classes for the youth section.[129] As a speaker he joined people like Fred Reid who talked on literature[130] and Rab Chalmers who delivered talks on socialism.[131] At a centenary demonstration for Robert Smillie in Larkhall in June 1957 the school presented extracts from Smillie's life while Abe Moffat, president of the Scottish NUM and a CP member, spoke on 'The Scottish Miner's are proud of Smillie's great work'.[132]

In the west of Scotland, where it was always stronger, the Socialist Sunday School was an important organization for many communists and it was respected for its equality and non-discrimination in gender and political terms. There were few attempts to exclude or discriminate against the CP and the causes it supported. In the postwar period, perhaps because of disproportionate influence from CP parents, the Socialist Sunday School was decidedly sympathetic to the Eastern Bloc and was susceptible to appeals from organizations associated with the CP or Soviet Union. That there were not even protests about these activities from other parties is initially surprising though it probably reflects more the respect for the Socialist Sunday Schools and a desire not to incur their disfavour.

Finally, if one looks at the gender division at the schools from 1940 one finds exceptionally high female attendance. Govanhill School, opened in 1909,[133] was in an area of one of the strongest CP branches in Glasgow in later years. A breakdown of the attendance roll from 1940 to 1955 illustrates the attendance of young women. From 1941 to 1950 girls and young women accounted for more than half the members in attendance with 26 of the 38 in attendance in 1946/7 and at times nearly three-quarters, with 30 of the 45 members for the 1947/8 session.[134] In the 1951/2 session there was an average of 30–34 children in attendance, 21 girls, in the 1952/3 session, 25 children, of which 15 were girls, in the 1953/4 session, 22 children, 14 girls and in the 1954/5 session 16 children, 8 girls.[135] The boys had reached an equal number. The school closed in November 1956.[136] As a long established branch, there is no reason to believe that Govanhill was exceptional, it was in a very strong working-class area of Glasgow and had been one of the longer lasting branches.

Having a membership where the ratio of female to male was equal, or in this instance higher, and in an organization that preached socialism, may be the lasting feature of the Socialist Sunday Schools. Most importantly was the effect on girls and young women whose socialist consciousness was developed with young boys and men in the same socialist institutions and where they were equal. On entering the adult world and the world of work, this unique environment would be lost forever.

Conclusion

For the last 30 years there has been a debate about the effects of the CP and whether or not its existence diverted socialists in Britain from following a truly socialist path. The drawn out negotiations, conflicts, doubts and resignations that occurred during that period should leave one in no doubt about how well scrutinized this decision was. This had come about first after having rejected purely formal parliamentary politics as represented by the Labour Party and the non-Marxist ILP left, and second by rejecting syndicalism and industrial militancy as forwarded by the SLP and some smaller sects whose limitations were obvious to all by the end of the 40-hour strike. Arguably, those active on the Clyde had the benefits of a diversity of groups and opinions that enriched their environment more than anywhere else in Britain. That there was an indigenous deficiency in not having developed a strong Marxist theoretical basis for the party's existence or a polemical tradition is rather obvious despite the proximity in activity and empathy of the SLP to the internationalism the dissident groups of the Second International displayed. Indeed, whatever its major faults and volte-face in the future, the CP in Britain, especially after the Second World War, would produce many noted trade union leaders and academic scholars.

The majority of women (or men) who attended a Socialist Sunday School joined the CP. Many went into the Labour Party. The women who joined the CP were used to being part of a minority anyway. They were a minority by being in the Socialist Sunday School and they were to remain in a minority party, but they seem to be the one group that continued to engage in political activity after leaving the Socialist Sunday School and joining the CP both before and after 1945. Party members still appreciated and utilized the Socialist Sunday School even when it was on the decline. Here was a legacy that began at the end of the nineteenth century and benefited the CP until the schools' successor closed in the early 1970s.

That the CP was less successful with the Young Pioneers in Scotland may be because the Socialist Sunday School was so well established that it rendered the Pioneers superfluous.[137] The Socialist Sunday School predated the revolutionary movement in Russia: it was a home-grown established asset that the CPGB would have been mistaken to have interfered with or ignored. Instead, it wisely kept a respectful distance by formally disassociating itself from it – a move that merely urged a positive response from the Sunday School board for them to continue sending their children to the schools.[138] After all, one could join the YCL as a teenager.

As in the later politics of the CP during the Popular Front period when the party offered the schools formal assistance and was refused,[139] the schools brought together children from all political households of the left. The adults were so dedicated to the schools that they worked together running the organization and taught the children irrespective of their own political differences in their respective parties.[140] The absence of any one doctrine being imposed on the children, which the CP could have decided to do, led to a unity and camaraderie that was invaluable. Respect for the schools was widespread on the left. The CP respected them because they predated its birth and honoured their independence because some party members had benefited from their teachings.

CP attention to education, especially formal Marxist education, made it seem like a continuation of the schools. There had been a natural empathy for Marxism in the schools, which respected and accepted Marx's contribution to socialist thought and the activities of the next generation of his followers like Liebknecht, Luxemburg and Mehring[141] from the German socialist movement, and lessons on the importance of the Paris Commune.[142] The YCL concentrated on practical social activity and did not expect any pre-knowledge of political theory; so, when people joined from the schools, there was no sudden rupture. The YCL, which one might expect to appeal strongly to women, was a logical next step, as was the party after that.

Having been involved in a small organization that rejected religion, encouraged its members to question authority, treated all people as equals and was 'different' from established social organizations for children, the experience of being against the tide and proposing a revolutionary philosophy inevitably led some women to communism. Organizing as a strong minority against the stream and firm in their belief partially insulated them from the enormous task of defeating British capitalism. They could find safety, comfort and comradeship among the small like-minded membership. At the schools they had been instructed in the precepts and formal drill of the agenda at meetings that young men from the schools might get from their work and an allied union involvement but that young women were less likely to encounter. Consequently, no one sex had an advantage over the other. The CP rules and discipline might just as well have been the elder of the Socialist Sunday School. The Socialist Sunday School was not a seminary for Marxism, at least not in any formal sense, but it stayed consistent to its socialist politics and did not dilute them at any time.

One might also be able to see how the Leninist theory of an elite party with a small dedicated leadership might seem acceptable to those who had belonged to an organization that educated its members and propounded socialism. It adhered strongly and consistently to supporting organizations with which it had always been associated through the First World War, the Second World War and the cold war periods. It did not deviate from its aims and its survival surely depended on staying true to its principles and not disillusioning past and present members who were its constituency. Finally, there was the one enduring benefit of the Socialist Sunday School that was taken for granted: there was no gender discrimination or role play that was deliberately or blindly imposed. For the first and last time women were treated as equals in a political organization.

Chapter 3

The Experience of Women Activists in the Party Structure, 1945–60

> The party developed me, enormously so. I always found the Communist Party a great support and definitely it developed me otherwise I can't explain how I could have done the things … I mean you thought you were right and that what you were doing was trying to better the conditions of the working class whatever way you were. That was the confidence you had.[1]

I need to emphasize that the women I interviewed did not see gender and the role of women as a reason to join the CP. Most joined it because they saw it as a strong political body that might change society *en bloc*. Their primary aim was to fight for socialism. Although some might have felt gender constraints, they were really interested in a collective approach to the class struggle and building the CP into the vanguard party in Britain. The issues that were being campaigned for in factories, working-class organizations and the community at large were their main concerns. The experiences of women who joined the party between 1920 and 1944 were noticeably different from those who joined later. They were still of a generation that felt the social constraints that had existed long before industrialization in Scotland and the rural and religious influences that compounded their restriction. One might subdivide the women who joined after 1945 into those who joined between 1945 and 1960 and those who came in after 1960, for the 1960s brought pronounced social changes that affected young people and were immediately reflected in the YCL. Yet, there were similarities in women's expectations of the CP and in the role they played irrespective of the time of their involvement.[2]

The party leadership did not deliberately confine women who joined the CP to any one area of work. Depending on their circumstances, they could decide whether they were content to play a role in the branch or whether they wanted to try to make a contribution to the party's higher structures. Not all male party members wanted to advance beyond the branches, but family life, domestic priorities and a limited initial awareness among party members of how to solve these problems did impose restrictions on women in the party.

From 1945

During the Second World War the CP reached its peak in membership with 56,000 in 1942,[3] yet there was a steady decline from the end of the war and by June 1947 it was down to 38,579,[4] followed by a recovery to 40,616 by 1949.[5] In Scotland the membership stood at 6869 in 1946 with women accounting for 22 per cent at 1521,[6] a very slight increase in the year 1945/6 despite the decrease in employed women.[7] People greeted the party's association with the Soviet Union positively for the first time, due in no small way to a recognition of the Soviet Union's sacrifice in war and to the work communists carried out in the localities and factories, though this did not always reflect the party's national policy.[8] With 158 party branches and 54 factory and pit committees in Scotland, a strong base had been built up since the late 1930s and the reduction in unemployment.[9]

After the 1945 general election great changes were anticipated from the incoming Labour government, whose large majority was an expression of support for measures it was hoped would leave the poverty of the 1930s and the horrors of the war behind. The CP shared in this enthusiasm but soon realized that the reforms being put through were not going to shift society fundamentally towards socialism, arguing that the radical changes merely strengthened capitalism through restructuring the economy. This analysis soon threw up in party literature the call for a more democratic nationalization and a greater redistribution in wealth, a call that emphasized the role that Parliament was to play in achieving this aim.

The British Road to Socialism, the new CP manifesto published in 1951, called for socialist nationalization of the major industries.[10] The aim was still to get rid of capitalism, but now with the emphasis on parliamentary changes and alliances with the working class. In the light of the cold war, the party's anti-US stance now foresaw possibilities within the structure of the British state to fight for a British identity against a perceived invasion of US influence and culture. *The British Road to Socialism* may also be seen as the policy the Soviet Union needed, for it stressed the need to fight off the most virulently hostile aspects of cold war propaganda against the Eastern Bloc. To counter the US military presence in Britain, the manifesto stressed that the party was fighting for the restoration of parliament's control of financial, economic and military affairs.[11]

Whatever its merits or faults, the 1951 edition, which was reprinted six times and sold 200,000 copies in Britain,[12] was a well presented and articulate document that critics on the left could not easily dismiss. Likewise, from 1945, the Scottish district came out with a radical economic programme for Scotland that emphasized the state of the traditional industries and the need for greater investment and public ownership. It was stated that, in war work, employment 'in many cases has meant improvements in conditions, and the issue of equal pay for equal work comes sharply to the fore',[13] a call for a measure that had been brought to the forefront of trade union activity during the war.[14] It was a measure that the party continually reiterated[15] after the war, included in its programme *The Socialist Road for Britain* in 1949[16] and would fight strongly for over the next four decades.

Scottish CP policy on the Scottish economy had developed from an optimistic outlook that declared 'never before in the history of Scotland has a more hopeful period opened in front of the Scottish people as a whole.'[17] There was a programme of demands after Labour's 1945 election victory[18] and a more developed critique in the late 1940s with the publication of John Gollan's book *Scottish Prospect*.[19] Gollan reiterated the danger of over-reliance on heavy capital goods industries and the lack of new light industries,[20] and provided a detailed breakdown of the state of industries in Scotland and what measures were needed to diversify and improve productivity with more worker participation. Critical of the Labour government,[21] Gollan saw the need for a reform movement that echoed those of the eighteenth and nineteenth centuries to achieve devolution.[22] The momentum had increased by 1949 with half a million people having signed the Scottish Covenant calling for more self-government and a Scottish parliament[23] and from the 1950s the party put more emphasis on the needs of a Scottish economy with a national political identity.[24] This had been a long-called-for measure from the party as well as the nationalists on the fringe.[25]

There was a call for 'a voice for women and young people'[26] and, to prove that the CP was cognizant of women, for a Scottish parliament with a women's committee.[27] In its submission to the Royal Comission, the CP's Scottish committee stated that more than 70,000 men and women were out of work,[28] that there was annual emigration of 20,000 men and women each year and that the 'dread disease' of tuberculosis was responsible for a high death rate, especially among women.[29] Suggested solutions to these problems were a 40-hour week, more holidays with full pay and, as stated, equal pay for equal work, which 'would be the rule throughout industry and the professions'.[30]

From the new programme and the radical reforms it forwarded, it was clear that if the CP was no longer calling for revolution, it was still pressing for strong socialist policies. These had been strenuously worked out and argued for in the party with a noticeable maturity in its approach to specific economic issues. The Scottish district was not just supplanting nationalism with socialism, but urging men and women to fight for better conditions and for a Britain where 'the bosses will be swept aside and the workers will take control'.[31] Over the next 30 years the CP would strengthen its calls for a Scottish parliament, though in 1950 Abe Moffat failed to get a commitment to devolution with the defeat by 234–78 of an amendment to a resolution for a Scottish parliament at the STUC annual congress.

The cold war

The late 1940s saw Western governments lose sympathy for the Soviet Union. Pro-Soviet governments in eastern Europe confirmed the divisions in Europe, while the USA used Marshall Aid and the Truman Doctrine to support its allies in western Europe. The CP saw the latter as relinquishing independence to US foreign policy.[32]

In Scotland, the cold war did not generate violence against communists, as it did in the USA with McCarthyism and the 'murdered' Rosenbergs,[33] but antagonism was not uncommon and the media were definitely anti-communist:

> At the time I stood as a candidate there was considerable anti-communist feeling because the *Amethyst* warship had been attacked by the Chinese, I think on the Yangtze River, and so there was considerable animosity towards me from various people. One man, a sort of ex-colonial type who came to a meeting, challenged me on

> the issue of the *Amethyst* and said, did I not feel ashamed to be standing there as a communist candidate when brave British sailors had been killed by communist action?[34]

Meetings were disrupted and some authorities attempted to stop communists renting public halls.

In 1949 a deputation from the CP's Glasgow committee lobbied the magistrates' committee to be allowed to use public halls for Sunday public meetings,[35] but still faced a ban. This was after being refused applications for a licence and having to resort to legal action. The party was refused a licence in December 1949 and CP women with sandwich boards had led a protest at the time.[36] A similar situation arose again in 1951 when the party accused the magistrates of acting in a political manner.[37] The change in the council's attitude to the CP occurred after district council elections in 1949 saw the Labour Party just retain control with a majority of one over the other parties,[38] which were mainly Progressives (really Conservatives). They were virulent anti-communists and with the two votes of the ex-officio, unelected, dean of guild and the deacon convenor they elected a non-Labour Party lord provost.[39] In July 1950 the lord provost hosted a meeting to institute the Scottish Society for Friendship with the Spanish People, which, though claiming to be non-political, called for full diplomatic recognition of the regime. Present were a representative from the Spanish embassy, businessmen, Progressive councillors, Labour MPs Alice Cullen (for the Gorbals) and John McGovern (Shettleston) and Labour councillor Mary McAllister.[40]

Outside a demonstration of mostly communists picketed the meeting with placards calling those inside 'Franco's Friends'. In Edinburgh the Trades Council banned the CP from participating in May Day[41] and even areas like Clydebank suffered hostility. 'I remember Jimmy Paterson … and we were gathered all around about but … *oh my God* we got *stoned.* … Aye we did and at that time they broke the windows in the party office a few times as well, threw bricks through.'[42] The party's most celebrated casualty in Scotland at this time was Willie Gallacher who had been a communist MP since 1935 and who lost his West Fife seat in the 1950 general election.[43] In July the CP was kicked out of the National Covenant Committee on which it had been represented.[44]

This all occurred as the war in Korea was developing, caused, in the party's analysis, by a breach of the peace by American imperialism.[45] Yet, it is testament to 30 years of party activity in Scotland that the most permanent effects of this period were that the Labour Party and trade unions at British level took measures to disenfranchise communists from holding office in certain unions. The party's ability to ride the storm of establishment opposition at this time may have had something to do with its influence in the engineering, shipbuilding and mining industries and their respective unions, most notably the NUM, and some communities. Certainly, party members immediately attempted to give a political explanation for events and when war did break out they were visible at parades and in forwarding 'Hands Off Korea' resolutions, which in Scotland were commended as a good counterattack to the public's perception of the war.[46] But even these solid efforts could not stop a certain amount of isolation, such as the ban the STUC imposed on the British Peace Committee.[47] The committee, along with the CP, was also banned from using public halls in Glasgow (and that year the magistrates refused even to give an explanation).[48] More seriously for the party's Scottish district, the STUC disaffiliated the Glasgow Trades Council in 1951 for going against congress policy and wound it up the following year for supporting (by a majority of 134) the call for the Five-Power Peace Pact.[49] As part of the World Peace Congress the British Peace Committee involved many CP members who campaigned for the World Peace Council's proposal for a Five-Power Peace Pact,[50] helping them collect 1,250,000 signatures, and also the Stockholm Peace Appeal for banning the atom bomb,[51] which collected 1,300,000.[52] The issue of peace would be an integral part of many party women's involvement,[53] including CND in later years.

Though there were defeats and some isolation in the STUC and unions, the TGWU imposed a ban on communists during this period.[54] There was always the CP's strength in the Scottish NUM. The NUM conference, whose executive committee comprised ten CP and ten Labour Party members,[55] condemned these anti-communist measures and retained a strong left wing that tried to counter the right wing in the STUC.

The Young Communist League

The YCL instilled a spirit of comradeship that had followed on from other youth organizations, though by the 1940s political activity was more intense and there was less naïveté about the tasks ahead. Rambles and socializing were still important, but the need to build the YCL into a politicized mass youth body would overtake them. Young communists were also aware of the work the party did in numerous areas, as well as campaigning on issues such as support for the Soviet Union and for liberation movements, which the youth would learn more about from the 1950s. But the cohesiveness of the earlier youth organizations and the communal activities that had been a part of youth social life continued and were still central, though a foretaste of what to expect in the branches was the emphasis on education, which was an important part of the YCL curriculum: 'It was at Marxist classes, we attended classes; it was expected of us that we should attend Marxist classes and day schools and weekend schools even, where, as I say, all these lecturers came and spoke to us. ... All sorts of people came and spoke to us.'[56] YCL branches also engaged in the labour movement's traditional activities such as the annual May Day march. The party always tried to have organized and well presented sections, especially on the largest march, in Glasgow, where contingents converged on the main march from all over the city.[57] The end of the war signalled optimistic expectations for the YCL, which, like the party, gained new members.

However, YCL membership never really took off, even within the party's limited expectations. The YCL Scottish district, along with Lancashire and London, could boast high sales of special issues of *Challenge* and in 1948 weekly sales were 12,500. There was a British membership of 2000, which was up 25 per cent[58] and this reached 3543 in 1949.[59] In Scotland not enough priority was given to building up the organization[60] and by 1952 there were only 673 YCL members. This was up from the 481 of 1950,[61] but it was still hard to recruit and sales of *Challenge* were low.[62] The YCL had a similar structure to the party, with committees at area and district level, so some women developed their political skills there through regular attendance and getting the YCL involved in broad-based social campaigns.

> You were always expected to work hard in the movement if you were on the Glasgow Committee or Scottish Committee of the League and we used to discuss politics, the political situation. The first item on the agenda was the political situation and each one of us took it in turn to introduce each week the political report which was then discussed among all the committee.[63]

From the late 1940s to the mid-1950s the party at the British level failed to foresee that, by keeping their traditional characteristics, children's and youth organizations would be less appealing than they had been. Youths between the ages of 14 and 21 were no longer entering into an adult life of marriage and family, for more opportunities in employment, better wages, education and lifestyle were slowly opening up the generation gap and leading to new and freer social activities.

Better economic circumstances in the postwar period only partly explain the CP's strength in Scotland in the 1950s and 1960s and any stabilizing of membership. Also, compared with the situation in Europe in the 1930s, with the growth of the Non-Aligned Movement and more countries with links with the Soviet Union, members internationally felt more confidence in the prospect of positive change. It was interesting to meet people from British colonies who were fighting for independence, and who introduced an alternative perspective.

> He was a doctor on the ward and at night we'd go out for a walk at nine o'clock when I'd finished. And there were new housing schemes in Edinburgh, big new housing schemes built and he says 'If Egyptian workers had houses like this they'd think they had socialism' and the other thing I can remember, he talked about the Soviet Union and his father was very influenced by the Soviet Union. His father was obviously quite a large landowner, grew cotton, and the old man had been to the Soviet Union and had been very impressed by what he saw there. [64]

There was a small but active YCL in Edinburgh and a diverse and growing student branch that attracted teenagers in the early 1960s and offered the contrasts of different nationalities' experience. The cosmopolitanism that university life offered and the influence of anti-colonial and socialist politics strengthened political belief in a way that was different from that of large industrial working-class branches in other areas.

Culture: the YCL choir

The YCL choir, which was founded in 1945, was very successful in Scotland and helped increase party influence. Jimmy Callan conducted the choir, which travelled widely in Britain and Europe, entering competitions and singing at international socialist music festivals, youth festivals and folk and cultural gatherings. Callan was involved with the Amalgamated Engineering Union choir in Glasgow and in late 1944 the party asked him to set up a YCL choir. After an initial disastrous meeting members were found: 'We went along the following Friday and about another five or six people turned up along with our two selves and the conductor. So that was the nucleus of the YCL choir and he handed us out Shostakovich's *Salute to Life*.'[65]

Callan had studied singing at the Academy of Music in Glasgow. The Orpheus was the most respected choir at that time so he took his new members along to show them what could be achieved. He taught the choir the tonic solfa music system so anyone popping along for the first time, perhaps expecting a sing-along, was introduced to a rigorous musical training and expected to work hard. Needless to say, those unprepared for such a commitment did not come back. Yet, nobody was ever turned away, for it was thought that everybody had a voice with which they could contribute something. A place could be found for anyone, not just YCL members, and soloists were encouraged – unlike the elitist Orpheus Choir, which held auditions to decide who was good enough to join them.

A good start for the choir was the contact made with composers Alan Bush and Rutland Broughton who were associated with the Workers' Music Association and who invited the choir to Edinburgh one summer. An unofficial festival was just being born and was presented as a more working-class alternative to the official festival; it would later become the more widely known Fringe Festival.

The choir entered its first Scottish Socialist Music Festival in 1947 and won first prize there in 1949.[66] It started having annual concerts. Paul Robeson and the 'Red' Dean of Canterbury attended their first one, which was held at St Andrew's Halls in Glasgow, and then another at the Usher Hall in Edinburgh in the same year. While visiting towns and villages at weekends, the choir members would engage in YCL and party propaganda work before the evening concert,[67] for they were determined to be seen to be doing their share of political work. However, much of its activity involved putting on regular concerts in Glasgow and throughout Scotland, and singing at trade union branches and factories to night-shift workers and Socialist Sunday Schools.[68] Not all choir members were in the YCL or party and naturally the composition changed, but it was a proud party institution with its own constitution,[69] and one that made its mark and was well appreciated for its musical ability. The choir went on to greater recognition in the 1950s when it won first place at various festivals and initially faced some hostility from the establishment during the cold war when the BBC insisted that left-wing organizations change their names:[70]

> they couldn't allow a CP organization to represent Scotland in the Festival of Britain. Anyone who won the Glasgow Festival was broadcast – any choir/singer could get a broadcast and we applied to be broadcasted and they said yes they would broadcast the choir if we changed our name, so we said 'no' we couldn't do that. So they said 'well we're sorry, we can't let you broadcast'.[71]

The party's national cultural committee sought to counteract the effect of American mass-produced entertainment, which it saw as undermining and cheapening indigenous culture.[72] As a cultural asset and great body for countering media hostility to communist politics, the YCL choir more than made up for some of the youth organization's deficiencies. During the 1950s it became the party's best-known institution and had a wide repertoire from around the world, including songs from the communist bloc. The Scottish party leadership recognized the choir's contribution, which was to raise the 'political consciousness of young people through Cultural Heritage',[73] and in 1953 stated that 'we cannot adequately express our appreciation for the very big contribution made by the YCL Choir to the work of the League and the Party.'[74] Callan's contribution was again recognized, as were those, among others, of Jim and Isobel Service. Jim Service later became the choir's conductor. This was also the period of its greatest success, playing at concerts throughout Britain and winning first prize at four Scottish music festivals in 1954.[75]

One of the most memorable appearances the choir made was at the bicentenary celebrations of the birth of Robert Burns on 25 January 1959 at St Andrew's Hall in Glasgow. More than 3000 people attended, with hundreds unable to get into what was probably the most successful single cultural concert put on by the CP in Scotland. It involved singing, theatre and speeches from party members and sympathetic artists.

In 1960 Callan moved on to form the Socialist Singers, for he felt he had spent enough time with the YCL choir. His influence on those close to him was obvious.[76] Whereas the party competed on highly unfavourable terms with nearly all institutions it faced – employers, state institutions, the Labour Party and some trade unions – the choir could prove its ability and high status over other choirs because success depended on the pure application and dedication of its members. Obviously, the wealthier elite choirs could afford more time and would have better facilities. But, allied to a cause in which they strongly believed and that took them around Britain and Europe, for a time the YCL choir became one of the best in Scotland.

Branch education

To retain its members the party had to start its education at a basic level in the branches and then offer advanced courses for potential leaders or cadres. This group numbered between 700 and 1000 in Scotland in 1948,[77] about 10–15 per cent of the membership. Party tutors regularly lectured to the branches. 'Willie Joss and Aitken Ferguson used to come down here on a Sunday morning and Dan always said, "You'd better go and you'll learn something." And I would go to the meeting and it would be a lecture on topical things that were happening.'[78] Aitken Ferguson had been a member of the Socialist Labour Party and was active in it along with Peter Kerrigan and Dan O'Hare and they had socialized as a group. Bill Joss had been educating party members in Scotland since the 1920s and was one of its most established and popular tutors, a role he continued until his death in the 1960s. The party was conscious of the lack of theory in the labour movement and saw this as a reason for the persistence of reactionary ideas. The education members received covered the basic theories of Marxism, dialectical materialism, political economy, the history of the British labour movement, contemporary works by Stalin, and official CPSU publications:

> there was a book issued by the Communist Party of the Soviet Union called *A Short History of the CPSU*, which everybody bought and of course there were chapters in it on dialectical materialism and historical materialism and, well you know that was an education. I mean I had no idea; you've got to understand our level of education. I hadn't heard of anything like that, even in the branch. Although we were always having education classes to try and help you, but that book was like a bible, it really was. I used to lie in bed and read it every night, it explained things, up until then I went against religion you know but that explained. It explained how what you might call evolution – I had never heard of anything like that and this book explained it all and it was really wonderful.[79]

Members gained their basic revolutionary theory by reading briefer, more popular works such as *The Communist Manifesto* and *The Origin of the Family, Private Property and the State*. The CP also provided works by writers like Emile Burns and Maurice Cornforth to make Marxism more accessible before the harder texts were tackled. There was thus an indigenous group of party theorists who could simplify and popularize

Marxism for education in the party. In the late 1940s Gallacher's *The Case for Communism* published by Penguin Books sold 100,000 copies, of which 65,000 were handled by the party bookshops.[80]

Teaching the dialectical process fundamentally convinced members of the truth of their cause and gave them the confidence to understand the processes involved in their lives, the economic bases of systems and a premise for arguing against and rejecting religion:

> Because you thought it was based on a material conception of life, that all life had sprung from some sort o' material, you nae longer believed in any sort of idealist conception o' mankind, so therefore it gave you this firm belief that because man had developed fae that stage and life had developed fae the amoeba stage probably, that inevitably there was this sort of progression of mankind and that inevitably, or so you thought at the time, it would lead to a better life and a more developed form of humanity.[81]

Not all women (or men) wanted to study in depth. The main priority for most party women who were not in full-time paid work was action on issues in their areas and having as much personal contact with people as they could. Those who were not involved in a trade union or were not used to public speaking, could feel reticent and unconfident at meetings:

> Well at first I used to not even speak at branch meetings and then I used to sit and think somebody was saying – it wasnae just right. And I said 'if I'm wrong they'll sort me out, I'll say what I think' and I did that and in our Cambuslang branch earlier on we had Mick McGahey,[82] you know who became a miners' leader. He was just a young man but he was doing a man's job down a pit and was very good. He encouraged the women. He'd say 'What is the women folk thinking about this?' In the branch he encouraged us to say what we thought too.[83]

A district and branch team headed by the propaganda secretary (the term was later changed) organized literature and a British-level central literature commission met monthly to direct work in the districts.[84] Each branch was expected to have a literature secretary and selling literature on stalls and in street sales was encouraged. A national syllabus guided education at all levels. It was continually updated and included detailed expositions of the party's policies and later *The British Road to Socialism*, which tutors would relate to branches. The party produced *Marxist Study Themes* – a series on various issues including a six-part study on *The British Road*. Its booklets, such as *The British State*, detailed aspects of the programme with contemporary examples[85] and explained it in more depth to members. The district committee kept and updated a list of approved speakers, and approved tutors were available to go to the branches.

The deeper theoretical works could seem complicated but were essential in widening members' understanding of how capitalism operated and the eventual inevitability of socialism. Once the prose was conquered, the works of other major figures were more accessible to members:

> It gave me an understanding of what Marx was actually getting at and showing how the problems of the world could be solved by economics. Some of it was over my head and it still is, I mean economics: I'm just inclined to shut off, somebody's throwing a lot of facts and figures at me. But on the whole I did find it, and particularly Lenin, I found he helped me a lot. *Lenin on Ireland* and *Lenin on Women*, those books.[86]

Women who wanted a Marxist education would be able to attend schools and devote (or sacrifice) more time to activity in the party's structures. Some were encouraged even though the time and effort might have meant more domestic inconvenience. There was also the human element – shyness, feeling intimidated by deep political tracts and the genuine fear of appearing in public.[87] 'I always shook like a *leaf* before I decided to speak but I always had something I wanted to say, some question I wanted to ask or something. So it was very difficult to get the confidence to speak, but I always felt I ought to.'[88] When the theory was presented away from the branch at a residential weekend school where women could feel less inhibited, they seemed to accept and even enjoy it. Having to face criticism from national tutors could put members off, whereas at residential schools they met in a more informal atmosphere, either at schools for women specifically or for the party cadre. Here they knew what to expect and a greater camaraderie often emerged:

> we went to one doon in Hastings and I must say I thoroughly enjoyed it and was instrumental in one of the young women who

> were there who was very reticent and didnae mix and I was the one who broke the mould; before we were finished she was taking part in the discussion and I was her buddy.[89]

The party branch: campaigning and the *Daily Worker*

The party branch was the main area of activity for nearly all women. At a rudimentary level, correspondence was read out and reports given from the leadership in Scotland, from the EC in London and from other party committees. The party centre was aware that not all members took an interest in or knew how district and ECs operated.[90] At local branch level an EC would oversee the administrative running of the branch. This body would make sure that decisions were carried out between branch meetings and would then report back to members. This was to allow the branch to discuss more important business and to develop a local-level leadership. Crucially, it was at branch level that the closeness and respect for other members developed. This would be a most important element in insulating members from the fact that they were in a small party with a lot of work to do to make any impact and who, at times, faced suspicion and hostility.

Much of the branch's emphasis was on promoting the party by selling the *Daily Worker* and running bazaars for the paper. Additional fund-raising was necessary to raise money, which, along with the laborious task of collecting dues, the full-time organizers depended on for their income and to pay for the cost of premises and publications. In Cowdenbeath the party branch met weekly. There had been a tradition of selling party publications and producing local papers for the pits even before the arrival of the *Daily Worker* in 1930. Later there was a Scottish edition of the paper and the Saturday edition, covering the weekend, afforded the best opportunity outside the workplace to push sales:

> we used to go out canvassing for the *Daily Worker* nearly every Saturday or we organized areas to sell the *Daily Worker* and we had members of the party that went out on a regular Saturday round themselves with extra papers on a Saturday. 'Saturday readers' they got and you tried to get the 'Saturday reader' to become a daily reader and my father went out as a 'Saturday reader' with the papers until he was nearly eighty.[91]

At the end of the war sales of the paper in Scotland reached 11,749 a day[92] and 12,463 a day in 1951[93] with increased sales at events and demonstrations. In 1955 the weekend sale was 7600.[94] Thereafter, sales in Scotland began to decline and from then on it was increasingly hard to keep up to the previous year's figure. To draw support from the wider movement, the PPPS was formed in 1946 with 1462 shareholders in Scotland by July.[95] Active party members had to keep up and increase their sales of the paper. If a member established a round then it would become a daily or weekly exercise to pick up the papers and deliver them to supporters and, if they could not be caught at the right time, some felt obliged to pay for all the papers they took.

Although fund-raising was hugely important for the party, there seemed to be an over reliance on women members to do the most mundane and, as far as political results were concerned, less rewarding tasks. The role of the bazaars was discussed at district conferences for women but in the 1940s and 1950s the designating of roles was not heavily questioned and there was still a culture that was to be challenged.

An immense amount of energy and organizing went into the bazaars; it was not as if women played a secondary role in the fund-raising, but it was not at the forefront of the party's political campaigning. Some women were aware of being pigeonholed and knew that it could be taken for granted, as it was at home. The question of fund-raising and the bazaars is a fundamental one pertaining to the postwar era. This was at the heart of the criticism that came to the fore in the 1970s about women's role:

> Well of course, I think it's nae use blaming the men for this because women themselves saw themselves as the tea makers and the providers, the knitwear at the bazaars and the baked things, because of women's traditional roles and because they can dae these things, it naturally follows that in these situations women did these things and it wasnae really a question of the men saying 'You're there to mak' the tea', the women accepted that role.[96]

Women with family commitments like looking after children, which they invariably still did, had less time to devote to the party, so baking or making items for the bazaars was a way of contributing and keeping in touch. This did not mean that women were any less politically developed, but it was essential for raising funds for the party.

Although most women attended their local branch, party couples always had a problem deciding who could go and who should stay at home if there were children. The importance the party gave to industrial work and the priority it placed on workplace branches meant that many women who worked in the home did not attend meetings.

Women were more present in less industrial areas with smaller branches. If they had been in the YCL, there was a natural expectation that couples would carry on with their equal level of involvement in the party:

> I was a member of the committee in Govan branch and when Kenneth was born I couldn't get out. ... So I wrote a letter to our branch committee and said I wished a discussion on the situation. So one of the women was sent up to look after the baby while I went to have the discussion and the decision at last of the committee was that they would co-opt me onto the committee and one week Bill would come and the next week I would come, and the week I was there Bill would look after the baby [*laughs*] – that was my night out once a fortnight.[97]

Although women were generally expected to stay at home, the party did introduce mechanisms like the women's advisory and women's sections to encourage them to get involved and to campaign on what were seen as women's issues. This was to address social issues rather than to develop any critique of internal exigencies. The party also tried to accommodate working women who wanted to attend meetings. 'We usually had a meeting every fortnight. I always attended them if my shifts were right, if I was on a late shift I couldn't but I attended them when I could.'[98]

The party recognized the importance of trade union and industrial work and emphasized this in its branches. The industrial presence in households and communities, and an awareness of the work conditions of relatives and friends, meant that it was impossible to separate industrial work from family and party life:

> My father, he went back to the yard when the war was on and went to work in the torpedo factory, he'd been away too long really in a way. For example, the hardship of his life, the terrible shifts that he worked but he had a job, my father was never unemployed and when my mother and father would go to rent tribunals, they were two people out of a street that was full of unemployed people and I knew then, and you kind of take it in by osmosis as I've said, that it was the employed who fought for the unemployed because when

> you're unemployed your morale goes ... in every way. And therefore people would come to my mother and father's door with trouble all the time and the CP people were seen like that.[99]

Correcting the imbalance

While non-industrial branch members deferred to the importance of industrial activity, steps *were* taken to organize and educate female members. The first advance in this area in Scotland was to set up a women's department in 1944.[100] This was run first by Agnes Maxwell and then Rhoda Fraser, who had a profound effect on women's work in the party for the next 13 years and on that generation of communist women in Scotland. An inaugural conference was held in April 1944 with 109 delegates.[101] Women's sections were formed and in mining communities miners' wives made up most of the membership.[102]

In the 1940s women's groups increased, the Women's Advisory Council (WAC) was developed at British and district level[103] and the party started to organize and recruit women in a more positive and meaningful way than before. By 1947, with 40 women's sections in operation, the Scottish WAC was holding regular meetings with representatives from nine areas[104] and the first district women's school was under its authority.[105] The 'considerable recruitment'[106] of women between 1947 and 1948 testified to the success of this policy. Membership increased by 20 per cent from 1408 to 1695, which took women up to an all time high of 26 per cent[107] of the Scottish membership. By November 1947 sales of the party publication *Woman Today* were 1650,[108] at least theoretically suggesting nearly one copy bought per female member.

The resilience of women at the base of the structure encouraged them to make a more politicized and organized contribution to the party. Women's sections were at one time more numerous in Fife, but the party also operated in some mining villages in Lanarkshire. Prior to gaining more statutory rights and massively increased state services after the reforms of 1945, in certain areas people relied on the CP to help them with a variety of problems that were more social than political. Communists saw it as their job and duty to help people with the most basic issues, such as disputes with the authorities:

> individuals came about ... housing, a lot of personal problems that people had with the establishment as it were, folk were having problems with what we called the 'parish' at that time and ... we

> dealt with a particular problem for somebody about the adoption of their daughter's illegitimate child and getting, before the adoption coming through, getting allowance for this child.[109]

Women, as an integral part of the branch, could win the trust and confidence of people, and this is where the party's strength and communities lay.

Area and city committees

The area committee covered the activities of local and industrial branches in designated geographical area like Lanarkshire, Dunbartonshire or Fife. The major cities had city committees. Delegates would be elected from branches and this gave women with the confidence to speak at meetings, and whose ability had been noticed, the opportunity to be elected:

> You took part in discussion if you felt that you could make a contribution. I was never terribly intellectual but I was able to ask questions for clarification and I think I must have made a contribution because as a result of my work in the branch I was nominated to go on to the city committee.[110]

The city committee was the next step up from the branch in the party's structure. It received reports from the Scottish committee, but was slanted towards administrative tasks and local concerns. It was still the starting level for future leaders and was the base from where full-timers for the area would forward the policies of the party to go through the branches:

> The area committee was a guiding arm if you might put it like that. ... They would discuss the aims, the general aims of what we should be doing. ... The political statement would be given by the comrade who was on the Scottish committee and he would bring the statement from the Scottish committee who in turn would be getting it reported from the national committee. So therefore it was a fairly direct line. But then there were a lot of local things.[111]

The Glasgow city committee covered all the branches in the immediate city boundaries that elected industrial and local delegates. Since the 1930s it had been a cohesive body that worked closely with the membership in local branches,[112] an advantage gained by having a full-time secretary and a couple of organizers, which not all area committees had. It was the first step up to a level where there was more political discussion, where a more comprehensive view of the party's work could be gauged along with the usual business on the agenda. There were city committees in Aberdeen, Dundee and Edinburgh, and area committee's where the party had a semblance of strength. These committees were the first step up for those who wanted to develop their leadership potential or specialize in particular areas. By being part of an advisory committee that reported to the Scottish committee, they could help formulate policy:

> There wasnae any use of just putting somebody to the city committee who wasnae showing any progress in their branch because the city committee helped the development of you from your own branch level, it helped you to develop as well because you heard other comrades, who were maybe much better than you were.[113]

The Scottish committee and the secretariat

The level of debate at the Scottish committee was very much higher, with more mundane activities given second place to political debate; reports of the national committee or 'executive', which met monthly in London, were given priority and discussed in depth. The Scottish committee contained delegates who were elected at congress to represent the party's membership and base. The authority of the party's hierarchy was enormous and the dedication and ability of many of its full-time organizers attracted the respect of many members. Even if the individual were disliked, the role of the organizer was seen as essential. Yet, it would be wrong to see the Scottish committee as meeting just to endorse everything that came its way from the highest body of the British party:

> The debates were fairly fierce and there were people in the party who didnae agree with everything … but they were listened to and if they could be corrected and were prepared to accept correction … we came to a kind of *fait accompli*. … People were allowed, not to have an anti-party point of view, don't get me wrong, but there was sections where people felt we werenae doing the right thing here and werenae doing the right thing there that maybe if you did it this other way we would make progress quicker.[114]

Thus there was a difference between voicing opposition openly and being anti-party. What seems clear from some women's experiences is that strong discussion was allowed and seems to have been far more a feature in the party structure than hitherto thought. Also, women who reached this level were treated as equals in what was a naturally elitist body, elected at congress usually through the recommended list, namely the party leadership's preferred list of candidates from the full list of nominees to the national or district committee.

The supreme body in the Scottish party was the secretariat, a group of around ten members from the Scottish committee. It was the leadership body and the party's ultimate authority in Scotland.[115] (It changed its name to the executive committee in the 1960s.) Constitutionally, the structure of the party allowed branches to debate matters openly and to express their views to their local area committee or to the Scottish committee.

Democratic centralism

The system of organization and accountability the CP operated, and that was embodied in its rules, was that of democratic centralism devised by Lenin. It had developed at the turn of the century when the tsarist authorities were intimidating nearly all opposition forces in Russia. Increased class conflict in Russia from 1917 and the success of the Bolshevik revolution were proof of the effectiveness of this form of organization, despite the odds stacked against it. The party's success lay in its ability to convert all the decisions of its hierarchical bodies into action. The ensuing civil war gave the Bolsheviks an even stronger, more disciplined and centralized party that was subordinate to the authority and actions of the leadership. Its effectiveness in sustaining the government in power during the hostilities, which ensured the survival of the revolution, gave it even more validity.

Although circumstances were different in more industrially advanced European countries, the argument for operating democratic centralism was a universal one. Once internal debate and votes had been taken it disciplined members to unite behind the final policies of the party and to go out and fight as a collective for them. It would be hard to imagine the CPGB having the impact it did on British labour history (namely a noticeable if limited one) had it not operated this system, so one has to see why there was an attraction to it. Within the party there was internal debate from the branches to the higher committees and then the final endorsement of congress on national matters:

> I was unaware that it was undemocratic, let's put it like that. I always thought that we discussed things and came to a majority decision and thrashed it out and that was it and I didn't have any inhibitions about that. Some individuals, their personality was such that they came down like [a] hammer, you had to take that along with other people who weren't of that temperament. But we had always the facility of discussing things openly and taking a decision and that was it, and everybody was committed to that decision. If you made a decision you were committed to it whether you liked it or not, if it was democratically decided. That was my experience.[116]

There was little dissension among those interviewed from this period about its necessity, indeed effectiveness and importance, for party members. The opportunity for local debate and decision making must be seen as critical or else there would have been little attraction in participating in branch life. The way local branches operated and the intimacy and trust between members contrasted with the top–down approach of the structure in which members might have felt they had little or no control. One aspect was when the leadership put requirements on a member or demanded sacrifices that the individual felt obliged, even flattered, to carry out:

> we always had communists on the council in those days. Johnny Kane was a very popular councillor and when he fell ill and wasn't able to continue, my brother Duncan was more or less directed by the party to give up his work in the trade union, which was really what he enjoyed doing, and he accepted the discipline … he got elected and was very well respected. That was the kind of thing that the party took decisions on and we as members went along with the decision whether we liked it or not.[117]

This aspect of democratic centralism could be unattractive and appear non-democratic. Some members feared the possibly adverse nature of the system, which some found hard to accept or could not agree with:

> I felt that decisions were being taken and you didnae really ha' a discussion about these things, there wasnae real ongoing discussions. We should have been forming decisions at branch level and local level which, in the end, like a consensus before we arrived

> at a decision. No, I didna agree with it, there was a whole lot of things I didna agree wi' in the Party.[118]

The ordered and effective nature of democratic centralism was evident in the manner in which the leadership, especially the Scottish secretary and full-time organizers, could direct members, branches and factory cells to carry out instructions on a daily basis. Often there was not time for debate on all issues and much instruction could only be contested retrospectively. It may well be apposite to consider the adverse and permanent effect of, for example, having to chair a public meeting with no experience. 'Never having ever done anything like that before I was terrified and I think that tied my tongue up for the rest of my life… it was a horrible experience which I blame the party for. … I could have said no couldn't I? Yes, but I didn't.'[119]

Congresses

Every two years the party held its Scottish congress in the alternate year to the biannual British congress, although extraordinary congresses might be called. Each branch devoted time to pre-congress discussion and there were aggregate meetings to discuss major policy documents. The composition of congress delegates was weighted towards male skilled industrial workers and the majority of women delegates were housewives. Even if women were in paid work they could suffer from the prioritizing of what were deemed more important sections in representing the branch.

This imbalance did change over the years. By 1957, although the largest single section of women delegates were still housewives, the majority were in paid employment and this reflected the importance paid work increasingly had on the position of women in the party, though they were in a range of professions[120] and lacked concentrated strength. The majority of male delegates in this era were employed skilled workers in blue-collar trade unions who could make an impact (if they were not banned) on union structures and on the shop floor. Anyone going to congress could expect intense political debate and the apprehension, if not fear, of having to get up to address their peers:

> Arnold Henderson was the organizer at that time and Arnold took us down, he was like a hen with his chickens you know, you got looked after, Arnold looked after you all the way and Arnold of course says to me 'you'll have to make a contribution, get your

> name down.' I said, '*God, I would die*', he said, '*Come on*, you'll get your name down and you'll make a contribution, that is what you are here for, to let them know about Clydebank' and I did it. I sat up the whole night in sweat and blood and tears trying to make a statement, which I eventually had to do, but Arnold was pretty good.[121]

It cannot have been only women delegates who were petrified at having to go to the podium. But since so many of the female delegates were housewives, especially in the first three decades of the party, and not used to addressing large meetings, let alone the largest delegate body, it was particularly hard. The nature of the congress, its procedure – with a variant of committees – and the need to fight for one's right to follow resolutions through or bring up points of order, could seem complicated. Yet delegates had to learn how to operate the system within a few days.

It was the highest body and the one event with guaranteed intense and often emotional debate. Even with the party machinery controlling events precisely, it was hard to equal congress. There was a good social life with the chance to meet national party figures, members of CPs from around the world and contacts in unions and British organizations in which the party operated. There were attempts to influence delegates in voting for the EC and then the anticipation of results to committees that were not always a foregone conclusion, especially since delegates often had to make a decision on the spot. Thus, to enhance the democratic process, delegates were not mandated, since 'if the branch were to mandate its delegate, what would be the use of discussion at Congress?'[122]

Influences

Despite all the logical steps to identify the path to political involvement of women in the CP, it would be wrong to dismiss or deny the importance of inspiration from individuals or through propaganda at local, Scottish and British level. Meetings and rallies were always used to impress individuals and draw them into the party and regular rallies in Aberdeen, Dundee, Fife and Glasgow during the 1940s and 1950s are testimony to this. The aim of public meetings was to explain and win support for party policy, enlarge the membership and commit the audience to future events.[123] To advertise meetings, streets were chalked as they were for the visits of speakers or political opponents. The aim was to fill the hall and make an impressive impact, which the party did especially when there was a Scottish district rally or the visit of the general secretary. Meticulous in its preparation for such events, the sequence and time allocated to speeches was strictly adhered to and strong chairing of major meetings essential.[124]

Women active between 1940 and 1956 experienced the influence of three great CPGB figures. Harry Pollitt, 'universally acknowledged as the Party's outstanding leader',[125] found that the CP met the level of personal commitment he believed was necessary to achieve anything and was a continuation of the commitment to socialism he had experienced in the BSP. His theoretical analyses did not match his inspirational oratory. However, his grounding in the trade union movement, as a boilermaker, gave him credentials beyond question and there would remain even in his communism 'the unmistakable imprint of the skilled worker'.[126] It was a characteristic by no means unique in the British CP, though the strong discipline of that union made the demands of political discipline more palatable. Pollitt's passion and, in party members and admirers' eyes, his basic forthrightness and honesty won him great respect and admiration: 'Harry Pollitt was probably the best speaker I ever heard in my life. I don't think there ever was or ever will be a mass orator the way Pollitt was.'[127]

Of the older party members there seems a consensus on Pollitt's skill to communicate with the audience and he continued the tradition of strong and impressionable public speaking, most noticeably at large rallies that the party held at St Andrew's Hall in Glasgow. Up until the late 1950s public meetings were still the main medium through which to hear political views.

Two other leaders also had the ability to inspire members. Willie Gallacher and J. R. Campbell had supported Pollitt when he argued against the Comintern's new line over the war in 1939. J. R. Campbell seems a slightly forgotten leader in British communist history. No major biography has been written about him but those who worked with him in Scotland remember his diligent work, voracious reading and analytical ability.[128] Gallacher's grassroots history of activity and involvement on Clydeside with the Clyde workers' committee was recognized and his approach to speaking at large meetings was like that of a pugilist going for the kill with direct, hard-hitting speeches peppered with an often sarcastic wit. Anxious to get on his feet he could be a bit insensitive in curtailing his juniors, so eager was he to get to the audience. He dabbled in poetry but was no lost bard, though his verse could be amusing and facetious.[129] To members Gallacher and Campbell no doubt added authenticity to the party's historical link with Lenin and the Russian Revolution. They were involved from the birth of the CP in Britain and had travelled to the Soviet Union and met its leaders in its first few years of existence. These leaders were the link to international communism, for at this time it was rare for members to have heard or met any major communist figures unless they had been to the Soviet Union or a major festival abroad. This undoubtedly added an aura to their authority. The regular closeness of the party leaders to families throughout the country inevitably influenced some children who later joined the party and were active from the 1960s:

> one of them bought my first dancing shoes. Willie always stayed with us when he was in Fife, even more so than Harry and they were totally opposites in some respects. Harry liked a drink but Willie would often argue the rights and wrongs of drinking. Gallacher of course recognized the importance of the participation of women and his success in becoming an MP in West Fife was due to the fact that he attended and addressed meetings of the Women's guild. He spoke to them and to other sections where women were involved and he encouraged women to play a bigger role in attempting to build a socialist Britain.[130]

It would be interesting to reflect on how the party would have fared had it not had Pollitt and Gallacher, both staunch socialists before the Russian Revolution but whose lives were forever changed by it. If R. Palme Dutt's theoretical contribution and measured approach is seen as contrasting with Pollitt's instincts in the party hierarchy, then Gallacher complimented Pollitt's campaigning among the party membership:

> Well the very first one I heard speaking in Rutherglen was J. R. Campbell. … And Willie Gallacher, he was smashing. Actually, … when I started to speak myself … I had to go to Willie Gallacher's branch in Paisley and Willie and his wife sitting looking at me, I thought 'What can I tell Willie Gallacher because he's such a good speaker?' I think Willie Gallacher would stand out really. I heard Harry Pollitt. In fact at that election in the Gorbals I spoke for five minutes and Harry Pollitt was one of the speakers and I was proud to be able to sit alongside him.[131]

Rather than being intimidated by great speakers, it was important for women to get beyond branch life and develop themselves in the party and become cadres. It was equally important that they be seen in the leadership as this inevitably encouraged others. Of those who achieved this there was the continued influence and encouragement of party figures who were established at Scottish district level:

> Kerrigan was one of my heroes and I think he returned the affection. The party had rooms in the High Street at that time, a shop, and … that's where Peter did his work. It was after I'd been to the Soviet Union, I came back and my mother died and I was very upset and Peter consoled me. I always thought Peter was so sincere and a real leader. He was always intent on giving leadership to the working class and I had that right up till he died. I had a high regard for Peter Kerrigan, yes I did.[132]

The paternalism of tutors and party leaders seems to have been greeted positively. Pollitt, Gallacher and Campbell's overwhelming influence show the inspiration their speeches imbued at party rallies and how little noticeable opposition there was to their leadership. The 1940s were their last decade of complete supremacy before the events of 1956 changed perceptions of the invincibility of party leaders.

Internationally, one of the most popular and celebrated figures of the communist movement was Paul Robeson, the African-American singer and actor who kept his sympathy with communist politics at the height of McCarthyism when people were being persecuted in the USA. He first gave a concert in Glasgow on 18 August 1938, which the Glasgow Trades Council arranged. He met those involved in campaigning for the Spanish republican government and also some who had lost relatives who had volunteered.[133] Having been denied the right to travel at the onset of the cold war, the Glasgow Trades Council supported Robeson in his campaign to get his passport returned after it was withdrawn in the early 1950s. In 1956 a committee was formed in Britain and 20 other countries to campaign for its return.[134] Robeson was articulate and well educated with a beautiful voice and wide repertoire of gospel, classical and popular music. There was a great reception for him when he finally returned to Glasgow:

> The St Andrew's Hall was packed and we just wouldn't let him go; he was singing on and on and he said look because of his voice he

> would have to stop but he would come back and he didn't care how many concerts he did as long as it didn't cost anyone more than a shilling to get in. So the Communist Party organized a series of concerts and he came back and sang. … It was exciting times, I must say. He was some character. ... He changed the words to *Old Man River* and St Andrew's Hall's roof nearly blew off with the cheers.[135]

After the St Andrew's Hall concert, which ran over time without any complaints from the audience, some of whom had travelled far and had to walk home, Robeson went to a restaurant off Buchanan Street in Glasgow where other party members got to meet him.[136] He made a few visits to Scotland, performing and speaking at demonstrations.[137] Robeson sang at the Glasgow May Day in 1960 and purposefully marched with the communist contingent. He told the crowd of 10,000 at Queen's Park: 'There can be no question that we, the people, in the deepest sense, create the wealth. We are building a world in which we can live a rich and decent life and our children should enjoy it.'[138] He led the crowd with a rendition of *Loch Lomond.* His visits left an indelible impression.

One exceptional woman, who worked at the heart of the party's structure in Scotland and later in the London headquarters, was Margaret Hunter. Born in 1922 in Bridgeton, Glasgow, her father had been a foundation member of the CP and was involved in tenants' struggles. He suffered unemployment and was an obvious influence on Margaret who was involved with the Young Pioneers in the Gorbals and joined the YCL at 14.[139] She worked at Barr & Stroud engineering company, became convenor for the women in the factory and spoke regularly at lunch-time factory meetings, including calling for a second front during the war. She became a full-time secretary for the party, worked in the Glasgow office, was on the Glasgow committee and became its secretary. For her the 1940s and 1950s were a period of intense party organizing and campaigning, a lot of which was done in the Glasgow office alongside Gordon McLennan, a full-time organizer, later Scottish secretary and penultimate general secretary of the CP. In the 1950s Hunter became a Scottish organizer for the party and sat on the secretariat. 'I remember Margaret. … she was very active she was very able she was very articulate and very determined. I mean she and Gordon had tremendous application and tremendous drive and they really grafted. They could work incredibly hard and they did a tremendous amount of work.'[140]

Margaret Hunter successfully applied for the post of national women's organizer in 1964, despite her and her husband's reluctance to leave Scotland. Her sense of obligation and admiration for General Secretary John Gollan, who specifically wanted her for the job, influenced her decision.[141] Prior to this she had no specific interest in women's issues. Once in London she still stood in Glasgow at general elections and influenced women well into the 1960s.[142] 'Margaret would stand in the street and speak through the loudspeaker and we would go around selling literature.'[143] Although an influence on women throughout Britain well into the late 1960s, Margaret Hunter's contribution ended prematurely. Ill health curtailed her continuing role in the leadership, yet her achievement in having held important positions and having reached national prominence in the party inspired future generations. Unlike Helen Crawfurd, who earlier had achieved the same, Hunter was of a rank of women 'born into' the party and who had progressed through it from an early age.

The Labour Party

Although the Labour Party and CP could work with each other at times (and this had been the case with the ILP during the 1930s), the former was held in some contempt. Its commitment to radical change was limited and the party was seen as complacent and too right wing. For communists, this was evident in the Labour Party's indolence over the Spanish Civil War in the 1930s and in fighting fascism, even in Britain. Yet the CP knew it was in its interest to build up a working relationship and this could best be done at elections in which the Labour Party was the dominant contender on the left. However, there was never a strong and permanent working relationship in Scotland and certainly no official policy of the Labour Party to encourage one even when approached:

> The Communist Party wanted to be affiliated to the Labour Party so we were not enamoured with a lot of the leadership, certainly not, and certain individuals within the local party you didn't have a lot of respect for but there were others, yes, that were fine people and we would have been very, very happy to work with them.[144]

At the British level, any attempts by the CP to affiliate to the Labour Party were always convincingly defeated. Although this objective was seen as essential for the advance of the CP's policies, failure to win affiliation was a good indication of how weak the CP and left wing of the Labour Party were in the labour movement. There was little need for the Labour Party to make overtures because it never faced any serious challenge to its electoral dominance from the CP. Yet, not all Labour candidates were hostile and members of both parties worked together on various bodies in their communities, though not always agreeing. Geographically, the CP could maintain strength in certain areas, such as pit villages where it had a strong core of members and some influence:

> we were the political force, very much so and also at the main place of work. You see the pit there, Douglas Colliery, was very much a focus point as well for politics and the Communist Party; people didn't talk much about the Labour Party, no. I mean [the] Communist Party at that time were in the forefront o' any political struggle.[145]

Thus, the Labour Party electorally dominated the very constituency in which the CP was based. In those rare areas where the party was successful locally there was mass campaigning and traditional ways of getting people interested and involved in local issues in order to sustain the party's presence on the councils. Such was the situation in the Vale of Leven:

> there was Dan [O'Hare], there was Davie McKim and Geordie Halkett, Hugh Macintyre, they were all communist councillors and Sam McDonald was a district councillor, it was all quite a number of them here. Somebody always took the meeting at the fountain on a Friday night and all the council business was discussed and it became a thing that everybody came if there was anyone interested at all; they came to the fountain to see what was being said.[146]

Women were encouraged to stand as candidates because the party needed people who were known for doing work in their communities. Despite council seats in Fife and Dumbarton and a few successes dotted around Scotland at different times, there was cynicism towards the parliamentary system. Most election campaigns were to advertise the party rather than realistically expecting an electoral victory.

Communist politics had long been considered beyond the pale in electoral terms. It was a salutary lesson for the party to discover that although it could gain the people's trust when working among communities, local groups and as shop stewards in factories, it could not win their support in council elections. This might explain why the CP placed so much importance on factory branch activity where it was more effective. As early as 1948, it said that 'the industrial base in all cases is out of all proportion to the general influence of the Party.'[147] In the workplaces the CP was better organized to face any concerted opposition; there was less of the supremacy of the Labour Party here and more room for the CP to win over members on the shop floor through strong organization and militant shop stewards' organizations. It also countered the apathy and conciliation that it associated with the right wing of the labour movement.

Conclusion

The importance of branch activity and the centrality of its role in the lives of party members cannot be underestimated. In the exceptional cases where the party had councillors, it obviously also enjoyed the strength of an electoral base and more institutional influence. By 1958 this legacy was weakening, but of the 36 communist councillors in Britain 16 were in Scotland so there was still a large party influence in a few places.[148]

Some women stayed in the party for as long as they did because of the close friendships they had developed in the YCL and party branches in the 1940s. In adulthood, when it became difficult for married women to attend meetings, the party sharpened the emphasis on its industrial role. Indeed, from this period its political influence depended on its industrial strength and this base gave it a strong presence well into the 1970s. Nevertheless, women still reached all levels of party organization, even if only briefly or in limited numbers. They were making an impact but their traditional domestic role held them back, especially on the Scottish committee where women's representation was lower than its percentage of Scottish membership. The highest percentage of women delegates on the Scottish committee was between 1950 and 1953 when women accounted for 17 per cent of the body's total membership. This figure suggests that if women were in work, they were not in the industrial areas of employment on which the party concentrated. That the traditional industrial sector was over represented reflected the party's strong position there.

Female members were not deliberately discouraged and many stress feeling equal with all party members. But the restrictions, which were mainly dictated by capitalism and were reflected in trade union organization, were so much an integral part of the British labour movement that it would have been surprising had some problems not arisen. One problem was that these were not recognized as endemic or integral problems. There was not yet a large critical body of opinion, as would develop in the party in the 1970s, that saw the need for major internal reform and a need to stress other areas, or means of struggle, that were more relevant to women. One can see the 1945–60 period promising more than the 1920–39 period when Sue Bruley states that women were still a small percentage of the membership and 'rarely held positions of power and influence'.[149] She also ascribes this to the weight of tradition and the CP being gender defined.[150] This was still so in the late 1950s, but slowly things were changing. Women were an integral part of the party's structure and were contributing a great deal to its fund-raising and community activities.

Some husbands were accommodating and modern in their outlook and the party hierarchy was interested in women's participation, especially once a firm policy and a women's department were established. One problem was the hostility of women who were not in the party but endured their partner's selfless, and selfish, devotion to it. Although some may have been disappointed by the inflexibility in family difficulties and women's domestic responsibility, this era also reflects the united stand behind party policy and the common goal of socialism that came before all else. There was still a positive response to the party and a belief that problems could be solved within its structures and that the degradation of women could be ended only with the achievement of socialism.[151] Members recognized that men at the point of production were also exploited and that this exploitation was reflected in the family.

There is no doubt that women were resilient and expected to contribute to and be an integral part of the communist movement. Facing a loud, confident and expressive meeting of mostly men could be daunting for some, though such initiations may also reflect the anxiety of any member, irrespective of gender. Those who were experienced in industrial work and union activity, where there were everyday issues to discuss in a workplace organization such as a shop stewards' committee or union branch, were usually more confident. As union membership grew the emphasis was on the workplace and, in the absence of organized Labour Party workplace branches, the CP was inevitably able to strengthen its membership. This was the one area in which communist influence could be greater than anywhere else. The starkest and most brutal conditions at the point of production often offered the classic recruiting ground for class-conscious workers presumed to be at the vanguard of any communist movement.

None of the interviewees from this period believed that it was primarily the fault of men that women were restricted or that the CP did not try and do things positively to alter the situation. While they did criticize the approach of some men and the party's failure adequately to tackle inequalities, their main reason for being involved was to promote left-wing ideas in the Scottish labour movement.

Margaret Hunter epitomized the modern communist woman leader. Being from a CP family, she was committed to the party as a whole, accepted its structures and worked integrally within them. In this way she worked perfectly as part of the leadership and, at the same time, in the context of the immediate postwar period, was a role model for women.[152]

Chapter 4

Sacrifice and Advance: The Scottish Women's Advisory Committee and Women's Sections, 1947–69

> 'We can produce women of the same calibre as our comrades in Europe and the Soviet Union.'
>
> *Scottish Committee of the Communist Party 1946*[1]

> 'There is not the appreciation in the Party of the great value of the Women's Sections, and the contribution the women can make.'
>
> *Communist Party Organization Report (Scottish District) 1949*[2]

Here we address the role of the Scottish Women's Advisory Committee (SWAC) and what it meant to women in the party. As will become clear, not all women in the party took a deep interest in its work. Given that very little has been written about the SWAC and that there are no major sources in any public archive or collection, oral testimony was central in gaining an accurate picture of this committee's work. Marion Henery's contribution was crucial to this part of the research because she had kept the correspondence and reports from her period as secretary from 1956 to 1968. This material was lying in folders in her house and its value was in that it led to further research and gave a graphic idea of the organization's work. This was an excellent example of an oral contributor having crucial primary material. From subsequent investigations I fear that much valuable CP material has been lost or will be discarded if it is not traced soon. In this instance the value of an oral history has been to unearth lost sources. This also applies to photographic material covering many aspects of party activity.

Women's issues

The Women's Advisory Council (WAC) came into existence at British level towards the end of the war in 1944 after an initial meeting of several women from the districts. After that there were meetings at least a few times a year to coordinate work throughout Britain.[3] The dedication those women who started the WAC, under the leadership of Tamara Rust, put into that body when the war was still raging and women's organization was still at a formative stage was impressive. Mabs Skinner, who later moved to Inverness, was a delegate from the party's Surrey district to the national WAC, which met in London:

> they said they needed to have a wider voice of communist women up in London. So I was asked by Tamara Rust to come up and she would see me and we would see about me belonging to the Women's Advisory Committee of the Communist Party. ... So I went up then once a month to London to the women's advisory council because this war was on and one of these times when I went up during the blitz, I got off at the underground and walked to King Street. And, oh, it must have been about just 100 yards in front of me, the whole flaming house collapsed onto the street, rubble and everything. I think it had been blitzed before you know and now it was crumbling. I thought to myself, 'my golly, just look at that, I just missed that', then I was off 'I've got to get to my meeting'. ... Then of course, when the meeting was over, I thought to myself, 'Oh lord, how am I going to get back? I've got to get back.' ... So, right, I had to get back to Waterloo station, which I managed. But when I got to Waterloo station they said, 'Oh well, you've just missed the last train out, there's no more trains, you'll just have to wait, there's no more trains leaving because the order has been given "no more trains to leave".' So I stayed all night in Waterloo station and I got the first train out to Surbiton in Surrey. And I got out of there and I eventually got home on another train and walked from there. Very late getting home I was ... and got a row from Tom because I didn't come home that night. Then I heard that the train I should have caught got bombed. So I missed two deaths in one night [*laughs*]. ... Because he was a communist, he knew that we were dedicated to our work so it was no use him saying that 'you're not going up anymore'. I still kept going.[4]

The growth of the SWAC corresponded with the Scottish district's elaboration of various social policies at a time when women members were expected to promote education and health. During the war the party raised the question of the effects on health of undernourishment and bad housing. The situation was noticeably worse in Scotland than across the border, with 22.6 per cent of Scotland's housing overcrowded compared with 3.8 per cent in England and Wales.[5] The infant mortality rate was 20 per cent above that of England and Wales and higher in western and central Scotland than in the northern rural areas.[6] Not surprisingly, the party supported 'Assumption B' of the Beveridge Report, which called for 'a unified, comprehensive free medical service'.[7]

War work and equal pay

As in the First World War, many women found war work liberating. The work was varied, it gave them a regular income and it was a politicizing experience. Agnes McLean, one of the foremost women trade unionists in Scotland,[8] had, unlike other women from the same generation in the party, joined because of her shop-floor experience and industrial work, which was unusual for women members. Despite recent attempts to paint a more cynical and derogatory view of the CP in Scotland during the war,[9] Agnes McLean had no doubts about why she came to join it:

> I found that the people who were ready to support the women and back them and stand by them and never let them down were Communist Party members. ...The result was that when somebody came up to me and said 'Will you join the Communist Party?' I wasn't for saying 'No'.[10]

Having been in the Socialist Sunday School, McLean took a job at Rolls Royce in Hillington, Glasgow, starting on Christmas Day 1939. She initially joined the TGWU, but later transferred to the Amalgamated Engineering Union, which had held a ballot in 1942 on whether to admit women workers into the union. Female membership of the AEU proliferated from their admission in 1943 and, within two months, 914 branches had women members.[11] With 750,000 members, primarily because of female recruits, the AEU then became the second largest union in Britain:[12]

> Thousands of women flocked into industry and they were quite

> brilliant at engineering. … And you've seen the skills developing and that's when the big battles started because as our skills developed, our labour power became more valuable and we were getting paid less than the rate for the job.[13]

At that time there were three categories of engineer – skilled or time-served, semi-skilled machine workers and unskilled. 'There was unskilled men and others, and we were the others, and we were below even the unskilled.'[14] On average, women were paid £2.3s a week while men earned £3.13s. For six months they worked 12-hour shifts six days a week. Any newly employed man who set the machines automatically got a higher rate than the women, who were not allowed to set the machines. This included the women who had trained the men, which McLean saw as 'disgraceful'. Also, young male workers did not have to go on courses whereas the women did. In 1941 the women in each department joined in strike action, but through inexperience they were 'chased back in'. Although the unions announced their intention to address the issue of equal pay, the women were dissatisfied with the slow progress being made throughout 1942/3, so in December 1943 they walked out. They faced hostility from people who shouted abuse and pelted them with tomatoes and eggs, but this time they were better organized and their determination finally won over their fellow workers: 'Once the men realized, first of all it was an injustice being done to women, for cheap labour and therefore a danger to the men … the men were absolutely fantastic.'[15]

It was during this industrial action that Agnes and her colleagues received full support from communists. Seeing the Labour Party doing nothing on the shop floor, she quickly joined the CP. The strike furthered the cause of the women, though Agnes knew there was still a long way to go: 'Not equal pay but nonetheless a good agreement. A lot of the women's wages were lifted right up and their skills recognized.'[16]

Skilled unions felt that employers were using the war to attack and undermine them. They were vociferous in their denunciations of engineering employers,[17] but, despite union resolutions for equal pay,[18] at delegate conferences there seems little doubt that action by women led by Agnes McLean pushed the issue to the fore. This remained a central part of women's struggle in the labour market, especially when they became more prominent in the labour force. Later, when CP women gathered at weekend schools, Agnes McLean, with her industrial experience and forthright open manner, often made a big impression, though there were regional and cultural differences within the Scottish party:

> She was very typically a Glasgow comrade and the Aberdeen comrades didna think much of the Glasgow comrades. We always thought they were very sure of themselves ... probably because Glasgow was a great industrial city with shipbuilding and railway engine building. Agnes was in engineering whereas ... most of the people in Aberdeen would be one generation removed from the countryside and it was very much based on just fishing and textiles ... the people in Glasgow had that much more industrial experience, that much more trade union organization, and Agnes could talk with so much more know-how and experience.[19]

McLean sat on the CP's Scottish executive and later on the (British) EC. This had much to do with her being a leader in industry and sharing the same important and respected position that was usually the preserve of men in the party. Her role in the fight for equal pay and proper union representation for women continued until the late 1960s (when she left the CP) and into the late 1970s when she retired from Rolls Royce.

Postwar social issues

In the 1950s, despite the Labour government's major social reforms, some social issues needed attention. Scottish education suffered from oversized classes. An extra 35,000 teachers were needed and many of those working were poorly qualified (or 'uncertificated'). One reason for this was that wages for teachers at the time were under £11 a week gross.[20] The party suggested establishing common secondary schools, abandoning selection and introducing advanced study courses to the age of 18, as well as a more common curriculum[21] and the abolition of corporal punishment. A lot of these issues meant that women could work together on a broader basis:

> Health was one of them. Child-care, nursery schools,[22] nursery education for under five's, we used to do a lot of that with Labour Party women because the Labour Party women were interested in that sort of thing as well. Crèches at factories, that was something else people like Agnes McLean were involved in.[23]

To these issues women's activity was directed. Budget leaflets criticizing changes affecting workers' living standards were distributed each year in Glasgow and elsewhere, and meetings were held to discuss them.[24]

If there were enough women in a party branch, a women's section was often set up to encourage them to meet among themselves. These bodies could be viewed as either pushing women to the side in their own little clique, or attempting to advance them in their branch and party. In mining villages they were frequently seen as a place to 'put' women, who were often treated with disregard at branch meetings:

> I think if a woman came along to a branch meeting if she had anything to say, she said it, but then I have known of branches where they had a branch meeting once and they were discussing a fund-raising function and after they discussed that, the person in the chair who was a male, said that the women could go if they liked, and that was a branch in a mining village and it maybe happened in other branches but that's the 1940s I'm talking about, I'm sure things changed.[25]

From the late 1940s, with women leaders in London like Tamara Rust and later Nora Jeffries, the sections were promoted more seriously. By 1946, 25 such sections were operating in Scotland and the Scottish committee reported that 'the developing political activity of women's sections of the Communist Party in Scotland is in tune with the rising role of the working-class woman in the country as a whole.'[26] Concerted efforts were made to get districts to adopt more policies on women, and, since women were in charge of the work, it did not seem patronizing or tokenistic:

> We did all sorts of things. Peace petitions, collecting at works for helping strikers and things but we also – then we formed a women's group and we met separately from the branch in a small local hall and we had speakers. On one occasion we had Tamara Rust and we got two new members that day. We had old Bill Joss, people like that at meetings, just for a period.[27]

Party officials and those who took an interest in the sections wanted to recruit more women (for their numbers were very low), and to integrate them into the women's sections and the CP using broad-based issues that were seen as of concern to women. Yet, a lot of women were interested in neither so-called 'women's issues' nor the activities of the SWAC. Women who had developed politically were reluctant to get involved in separate sections, away from the main branches:

> I never saw any reason to become involved in women's politics; to me it was the political situation and what needed to be done and how we could advance to a better socialist system of society. I dare say it is not a good thing on my part, I probably should have been more involved in the women's side of things, but I just accepted that I was an equal part of the organization and at that time I didn't have children and I wasn't tied down, I was free to do whatever I wanted to do so I mean I suppose it was different for people that maybe had conflict within the family, about who would be active and who wouldn't.[28]

Some women who had found they were treated equally at branch level felt it had taken them enough time to achieve this, and saw it as a retrograde step to concentrate on organizing women separately. Despite their intentions and results, some saw women's sections and the WAC as doing exactly what they were set up to oppose, namely pigeonholing women's issues so that they were excluded from 'real' politics.

On the other hand, enthusiastic women activists could make the running in the sections and 'sometimes it would be too advanced for some women'.[29] Some quite simply were not interested. For those who were interested and who were also involved in other areas of party work, the commitment to developing women's sections and giving their profile a much needed boost meant more work elsewhere.

This may be one reason for the initial slow growth of separate women's groups/sections.[30] However, there was development and in 1950 there were 28 organized in the following eight areas of the Scottish district: Glasgow (12), Dunbartonshire (3), Renfrewshire (1), Lanarkshire (5), Edinburgh (3), Fife (2), Dundee (1) and Ayrshire (1).[31] By 1952 there were 35 CP women's groups involving 560 of its 1400 women members.[32] Still, not all women were interested or involved and Nora Jeffries pointed to the overall problem in Britain: 'we cannot shut our eyes to the fact that in spite of big changes in the party there is still a widespread attitude among comrades that there is no need for special work among women.'[33]

After a 1952 conference for party women, which stressed the growing independence of women's groups and the need for independent activity and education, the WAC was taken more seriously. By 1956 there were only 22 active groups with only one in Fife, one in the northeast and none in the southeast or West Lothian.[34] This does not mean that female membership was falling or that there was less activity in this sphere; what remained a problem was the number of women's sections and promoting their growth along with a higher profile for women's issues:

> I thought the Scottish Women's Advisory Committee was a great organization because we dealt specifically with women, only with women, and we would try to work out what issues women could be active on. ... You always felt a tremendous responsibility when you went up and would be doing this and this and you felt you had to do it well. ... But there was always controversy over whether or not these should be separate, a separate meeting.[35]

The constitutional role of the SWAC was to campaign among women, organize and educate them through the sections and put recommendations forward to the Scottish committee. The party's other advisory committees had the same constitutional role. The word 'advisory' was well chosen because these committees' recommendations had no statutory right to be accepted, although their work was valued because it was central to generating responses of party members to different areas of activity.

The first Scottish district women's conference under the WAC took place in February 1946, encouraged by the recently formed World Federation of Democratic Womanhood. The conference discussed ways of making a noticeable impact on International Women's Day, also the development of Marxist education and the new national syllabus for women.[36] The role of the SWAC was vital to developing the activity of women and, irrespective of which views dominated at certain times, was invaluable for widening the role and involvement of women in the party.

When the SWAC was first set up women were confined to certain areas more through lack of expectations than by design. From the 1950s onwards, the SWAC was run by women sent by their party branch or encouraged by the party leadership to attend. The secretary was essential to the effective running of the committee and the SWAC was given a free rein to formulate and initiate policies without obvious interference from the party hierarchy. In the late 1940s and early 1950s modern young women emerged who broke the traditional mould by not being a party member's wife and not expecting to play a secondary role. They were bold and confident:

> Sarah Sheddon intimidated me a wee bit I think ... in today's parlance she would be a 'new woman'. I remember one instance where she was speaking ... at Clydebank. ... Peter Kerrigan was the main speaker and Sarah turned up with her nail varnish on her fingers and on her *toes* and Peter got rather annoyed. ... She was being '*frivolous*' in front of the workmen.[37]

In 1944 Rhoda Fraser (née Jupp)[38] became the Scottish women's organizer and secretary of the SWAC. Always actively campaigning, Fraser, with 100 women from the west of Scotland, occupied the Board of Trade in February 1947 demanding lower prices and better quality goods.[39] In many ways she started to broaden the activities of party women and campaigned on what were seen as women's issues – fighting for lower food prices (as in an open letter to John Strachey in 1947)[40] and rents and for crèches. She organized women on demonstrations and pickets to get the maximum effect and publicity. Such action was also in opposition to the right-wing Housewives' League. Fraser, who was from Edinburgh, was popular among women, for she had great enthusiasm and concentrated a lot on social activities. She organized a peace bus to tour Scotland in June 1949 with Scotland's first woman communist leader, Helen Crawfurd Anderson:

> I have a photograph in the house and I believe it was the last public appearance she made; she was a very old lady. I remember she had a long black cape on and a *huge* black hat, which very nearly covered her face. It was a peace bus that the women in the Communist Party, Rhoda Jupp in particular, was organizing and it was travelling all over Scotland bringing the message of peace to the people of Scotland and Helen Crawfurd Anderson was doing the sort of official send-off of the bus.[41]

Broad-based campaigns among women were at the heart of Fraser's perspective on how CP women's groups should grow. She also directed a lot of women's energy into new areas, most notably the women's assembly – a broad-based national body:

> I was the secretary for a while. Rhoda Fraser was the one behind it. ... It was a separate organization because we had women in it that werenae in the party at all and we had wee groups here, there and everywhere ... it was a great organization at that, it was an organization that served its purpose at that particular time.[42]

In 1953 Fraser organized the first Scottish national assembly of women and saw this as a move 'towards a united women's movement in Scotland, releasing as it did a flood of new ideas, enthusiasm and a sense of solidarity that inspired everyone taking part'.[43] By 1956 there were committees of the women's assembly in Glasgow, Aberdeen and Dundee, but the party was self-critical about having failed to value the potential of this organization from its inception.[44] This had been a major point of disagreement between Fraser and the Scottish CP and in 1955 she was deliberately replaced as secretary of the SWAC[45] and came off the EC, which she had been on since 1947.

As well as seeing the need to support women in industry Fraser implied that a move towards politicizing the women's movement as a whole was required. She saw a need for more attention from the branches, areas and district and 'from all our women cadres, more self-study, more self-confidence, more Communist perspective is needed'.[46] In seeking to politicize party women but at the same time develop the party's influence in broad-based bodies, she was at least a decade ahead of her time.

The Scottish party reiterated the complaint about the small size of women's groups and observed that only a few activists did 'outdoor work'.[47] Another criticism was that 'political weaknesses resulted in the partial failure of our women's groups to fulfil their main functions of training our women members to lead others and strengthen and build the party amongst the women'.[48] Women's groups were seen as 'things in themselves' and were left to do their own work. This was a cold but honest assessment given that by 1953 there were now 44 women's groups and an optimistic belief that they could reach the 50 for which they aimed.[49]

Marion Henery, an established and popular women's activist,[50] took over the SWAC in 1956. She too saw the value and strength of the committee:

> Now I took over from Rhoda Fraser who was an up and coming communist and a very highly intelligent person. Rhoda was, I think,

> trying to find her way to a broader concept than the Communist Party and she got involved with the peace, with the women's assembly. They also had at that time women's groups of the Communist Party, but my opinion was, and I think the opinion of the comrades was that we should be strengthening and developing the women's groups of the Communist Party; but Rhoda, her line was rather different. She saw the movement progressing through the women's assembly, broader groups, peace groups, all that. I gathered that the party leadership felt this way. ... Now I don't know whether there was any pressure brought on Rhoda about this or not, but Rhoda, she either left or she was pushed and it wasn't until later on that I found out from Marion Robertson that she had actually been offered the job of Rhoda's and turned it down. I was unaware of this and I was offered [it] and I decided to do it.[51]

The above quote suggests that the leadership sought primarily to strengthen the party women's groups and certainly Marion Henery agreed with this strategy, though she had always appreciated Fraser's role. Fraser phoned Marion Henery to tell her that the secretariat had put her name forward.[52]

The events of 1956 cut short Fraser's time in the party. First, party members in Glasgow underwent some traumatic meetings and much soul-searching following Khrushchev's revelations. Then there was the invasion of Hungary. The revelations proved too much for Rhoda Fraser and she decided to leave the party. Her promising contribution to communist politics had ended, though her inspirational influence is still remembered among the generation who worked with her. She left the party, as far as people were aware, primarily because of international events and not over her conflict with the Scottish party leadership.[53]

Although now going their separate ways through irreconcilable differences over the Soviet Union's actions, there was no animosity from any of the women towards Rhoda Fraser (and vice versa) but a great regret that she, and her work with the SWAC, was now over. Unfortunately, there is a sadder postscript. Having moved back to Edinburgh, Fraser joined CND in the 1960s and campaigned vigorously against the Vietnam war. In Edinburgh in 1969 she interrupted a reception for the ambassador of South Vietnam and denounced the actions of his government. However, her personal circumstances were very unhappy and, after suffering from much depression, she took her own life in

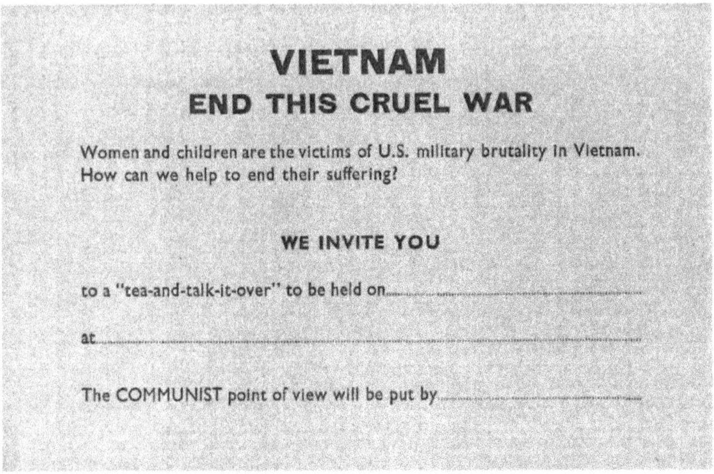
VIETNAM
END THIS CRUEL WAR

Women and children are the victims of U.S. military brutality in Vietnam. How can we help to end their suffering?

WE INVITE YOU

to a "tea-and-talk-it-over" to be held on..........

at..........

The COMMUNIST point of view will be put by..........

5. Cards handed out by CP women's groups to attract women to meetings.

1970. Although it was well over a decade since she had left the party, many members, especially the women who had worked with and been influenced by her, were shocked. Some wept at the news. Many still spoke of her with great affection 25 years later.

> I didnae know her terribly well but she was very friendly with a friend of mine, a close friend of mine in Aberdeen called Dolly Shearer, she and Rhoda were very friendly, but I wasnae all that friendly with Rhoda but I knew her and she was a very capable person, very honest, sincere sort of person, possibly too sincere: well you can nae be too sincere but maybe she would feel that she would be easily knocked off balance, she felt she'd been let down, if she felt disillusioned about people or circumstances or politics, and it would be easy to get like that I think.[54]

Her contribution to the CP in Scotland had been to get the SWAC operating as an effective campaigning body and to open up new routes of campaigning among women. She was no less demanding of women comrades than the party organizers and had many of them rushed off their feet. Those in women's sections benefited most from her enthusiasm and encouragement. They gained more confidence in that environment than at the party branch:

> She encouraged me too and during one period of election[s] when Peter Kerrigan was standing in the Gorbals and we were all helping there I was asked to go and speak to a women's group. You know, they had a women's meeting in their rooms and I spoke to it. Then I had to go and speak in a school and I had my speech all written out. I had remembered somebody doing it on postcards but I started to speak, we were all sitting at school desks, and when I looked down I had mixed all my postcards up. However, I managed my speech all right and from that I spoke at meetings not as a big speaker but I was able to get up and say my piece when necessary.[55]

That women's work was still sectionalized may have been a fault but one must see this in the context of the SWAC being formed to raise the profile of women in the party. What differs over the decades is the attitude of women to the SWAC and the way women used it until the party's demise.

Like any other body in the CP in Scotland, the SWAC relied on those deeply committed to its specific remit who realized that if it were to be successful, then most of their time would have to be devoted to its work in addition to that of the branch:

> You went from *door to door*, it's a lot simpler in a small village going from door to door: you know people physically, it's not as hard as in the city running up and down tenements, and you could go down a street in no time unless you blethered of course, which happened pretty often, and we used to sell about 100 *Woman Today* for instance, which was the party publication at that time.[56]

Although targeted at increasing women's membership and broadening the party's appeal, *Woman Today*, edited by Tamara Rust and launched in the late 1940s, did not last beyond the 1950s. The publication targeted women's issues, was highly political and not at all condescending, but it seemed imitative in presentation of 1950s women's magazines and to some it may have seemed unattractive. It lacked permanent sales, despite healthy Scottish ones initially,[57] and was cut back in regularity before being wound up. The CP was unwilling to subsidize the journal for too long and members were obviously showing a preference for publications dealing with a breadth of issues generally. *Communist Review*, *Labour Monthly* and *World News* filled this niche and were still popular.

Working for the party

Such was the commitment of many members that they were more than willing to work in the party offices, both at area and district level, if they got the chance. Usually one of the party cadres, the leading members, would be chosen for a paid position in the party structure. But any enthusiasm to become part of the leadership could turn to disillusionment if they were taken for granted or not treated well. 'I was like a fish out of water in the Glasgow office … the organizer … had a bad attitude. … I was badly treated and I don't think I was helped very much by the people.'[58]

In this case fellow comrades spoke out at the unfair treatment and the official concerned lost the respect of a few members who knew how he had mishandled the situation. Those who had often sacrificed the chance of better wages elsewhere expected the CP to treat its employees well and to experience camaraderie in the branches. This was often a mistaken assumption because, whatever united members ideologically, mundane administrative party work still had to be done and party organizers could be as demanding and as insensitive as any employer:

> Some of the Scottish office people asked me, they were looking for an organizer for Ayrshire and they were looking for an organizer for Aberdeen and they came and asked me if I would do it and I said no I wouldnae work for the party ever again, no' with the treatment I got, and I told them and I says, 'I don't think I got any great support from you people because you werenae prepared to stand up to the individual that was making my life a hell latterly,' I says 'I was doing my best for the party.'[59]

Such problems, however, often came not from the leadership at the top but from colleagues at district and area level who were also on low wages and worked long hours for the cause. Some organizers, often the most committed party workers who were run off their feet, may have been trying to disguise the deficiencies in their office skills. It would be unfair, however, to make a blanket judgement about all full-time officials. Many were considerate and did address women members' concerns in the party. It is illuminating to see how organizers, often articulate and bold people publicly, could be so disorganized behind the scenes.

Another area in which the contribution of women in the party seems to have been undervalued is as the partners of party organizers sent by the Scottish district or area committee to build up party membership elsewhere. Officials were often sent to places for a period until the party needed them somewhere else, or sufficient party activity was occurring for their work to be transferred to new activists. If a married couple were both party members then there was a joint commitment to accepting the party's priorities, often meaning low wages and poor conditions. But they were at least assured of an income of sorts:

> the guarantors system where members would guarantee to give two bob a week or something above their dues and a lot of income came from that, well you had no guarantee, they had a set wage I think about £4 a week or something at that time. I didn't have to pay any rent for instance, I cleaned out the party premises, the offices and the function room and I got rent free for that and two or three times a week you would get a pound then ten bob as money was coming in, some weeks you would get full wages, other weeks you wouldn't but I took charring jobs.[60]

But there were compensations. If the party depended on a couple to carry out full-time work then their most basic needs were prioritized – basic accommodation and amenities would be found through appealing to the membership and making known the need for funds. This appeal often elicited the desired response because members were usually aware exactly how much the full-timers sacrificed to work for the party.

With so few women full-time officers, the burden of the family often fell on women party members. They had to be understanding for the marriage to survive because even the demands of ordinary party members could cause family problems: 'we wouldn't let these things interfere, but I know a lot of comrades, *particularly* where the woman was not in the party, caused *a lot* of trouble.'[61]

Women's schools

The introduction of weekend residential schools for women increased the confidence of women members and strengthened their commitment to communist politics. The congenial atmosphere of a hotel or large house, sometimes belonging to a party member, and a more relaxed approach meant that more theory and discussion could be digested than in a two-hour meeting. Women's schools had been run successfully but intermittently in the party[62] and these had been on an area basis. Schools were organized for district women cadres, but they were restricted to those who were seen as the prospective leaders among the women. Expecting the highest standards from those attending, the sessions, spread over two days, concentrated on the rise of capitalism, the development of the labour movement, imperialism and the world transition to socialism.[63] This was a broad approach but one that covered domestic and international communist and social democratic ideas up until the present day. The cadre schools were for those who devoted more time to trying to take a leadership role in the party or in labour organizations and who were prepared to tackle the harder and deeper theoretical issues.

The central propaganda and education department in London also ran residential schools for women cadres at the British level. Cadres were told that 'the value you get from this school depends to no small extent on the preparation you make for it.'[64] There was essential reading prior to the school and further recommended reading. For these schools there were lectures, discussions and then group discussions. The broad variety of British and international socialist history, especially discussion of the Soviet Union, went into more depth during the course of a week. The schools left no time for anything but reading and sleeping as they started properly on the Sunday morning and ended on the subsequent Saturday. Each day's sessions lasted 12 hours from 9.30 in the morning. The sacrifice and commitment needed from the women who managed to attend these schools is self-evident.

There was a need to bridge the gulf between women who were in the cadre category and those who wanted to advance their knowledge, and so discuss and understand the basic historical issues so important to the party, but due to practical party work or family commitments did not have the opportunity. Fortunately, there was a solution to this problem.

Following the example of the Yorkshire districts' successful residential schools for women,[65] the first women's residential weekend school in Scotland took place in 1955 at the Bridge of Allan and 74 women attended. Prepared well beforehand, all sections of the party were asked to encourage women to attend and while the women were expected to meet most of the costs; branches were encouraged to raise funds to pay part of the cost for those who could not afford the two days. Although open to all they were geared more towards women 'already interested' in party policies.[66] The syllabus, sent out well in advance, was discussed at women's groups. The school was an opportunity 'for a weekend without the boss'.[67] 'The school showed an amazingly high level and proved how

6. CP women's school at Balloch, 1963. Jack Cohen was the tutor again. Marion Robertson is second on the left sitting. Edith Monroe is far right standing. Isa Porte is standing at the lowest point, third from left. Agnes McLean is in the white dress, sitting at the centre.

women already under capitalism, are emancipating themselves from the soul-destroying dullness that accompanies the drudgery of the kitchen and the monotony of factory repetition work.'[68]

A second school took place the same year in Edinburgh with over 100 delegates – Rhoda Fraser organized both. Being well subscribed and receiving positive responses from the participants, they were considered very successful. As well as hearing of contemporary events, such as a strike at Rolls Royce by 500 women engineers for higher pay, there were also classes on Scottish history.[69] The schools were open to non-party members and the involvement of a few Labour Party women made the proceedings more optimistic – 'we were seeing our work *together*, in a simple but profound relationship of completely mutual confidence between tutor and students.'[70] After the first day's work there was always a social event to look forward to in the evening.

The effects were beneficial, for in this informal atmosphere the women felt relaxed. This might be as much to do with the short, intense but usually enjoyable curriculum that filled the two days. It also gave women a chance to meet people from other parts of Scotland and to 'sus' them out in a jocular way. Women from the more rural areas came to the industrial west and Glasgow:

> In Aberdeen we had a sort of peasant culture really, and we kent things like corn-kist, that sort of thing was very much the background to Aberdeen culture whereas in Glasgow it was the street culture. Agnes McLean would tell you aboot lying in the beid and being able to put out her hand and switch off the cooker and switch off the light, you caud dae a'thing fae yer bed because the room was so sma' and aboot the people being raised in a room and a kitchen or was it, there's a term for it in Glasgow, just the one room and the kitchen, and the lavvy in the stairs, it was the cludgie! So there was this Glasgow culture which gave them a sort of brotherhood and sisterhood which we didnae have in a more rural area, so we might resent them and possibly they would see as well, we didnae have that industrial/trade union/political experience.[71]

The school's success led to regular area schools and biannual district weekend schools. In addition, British women's schools were held biannually in the 1950s and then annually in the 1960s to which one or two women would be sent by the Scottish district.

The choice of tutor for the schools was important because if people were bored or a tutor communicated badly then there would be a lack of interest in future schools. Many tutors were able to relate the history and theory well to their students having done so at numerous party meetings and in some cases as academics. They were experienced at pitching their material at different audiences. James Klugmann, the party historian, was very popular and took two residential women's schools in Scotland.[72] District schools for women increased in the 1960s and there was one usually every two years (two in 1963).

Ayr became the regular venue, with Balloch and Glenshee having been used previously. At the Balloch school in 1963 the tutor, Jack Cohen, wrote in his report of the school (after a collective report from nine of the women brought out some of the problems women there had in the party):

> It was stated that one of the big problems that party women face are the men – their husbands. 'The men are not interested in women, in their wives working actively in the party:' 'Some men

> don't want their wives in the party,' and this was echoed later in the class discussion.[73]

Raising the issue of women's organization in the party, he continued: 'There seemed a danger to me that the women's groups were being counterposed to the branches, as the place where women found their place in the party.' Women had said that they preferred the women's groups and had felt freer to talk there; in party branches 'they felt inhibited by the many contributions made by the men.'[74] Despite these problems, Cohen was impressed by the level of debate in the group's report back and following discussion. There was also a feeling that if a husband and wife were in the party then the husband invariably attended meetings and there was 'more than a danger that the women's groups were being seen as the only place where women in the party had their party life, and not the branches'.[75] These were important points on the problems women faced and were now being aired openly, though only in the collective company of party women.

In 1969 the district women's school discussed the latest revised edition of *The British Road to Socialism* with Joan Bellamy as the tutor. There was a slight criticism that those attending had not done their reading for the weekend.[76] The majority at the school were housewives, only two were students, and the others were in paid work, which possibly explains why many had difficulty finding time to prepare for the schools.[77] It was encouraging that nearly half the women at the school had been in the party for fewer than five years and half were under the age of 40, a sign that younger women were taking an interest in the SWAC's work. Deemed a success by the SWAC and the district, the schools were only attended by a small percentage of party women. The highest attendance during this period was 50 (1963) and the lowest 14 (1964). Usually the average was around 30.[78] Despite the effort and encouragement, there was a degree of apathy, with attendance from some areas sparse or non-existent.[79]

The schools continued well into the 1970s and 1980s. In these later years schools were aimed more specifically at women's issues, which by now had changed markedly from the first two decades of the SWAC, and were trying to challenge the accepted view of women in society and even in the party. They would become central to articulating the new approach to education, which was not just about the injustices of capitalism but also about the need to challenge previously accepted views of women's organizational role in the party and the neglect of gender and sexual issues in the movement. Even the original format of women's education and the schools would be altered to emphasize this new thinking.

The Scottish Cooperative Women's Guild

The cooperative movement had a mass membership in working-class communities. Having 11 million members by 1954 meant that 'half the families in Britain are connected with the Co-ops'.[80] In Scotland membership was proportionately higher than in England. It was a working-class way of life. Many families had grown up with the services of the cooperative movement because it was purposefully set up in the nineteenth century to look after the basic needs of the working-class population. For many CP women, membership of the cooperative guild, split into gender, was more natural than trade union membership, with 1108 of its 1695 female members being cooperators in the late 1940s.[81] In 1949 the Scottish Cooperative Women's Guild had 481 branches and 38,426 members.[82]

The CP saw the benefit of encouraging its members to be active in the Cooperative Women's Guild because party members could influence the guilds naturally through their local association and knowledge of its workings. It was also the one meeting women communists could attend if their partners, whose industrial position (and therefore gender) gave them priority, discouraged them from going to the party branch.

The culture of the Cooperative Women's Guild belongs more to the pre-1960s generation of communist women. It was used to promote the cooperative movement's interests and original ideals and its officers as capable individuals in the community. This inevitably benefited the CP as well. Recognizing it as a natural base from which its hard-working members could be respected for their dedicated work, the CP encouraged its women to influence cooperative movement policy as much as possible. There were two obvious reasons for this. First, as the party continually pointed out, the cooperative movement's officials were lazy and complacent. The CP thought that more could be done to represent members' interests, for it believed that the inactivity of the cooperative guilds was a reason for its declining membership and loss of influence over new wholesale and retail competitors. Second, there was a need to counter the labour movement's right wing, which had continually denied the CP affiliation to the Labour Party, had excluded its members from some unions and supported policies the CP saw as reactionary and anti-socialist, most notably its support for the cold war and consequent hostility to the Soviet Union. At least party members could work in the co-ops for the benefit of working-class communities without being discriminated against.

Many CP women supported their local guild irrespective of whether the party could influence it. That party women dedicated time and effort to running guilds in their communities and trying to promote their activities is a testimony to their commitment and integrity. Their work was in the interests of women and the wider community and not necessarily a deliberate attempt to bring the two organizations together.

In 1948 the Cooperative Women's Guild, and cooperative movement generally, brought in a new regulation known as the political rule. Introduced as the cold war was reaching its peak, it excluded communists from holding office in the guilds.[83] This tied in with the discrimination against CP members that occurred in other labour movement organizations.

> The same as the TGWU, they had an embargo on Communist Party women holding office but the unfortunate thing was, the Cooperative Women's Guild in some cases could not practise that, couldnae operate it because it was only some of our women that were prepared to take office and my very dear friend in the Townhead area, Margaret Reid, was the chairperson, the president of her cooperative guild and Margaret was a communist, but they couldnae do anything about it because it wasnae body else would do it ... in many cases I was denied the opportunity to do certain things because I was a communist.[84]

Potentially, it was a severe setback and challenged the strength of party women in the guilds. It could also adversely affect the work of the guilds locally, for party women were naturally active in them and had often played a useful and important role. Some guilds protested against having to replace capable women who had to relinquish their positions because they were communists and the measure seems to have elicited sympathy more than successfully isolating communist women:

> Those who were members of the co-op guild naturally discussed questions arising out of their membership of the guild with the Communist Party and that was fine and everything was all right

> until we had this introduction of the political rule … and when this was introduced in Kirkintilloch, there was a deputation there and this woman from the women's section, a higher body than the local, came out and said that every guild had to adhere to the political rule and therefore, if the branch was not going to adhere to the political rule then they would no longer be a branch. Of course there was an angry reaction to that because I had been the first secretary of the co-op guild after the war when they built the organization after the war and I enjoyed it very much.[85]

This shows how much party women were operating impartially in that they were 'naturally' members of the cooperative movement often before joining the party. They were often closely involved with cooperative work, so cutting out communist women was often recognized as affecting good cooperators. Marion Henery was secretary of the Cooperative Women's Guild in Kirkintilloch for four years before having to relinquish the position. She was re-elected as secretary in 1955.[86] There were long involved party members such as Nan Wallace in Clydebank who concentrated her work in the women's guild and was re-elected to the local cooperative board from which communists had not been excluded:[87]

> Nan Wallace was an outstanding member of the cooperative movement and she was a member of the local board of management and that was not usual for our party women to be as high as that in the cooperative movement. But Nan had that status, so she was not only a member of the local Co' guild but she was also an active member of the local society. There wasn't any organized direction that we gave to our members, to join the Cooperative Women's Guild because, already, a lot were members of the Co' Guild see.[88]

The attempts at exclusion were only partially successful at local level and of no benefit to anyone except those who wished to see inefficiency introduced. There had been no large mandate from the membership for these measures and there was absolutely no proof that it was popular. The party pointed to the fall in guild membership of 4936 within a year of the rule being introduced and cited the rule as a contributory factor. This might have been a reason, though it was stretching the point a bit. Membership was in terminal decline and, not surprisingly, it was a contention denied by the leadership of the movement.[89]

What seems evident from the conference agendas of the Cooperative Women's Guild during the years 1948–52, the height of communist isolation, and thereafter during the 1950s, is how effective communist women were in getting their ideas over and winning through some of their policies against the right-wing establishment.[90]

At the 1949 women's guild conference at Dunoon, Anniesland branch submitted a resolution on international cooperative unity that called on the government to 'strengthen its relationship with the Soviet Union and the democratic countries in Eastern Europe and thus build up the peace front of working-class men and women against the unbridled imperialism of America'.[91] The boldness of pushing party policy through a guild branch was not mere folly; it indicated the extent to which party women had got their views over in their localities. In 1951 the national committee of the Cooperative Party defended rearmament and, the CP felt, 'the peace movement was treated as a Communist plot, and the witch-hunt was in full cry.'[92] The cooperative movements in Poland, Hungary and the GDR were excluded from the International Cooperative Alliance mainly at the instigation of the British representatives, the reason given that these movements received help from their governments and were now integrated into the planned economies. In 1952 the central council's peace resolution supported Labour government policy but they 'deplored' the release of Nazi war criminals, opposed German rearmament, and supported efforts to bring about the unity of east and west Germany.[93]

The following year the Anniesland and Kirkintilloch branches were at it again with resolutions to conference that CP women merged and then supported on the floor. These resolutions, passed at the international guild conference at Copenhagen, called for a meeting of the 'Five Great Powers' in the pursuance of peace.[94] The central council of the guild opposed the resolutions stating that work should be done through the United Nations. The resolutions were defeated but others were won on education and opposition to attacks on the health service. This was safer ground but again it was party women who moved and supported these measures.

If they could not win the guild conference for pro-Soviet positions or peace then domestic militancy was safer ground. The congress pledged 'to actively continue the struggle for socialism to organize our women for mass demonstrations, and protest against those acts destined to destroy socialism and combat at all times those who would bring misery and suffering to the people of Britain'.[95] It ended with a call to 'rally the non-political and unorganized women' for future struggles. A lot was left to interpretation. Socialism could only be destroyed if it existed and if, for most guildswomen, this meant the local 'co-op' then for CP members it could also mean the rather large expanse of communist run countries in eastern Europe, which were in conflict with the Western powers. While the intention to mobilize the non-political may have been seen as knocking on doors and informing housewives of prices, party women could no doubt interpret it as a call to politicize the membership towards a more militant approach.[96] Any Bevinite would have sighed resignedly at the irony of it all – victory against overt CP policies, defeat against semi-covert measures. The conference also agreed to support unions in dispute against the non-union paper magnate D. C. Thomson in Dundee and Glasgow. All guildswomen were asked to boycott the company's publications.[97]

By 1952 the Scottish Cooperative Women's Guild had 33,392 members in 498 branches.[98] The Scottish men's guild had only 1100 members,[99] which showed how much the movement depended on women for its local activity. However, a fall in membership the following year to 31,366, despite an increase in branches, evinced party criticisms of the failure to stop the continuous ebb.[100] After 60 years the organization was on the wane and between 1948 and 1954 it lost nearly a quarter of its members.[101] Women at the 1954 congress supported resolutions condemning aggression against the People's Republic of China[102] and opposed sending troops to Korea.[103] Also, despite opposition from the president who opposed the measure, congress supported calls for the abolition of capital punishment.[104] The Scotstoun West, Anniesland and Whitehill branches of the guild, where CP women were well established, moved 12 resolutions sympathetic to CP policy. Given that there were only 23 resolutions in all, this shows both the dedication and success of party women committed to the guild. It is also illustrative of the effectiveness of the party's method of organization and its dedicated aim to formulate and change policies in comparison with Labour Party women in the guild.

When Scottish guildswomen visited the Eastern Bloc in 1955 they saw the horrors that war had wrought in Poland.[105] Visiting the Soviet Union they extolled the virtues of the cooperative system where shop workers acted for and reported to shop committees – on which 90 per cent were women.[106] The delegation was clear that it had not been coerced in any way and, having also seen amenities such as crèches, kindergartens, schools, hospitals, a new university and housing estates concluded that 'one lasting impression of the visit was the equality afforded to women in almost every walk of life.'[107] As the central council proscribed even the Scottish–USSR Society as a communist body,[108] such a response could only strengthen the will and likewise the acceptance of party women in the guilds. There was a commonsensical and effective way of getting the socialist message across in the cooperative movement:

> They werenae in there to dictate Communist Party policy but they obviously had to discuss issues that were coming up at the Cooperative Party congress, the Women's Guild congress and brought a lot of good stuff intae the likes of us and it was the same with us in the trade union movement because there was women in the trade union movement who had to be developed to put forward the fight for women's rights in the trade union movement.[109]

By getting involved in the women's guild in their area, attending meetings, holding positions and doing administrative work, communists could make an impact, and found it easy to do so in this organization. It would be hard to see it as overt infiltration, for the cooperative ethos was the basis of socialism. Since most party women were not involved in industrial unions, they directed their involvement to groups in the social sphere.

It was Rhoda Fraser who when asking 'Do you want a man's Party or a mass Party?'[110] pointed to the 'largely buried treasure'[111] of half a million women workers in Scotland. She believed there was a need to bring women in different organizations of the labour movement together: 'We can't transform the Scottish labour movement without also transforming the policy and outlook of the 100 women's sections of the Labour Party and the 400 branches of the guilds with their 28,000 membership.'[112]

Had Labour Party members been as ideologically committed to the cold war as its leadership was, or even if it had a more definitive belief in a form of socialism, surely there would be evidence of a greater political contribution from its membership? The Labour Party had the allegiance of many working-class communities, but there is little proof that in Scotland, prior to 1956, this depended on its anti-communist stance.

Once there was a thaw in the co-op's exclusions, the CP became more critical of the movement's lethargy and lack of drive. Communists felt that the cooperative was not doing enough for its members or utilizing its resources to counter competition from private traders. Women in the party who became specialists in this area coordinated work in the districts:

> we had an outstanding married couple in the Communist Party. … I always remember she took this school on the co-ops … from the point of view of production. I kept thinking about her, Elinor Burns was her name and she came and she took the school on the cooperative movement as such. Emile Burns was her husband.[113]

Burns stressed the very slow growth in the movement's share of retail trade and how few of the goods sold in co-op shops were products of cooperative factories and farms.[114] In Scotland and northeast England, where co-op trade was highest, 80 per cent of purchases of consumer goods went to private trade.[115] There was much emphasis on encouraging activity among women party members in the guilds to explain the greater role the cooperative movement could play in countering the business community and offering lower prices and higher wages.

An independent commission of inquiry into the cooperative movement was appointed in 1958 and the CP attached great importance to its findings. In the guilds the party saw the cooperative movement as having a 'priceless advantage which their monopoly competitors cannot share'.[116] With more than 30,000 shops, 250 factories and the largest wholesaling organization in the country,[117] the party felt 'the wholesale societies should be serving the needs of the retailers, and not dominating and controlling them'.[118] There was a need for the co-op to undersell the multiple stores and yet it was not doing this because of a lack of any organized and coordinated strategy throughout the movement, both wholesale and retail. The party detailed plans for a more professional and elected management structure covering the boards of wholesalers.

The wholesale societies rejected the independent commission's report, but made some democratic reforms in the composition of the cooperative union's central executive.[119] By the early 1960s the party was critical that 'too many local societies have lost their identity and independence too by going into the Cooperative Retail Services – owned and controlled by the Cooperative Wholesale Society.'[120] It was still recognized, however, that women easily constituted the majority of co-op customers and party members were expected to be members of their local co-op society 'as a movement to defend the working people from the robbery of capitalism'.[121]

Advisory and social issues in the 1960s

By 1958 the SWAC was meeting monthly and the Scottish district of the CP recognized the need to improve its work among women.[122] The party believed it had strengthened its influence in the women's assembly and cooperative guilds despite political proscription.[123] By the 1960s the role of the SWAC was firmly established as an integral campaigning body of the party. With its dual role as an advisory body that formulated policies to the Scottish executive and in organizing women's sections, it was also intrinsically part of the party and was the most important advisory body because it had this vital twofold role. The SWAC's work was coordinated from the party office in the Scottish district but it was also linked with women's advisory campaigns at the British level.

The SWAC engaged in some specific and, for women, extremely important campaigns in the 1960s. By 1964, in expectation of a Labour government, a Scottish *Women's Bulletin* had been produced. This informal news sheet carried information about the SWAC to members in Scotland and it lasted for only a few issues. Again the emphasis was on domestic topics in the women's sphere – 'high rents, bad housing, soaring prices, scandalous maternity services'.[124] It was in this context that it was said 'our Party is now leading a real fight in Britain for women's rights – as a citizen, mother and worker,'[125] an example of the existing unitary approach in the party as a whole to women's issues.

Much branch activity focused on fund-raising, education and an occasional film about the Soviet Union. International Women's Day was celebrated and work continued with the women's assembly.[126] As if to stress an awareness of the need to politicize women, the *Women's Bulletin* carried a quote from Lenin's *Letters from Afar* – 'If we do not draw women into public activity, into political life, if we do not tear women away from the deadening atmosphere of household and kitchen, then it is impossible to secure real freedom; it is impossible even to build democracy, let alone socialism!' With not even all party women in the SWAC, one wonders how many other party members knew of this quote.

The issues on which the SWAC campaigned were producing noticeable results. It was strongly supportive of the right to equal pay, a main concern of the advisory and women's groups. It produced regular district leaflets on the issue and women party trade unionists were encouraged to work in this area.[127] The campaign was to reach its height at the end of the decade, prior to the introduction of legislation in the 1970s.

The SWAC and women's sections got heavily involved in the prevention of cervical cancer and the need for more screening facilities. Their broad-based campaign elicited important statements from the government and results from the health authorities. This was SWAC's central concern in 1964/5 and much time was spent developing a strategy to put pressure on the authorities and various administrative bodies concerned. Medical opinion was that women over the age of 30 should be screened at five-yearly intervals.[128] Cooperative women's guilds throughout Britain had already raised the need for tests, treatment and 'the provision of mobile units'.[129] The Women's Liberal Federation had also been vociferous on the issue as had the Labour Party women's conference meeting in April 1964. Women in trade unions soon got motions to conferences on the issue[130] and the TUC promptly supported the campaign. The NWAC (National Women's Advisory Committee) wrote to the minister of health about the need for preventive measures, stating there were over 4000 deaths from cervical cancer each year. The minister called the figures inaccurate but said 'we accept that routine screening against cervical cancer should be available to all women at risk'.[131] The NWAC's reply was specific about the mortality rate: there were 2511 deaths from cancer of the cervix of the uterus in 1963, in addition cancer of the body of the uterus killed 1504 women, a total of 4015 – accounting for 10 per cent of the annual total of cancer deaths.[132] The possibility of mobile cytology units was also raised. The SWAC wrote to the Department of Health for Scotland urging more facilities and funding be made available.[133]

Aware of the importance to women of health facilities and preventive measures, the SWAC encouraged women to campaign with other groups and guilds. Thousands of women were dying each year from cervical cancer and it was preventable.[134] The SWAC also began to educate itself and the party women's group about the intricacies of cervical cancer. Medical journals such as *Nursing Times* were read and excerpts from a sympathetic editorial from it stated that: 'it is now possible to save an estimated 4000 women every year from the mutilation of their bodies (and their minds) from the sickening misery of radium, from death.'[135] At British level the NWAC wrote to the Ministry of Health, which replied that regional boards decided on what priority was given to cytology, that there was a shortage of pathologists and technicians and that five hospital boards were to run courses for training. There was now a strong angle for the SWAC to pursue in Scotland. It learnt from the Scottish Office that the secretary of state, who in January 1964 had asked what steps were being taken to provide routine cervical smears and cytological service facilities, was stressing the importance of the matter to the regional boards. Nevertheless, the SWAC was critical that the government, which could give it priority, was not doing so. Women were urged to write to their MPs and local medical officers and to illustrate to women 'how very low our present Government places the health of the women on it's list of priorities'.[136] By November 1964 the campaign, which the British Medical Association, the Royal College of Nursing and the Socialist Medical Association backed, was firmly established and gathering momentum. The SWAC called for a nationally sponsored government campaign to allocate funds to regional hospital boards[137] and for a national campaign to convince women of the need to have a smear test. The SWAC advised its members: 'All women among whom we live and work should be urged to go to their GPs and ask for a smear test.' They believed that leaving the impetus to hospital boards and limited funds would delay proper action.

By 1965 the secretary of state was demanding more action from the regional boards with greater resources and training given to the more rapid screening of women. More facilities were forthcoming and 'a number of married women doctors'[138] became involved in training staff. The campaign was now getting prominent coverage from the press. Despite the assurances of Judith Hart MP (parliamentary under secretary of state at the Scottish Office), there was criticism that the 'official bodies' were not treating the service as a matter of urgency. An intensive three-month cytology course was needed.[139] The SWAC wrote to Judith Hart, always seen as a sympathetic left-wing Labour MP, and asked for an assurance that the regional boards would allocate the necessary funds and carry through educational work among women. The SWAC pointed out that in 1962 the Scottish Health Council had asked the regional cancer committees in five hospital regions for comprehensive cytological services.[140] The reply from the Scottish Office stated that there was 'slow progress in extending facilities'[141] to cover all women at risk and that there was a need for 'an emergency provision of trained personnel, laboratories and clinics',[142] and that training of GPs was also needed. There was to be a conference of all medical groups concerned.

The campaign had highlighted the scant attention paid to the availability of facilities for screening for cervical cancer and had put pressure on the appropriate authorities. Elizabeth Bowman, a CP member involved in the campaign in Dundee, reported how a woman doctor running the cytology clinic in Maryfield Hospital (who tested women by going around hospital wards and telling them about its availability) had screened her and found her to be positive: 'I got such a shock because I had no symptoms that would even raise doubts.'[143] Here was a graphic example of the campaign's relevance and importance. She continued, 'This situation where it is left to the woman to go and seek the test, should really rouse us to anger and action.'[144] There had been an increase in provision because of the effectiveness of the broad-based campaign. Party women engaged in it and prioritized the issue, which showed how effective the SWAC could be in mobilizing its small, active membership.

It might be pertinent to see this as a moral issue, for views about what was considered acceptable behaviour were still old fashioned. The SWAC tackled the issue of cervical cancer from a critical standpoint, pointing to the general lack of concern about female mortality rates and avoidable deaths. On other health issues concerning women there could be a conservative response. In the late 1960s legislation was introduced that dramatically affected women's reproductive rights:

> I got quite a big surprise when we were all talking … about abortion and I took it for granted … that although it's horrible and I've seen it in 'gyny' wards where there's a woman desperate to have a baby and can't have it in one bed, and next to her is a school kid who's had an abortion, and no way it's nice … but it's a woman's right to choose whether she has a baby or not. And I thought *stupidly enough* that all party women would think that, but of course they don't.[145]

The provision of nursery education was raised in many areas and was still seen as the specific work of women's groups. Although predating the 1960s it also developed in this decade. A national campaign committee for nursery education coordinated the work of local organizations trying to pressurize the government to provide nursery schools and crèches.[146] The SWAC could report that the fight had been successful in Paisley and Glenrothes. Allied to this was the question of school meals and milk. Deputations with the Scottish Office were requested but rejected. As the SWAC argued, 'in all parts of Scotland there is some concern about our children's welfare'.[147] There was an attempt to link school meals and milk to wider matters, including unemployment, the wage freeze and price rises.

Prior to the election of the Labour government in 1964, the SWAC campaigned for the few CP candidates who stood. Emphasis was on the small things that affected people a lot, like the cost of a loaf of bread. The profits of the largest food companies were displayed and there was a call to support co-ops more, and to limit the big monopolies' price rises and profits.[148] Women in the party lobbied their MPs and called for price restraints against profiteering companies. Party women led delegations from throughout Britain and presented petitions. Despite Labour MP Willie Hamilton's anti-communist rhetoric,[149] the lobbying succeeded in getting most MPs' sympathy, and raising the profile of the party women.

On local issues the party highlighted the annual rates increases and, though the Labour government introduced some ameliorating measures, it was still criticized for not granting enough relief to poorer households.[150] The party's call was for a local income tax. It was about these issues that the SWAC, with Margaret Hunter as national women's officer, was concerned.[151] The work of the women's advisory committees was vital and there were around 50 in Britain altogether. The aim was for one in each town and, if possible, one in each branch. This was important for the new housing schemes thrown up in the 1950s and 1960s in all urban areas, which often left people isolated.

Elizabeth Hamilton built up the Castlemilk party branch and the women's group, which met every Wednesday[152] and was central in forming the local tenant's association in Castlemilk, one of the biggest housing schemes in western Europe:

> I joined the Castlemilk branch of the CP and … the women's group used to meet once a week and I didn't or I couldn't manage to go to them all the time. … I used to go round trying to recruit other women into the party and all that and we used to help the *Daily Worker*'s bazaars. We would make lots and lots of things, either knitted things or creative things and baking things for the annual bazaar every year and they did lots of fine work. … We always met in someone's house and every so often it would be your house to have a turn to have the women's group in. So that was my involvement with the women's group advisory committee.[153]

When the delegates to the national women's conference met in London in October 1966, just after the return of the Labour government, Margaret Hunter was still prioritizing the problems of the wage freeze, price rises and the need for the government to build 400,000 council homes.[154] There were also important international issues like Vietnam, Zimbabwe (Rhodesia) and South Africa. There was now more emphasis in the party on solidarity work generally, which continued through to the 1980s.[155]

Conclusion

There seem to be three discernible periods in the evolution of the SWAC. First, an innovative stage in the late 1940s and 1950s when it was built up methodically branch by branch with the enthusiasm of the secretary Rhoda Fraser; second, as an established and publicly campaigning body under the diligence of Marion Henery up to the late 1960s; and finally, with Pat Milligan as secretary, as a structurally reforming and more noticeably feminist body in the 1970s and 1980s. This latter period also saw it merge more in aims and work with party members who supported some of the new ideas. There was a determined effort, which was successful, not to separate the actions of the SWAC from the rest of the party. This was a noticeable change from the late 1960s when, with Margaret Hunter now active at British level, the emphasis was on women in the domestic sphere. For instance, the SWAC attacked the Wilson government for not dealing with housewives fairly over nursery provision, and its campaigning role was still primarily on social issues such as rents, rates and price rises.[156]

There was thought to be no underlying problem in the party's approach to women that more attention and better organizing could not solve. In the 1960s high priority was still being given to discussing the SWAC education syllabus and the work in the co-ops.[157] Most international protest was against the war in Vietnam.[158] While party members complained about apathy and indifference generally, this was not directed to the SWAC's work, or to its overall historical interpretation of events and definition of a women's role as a part of the class struggle. Any conflict of ideas within the SWAC was not about its existence but about what it existed for. There was disagreement over the direction but not the need to organize women and encourage the section's growth.

In 1968 the women's school in Ayr discussed the women's movement[159] and the place of women in past societies. Younger women could understand the evolution of women's oppression. 'I can remember Marion Henery … organizing weekend schools down to Ayr[160] with really good speakers and talking about the origins of women's oppression through a feudal society and also making points that it wasn't always like that.'[161]

At the end of the 1960s there was a new generation coming into the SWAC and into the women's sections that would highlight the extent of women's oppression in contemporary society and promote the need for more attention and appreciation of gender inequality. This came too late for those who had left the party a decade before and had not been impressed by women's sections and saw little progress in their role:

> I wouldn't say they did any better than when I joined the Labour Party and there were still women's sections from the same period. They were stuck I think in the 1930s, which had been a decade of real antagonism to women's separate demands or women expressing their own demands, there'd been a real hiatus in the women's movement and I think the Communist Party was in that sense like all other parties so I don't think they were any better about women but I don't think they were any worse than the Labour Party or the co-op movement which had the Women's Cooperative Guild which actively organized working-class women.[162]

Yet, it was the development of the women's schools from the mid-1950s and the intense two-day programmes that advanced members' understanding and boosted their confidence. There were more schools in the 1960s and they were more theoretically based. However, if the SWAC was responsible for a high level of education there was still the issue of its relevance in the party structure, especially as the younger generation was more inclined to question traditional methods. Party members were now being asked 'are women's groups out of date?'[163] The criticism was that they were solely concerned with domestic issues. By this time aspects of the SWAC's role, even though it was barely 20 years old, could inevitably be seen as slightly outdated or even archaic to younger women of the 1960s generation. There was discussion about strengthening the work of the SWAC[164] although it was nowhere near folding and still had a very active body of younger women involved. There were regular monthly meetings and two Scottish district meetings a year for the branches.

Though it might seem as if women only became aware of their exploitation in the late 1960s, this was not the case. It would be wrong to underestimate just how aware and self-critical the first generation of activists in the SWAC and the sections were about their limited role, or indeed to believe that the party failed to recognize the specific problems women faced. As early as 1952 Elinor Burns wrote that 'the least glance below the surface shows that the degraded position of the women still remains, and until women themselves understand *why this degradation will end only with the change to socialism* they are held back from using their full strength in the struggle for emancipation.'[165]

From the developing feminist viewpoint, the argument 15 years later was the other way round: there could be no change towards socialism until all communists recognized the need to end discrimination in the party. But that was not the predominant view in the SWAC until that time. Burns stressed the need for a united movement of which the women's movement must be a part. There was unequivocal recognition that women were more unequal than men, but the class struggle and accepting that 'the real enemy of the women is capitalism' were still paramount.[166]

From the late 1950s the Scottish district declared it had made a more serious effort to address the problems affecting women and was trying to increase women's involvement in party campaigns.[167] In October 1958 the NWAC adopted the statement *On Work Among Women*[168] and by 1959, as if to prove the success of giving due recognition to the issue, one-third of all recruits to the party were women and thousands of leaflets on women's issues had been distributed.[169] By the 1960s more attention was being paid to the role of women and the party leadership was giving the SWAC a lot of encouragement.

Because its membership was specifically gender based the SWAC transcended the usual role of an advisory committee. It had a swathe of members for whom it was responsible, so had to fulfil an important role in sustaining and increasing membership. It is well to remember that it was a new body and, with new women coming into the party, its development also necessitated its change. That it had encouraged so many women and had politicized them more than the party branches appeared to do is testament to the need for a specific structure in which women could organize. As early as 1955 it was observed that, concerning party women, 'most of them have not been able to take part in branch life'.[170]

One should not forget those women who never at any time took an interest in women's issues. This accounted for half the female membership and included those who opposed separate organizations for women or specifically women's issues: 'There was always this discussion about whether or not to have a women's section, *not* among the male comrades but among the women. Some agreed with it and some didnae agree with it. It always went on. I was always for it.'[171]

There was little actual criticism until the late 1960s that the party was going the wrong way about tackling women's issues or indeed that its definition of women's issues was limiting and not extending the role of women.[172] One reason was that there was little interest in separate women's activity and in attending women's sections from those who might do battle with these new ideas at branch level. A conflict between the two would not occur in the SWAC or women's sections, as the traditional 'vanguard' element did not consciously operate in them. By the end of the 1960s the CP's traditional way of operating was not automatically accepted. Party structure and party theories needed to be looked at from within. This momentum gathered pace with the CP women's conference in October 1970 criticizing past practice and recognizing the impact of the Women's Liberation Movement (WLM).

Finally, in 1968, as if to illustrate the success that persistence sometimes brought, the SWAC proudly reported the election in Inverness of Mabs Skinner to the local council. It was nearly a quarter of a century since she had manoeuvred through wartorn streets to help in the formative stages of the NWAC in London. That a woman, who was a communist, who was English and lived in the Highlands, could win an election in this area of Scotland was quite astounding. Some things had changed.

Chapter 5

Solidarity with the Socialist World: The Soviet Union and the Eastern Bloc, 1917–64

> I thought we all looked up to the Soviet Union. It was the first country in the world that threw the capitalists off their backs, so we had to look up to it. It was important.[1]

The USSR 1917–45

The Russian Revolution and the fight to retain the new republic in the first few years shaped the consciousness of many party members and determined at times a fiercely loyal, albeit uncritical, attitude to future events. After the 'war on 23 fronts'[2] with countries and internal opposition hostile to the Soviet republic came the years of famine and the economic restraints on trade that made it seem doubtful if the revolution could survive. That the Soviet Union did survive such open hostility no doubt coloured party members in supporting measures of dubious legitimacy. In this chapter I attempt to set out and explain the attitude of women party members in Scotland to the Soviet Union and their experiences and perceptions, including the dramatic and for some traumatic events of 1956.

More than three-quarters of the women I interviewed had visited one or more socialist country and, more often than not, the Soviet Union was prioritized. The history of the USSR was tied up with its affiliated parties. Most gave unquestioning allegiance to the CPSU through the Communist International. Lenin's legacy and, from the mid-1920s, Stalin's dominance were seen as central to world socialism. Many workers had acted in international solidarity before the appearance of communist parties: 'It was the first country that had been taken over by the workers and everybody looked towards the Soviet Union for leadership because it was the first workers' republic. In this area there were 'Hands Off Russia' committees set up so that Russia wouldn't be defeated.'[3] These early acts were etched on the minds of many future CP members and would be important in continued support for the Soviet Union. The deprivation during 'War Communism' and the economic retreat from socialist policies that was seen to be necessary under the New Economic Policy did not spell the end for the new republic. The appeal of Lenin's arguments, his supremacy in the Russian CP and the dissemination of his work among party members and in the Communist International, led members to expect that the Soviet leadership would always be of the same calibre.

The first chance for ordinary members to get to the Soviet Union was to be sent to the Lenin School in Moscow or to go as part of an official delegation. The five-year plan in the late 1920s was the first major attempt to expand the industrial sector and to subordinate agricultural production to this process. Even at this early stage there were noticeable advances. Mary Docherty from Fife visited a Soviet motor vehicle factory in 1929 at the beginning of the first five-year plan:

> When we were getting introduced, interviewing some of the committee ... we seen young fellas passing and we asked 'what are all the young fellas passing for?' and they said 'The night school are starting and they're all going to sign on for night school' and that was 1929, they were that interested ... it impressed me because ... it wasnae for their sel', it was for everybody because everything belonged to them and you felt that when you were in it, that everything belonged to you. Even when I was there I used to walk up and think 'fancy, this belongs to me too, I'm here, I'm a worker.' Everybody was working for one another as it were.[3]

This sort of experience convinced people that the road to socialism was being built. After Lenin's death in 1924 Stalin was quick to eclipse his rivals for the leadership, but at this stage the long drawn out battles between the various opponents were not self evident to ordinary party members abroad. There had been bitter disagreements in the CPSU central committee, but it retained the impression of continuity and strong leadership. Soon Stalin was seen to embody Soviet socialism:

> When you were there you looked up to Stalin. In fact, I could hardly believe the things they told us years after that had been

> taking place; there was never any sense of that when I was there, never got any inclination that that was going on. In fact … Stalin was to be at that meeting but he had something on and couldnae come and [it was] Budenny that come to the meeting.[4]

Budenny was no minor replacement. He had been a commander in the civil war and was one of its heroes. He was a founder and later inspector of the Red cavalry in the 1920s. In 1935, firmly a part of the hierarchy, he became one of the five marshals of the Soviet Union.[5] Industrially, there were already notable advances. From 1926 to 1927 there was a 31.7 per cent increase in the total volume of investments, and in construction it nearly doubled.[6] The five-year plans, the first of which started in 1928, sought to industrialize the economy rapidly and so catch up with the output levels of advanced capitalist countries. It was seen as the only way the Soviet Union could progress. In the treatment and upheaval of people from the countryside and the shortages that were incurred, the effects of the first plan were horrendous,[7] though perhaps inevitably so:

> Obviously you saw a lot of evidence of privation. I mean the footwear, there was so many people going about with felt boots on, they didnae have money to buy leather shoes. Also, as far as food was concerned, it was basic, very very basic … there was a lot of privation leading up to the end of the five-year plan at that time.[8]

At this stage one must recognize that communists in Scotland (and elsewhere) felt a physical attachment to the Soviet Union. The economic depression that cast a shadow over the major industrialized nations at this time brought staggering reversals of fortune for even dynamic economies like the USA. In Britain, unemployment reached historically high numbers at a time before the automatic safety net of a welfare state. Worse, the Labour government penalized people who were out of work. In Scotland, mass unemployment and deprivation drastically lowered many workers' living standards, especially once the means test was applied and the plight of one member affected whole families.[9]

It looked as if the Soviet Union, despite its backwardness and primitive level of industrialization, was making headway and employing its people to advance the living standards of the majority. It was certainly at the expense of the peasants who had benefited from the

New Economic Policy and who were said to be a nascent bourgeoisie. The offensive against the Kulaks was brutal, but, it was argued, they were profiteers who did not deserve the sympathy of communists and who were seen as being detrimental to the revolution and its purpose. 'And you had sabotage from the rich Kulaks and all that was very worrying. In the countryside there was a special class war going on and I think this was a very difficult thing.'[10]

There were of course different views on the speed, time and necessity of the policies implemented during this period. Industry was central to an advance in living standards in either economy, and the industrial working class was pivotal for furthering the advance to socialism in the USSR. For women, advances in social relations were announced in official statements proclaiming equality in law of men and women and the right of one partner to dissolve a marriage.[11] In employment there was a large increase in female unskilled labour, though medicine and teaching were seen as the almost exclusive preserve of women.[12]

In the run-up to the Communist International congress in 1935, the CPGB had sent Peter Kerrigan to work in the Soviet Union and the influx of visitors and delegates presented family problems. Rose Kerrigan found she could not get facilities for her youngest child Rose:

> I had nobody to take her and look after her so I just had to stay home and we went out a lot together, tried to learn some of the language but even then things were against me because that was the year of the seventh world congress and all the interpreters ... were all occupied and I couldn't get anybody to teach me! ... [Peter] was the one that had to organize a delegation from Britain and everything because we were living there and he was supposed to stay there a year and if he had I would have learnt the language but everything was against me.[13]

The mid-1930s was also the time of the great purges when Stalin eliminated his opponents. D. N. Pritt, a Labour MP, and Pat Sloan,[14] who worked for five years as a lecturer in the Soviet Union, were eyewitnesses who defended the 'fairness' of the 1936 trials.[15] Party members were told of the Soviet party leadership's success and that 'socialism has been built in the Soviet Union precisely because Trotsky's wrong policies have been defeated'.[16] Some members developed doubts about Stalin, but there was no universal questioning.

The 1936 'Stalin Constitution' claimed to make 'the Soviet Union the fullest and most complete democracy … the world has ever seen'.[17] Few people in the CP at this time in Scotland had any criticisms. The Soviet Union was a source of inspiration because it seemed to contrast full employment and progress with stagnation and depression in the West.

The dramatic change in Soviet foreign policy in 1939, which resulted in the Nazi-Soviet Pact, caused ructions in CPs and precipitated a crisis in the CPGB. Harry Pollitt, J. R. Campbell and Willie Gallacher strongly opposed the Comintern's change of line,[18] which amounted to a shift from an anti-fascist position on the Spanish republic and war against Germany to seeing the conflict as an imperialist war. Party members in Scotland knew about Pollitt and Campbell's stand (Gallacher supported the change) because the matter was discussed at meetings. May Annan, who had joined in 1938, remembered: 'That was the first controversy that I met in the Communist Party.'[19] Alice Milne, who had joined the YCL the same year, was slightly bewildered by the arguments. 'I couldna understand it. I couldna understand why one minute we were for the war, the next minute, well maybe I've got this wrong but it seemed to me a remarkable turn around in a very short space of time and I couldna understand it.'[20]

Pollitt was consistent in having always opposed fascism, as had J. R. Campbell. The imminence of war may explain the lack of resignations over this issue. There was a massive vote of Scottish members supporting the new party line.[21] The testimony of women party members shows that the issue was by no means quietly accepted by a compliant membership and that as well as among the leadership, much soul searching went on in many Scottish branches. Having heard the facts at a meeting, Effie O'Hare and her husband Dan discussed the issue:

> When I came home I started to talk to Dan and we argued and argued until four in the morning and Dan said 'Oh to hell with this, I'm going to bed.' … I supported them instinctively, I wasn't very good at explaining why. … I thought it was wrong because you don't fight for years up to 1939 against fascism and suddenly turn. To me that was wrong.[22]

The confusion and a dramatic change of policy was evident at Scottish district level when Bill Cowe, a party organizer, wrote *Scotland and the War* in opposition to the war in 1940[23] and then, a year later, in *Scotland for the Offensive: A Call for a Fighting Lead*, stressed the urgent need to support the war effort.[24]

Once Hitler turned his forces on the Soviet Union and swept across its Eastern Front, there was wholesale destruction of villages, towns and the annihilation of vast numbers of people. Isolated, faced with devastation and in need of help, the defeat of the Soviet Union seemed a distinct possibility between 1941 and 1942. Whole factories and resources were removed. From July to November 1941, 1523 industrial enterprises were evacuated, 1360 of which were said to be large-scale. Ten million Soviet citizens were moved eastwards.[25] Also, more labour was mobilized (in millions), work hours were increased and food was strictly rationed.

In Scotland, women in various organizations in Coatbridge and Airdrie (starting with the actions of women in the Airdrie 'Russia Today' society) responded to their perception of the stark conditions in the Soviet Union.[26] The Airdrie CP women's section, the Cooperative Women's Guild, churches, political parties and youth associations showed their solidarity with the women of Leningrad during the siege of the city from 1941 to 1943. Led by Agnes Maxwell of the local CP branch, along with a concerted effort by other party members, such as Minnie Aitken[27] and many sympathetic people in the community, women in Lanarkshire compiled an album of their locality for the women of Leningrad as a gesture of solidarity. It told of their history, how they lived and what they were doing for the war effort. Signatures and messages of support were obtained from women in workplaces, women's organizations, churches and youth groups.[28] The initiative was enthusiastically taken up and a similar album was sent from Leningrad. The Scottish album was presented to Madame Maisky of the Soviet embassy in February 1943 at a reception in Glasgow of 500 people.[29] Having learnt of the dreadful conditions the people in Leningrad were facing, the starvation that had ensued by being cut off by the German invasion and the lack of established and reliable supply routes into the city, one might presume that Scottish people were made well aware of the tragic state of affairs in the Soviet Union by this well publicized act. The final death tally for Leningrad was 830,000, including combatants.[30] The solidarity in this one instance had a lasting effect for those involved and possibly countered some of the dehumanizing images that developed with the cold war.

Visiting the USSR and the people's democracies

From 1942 the call for a 'Second Front Now' was evident on many demonstrations; keeping up with news from the Eastern Front and the intense fighting brought greater attachment to the cause: 'Stalingrad was a terrific epic o' gigantic world proportions and that affected me very deeply and in that sense the war did affect me very deeply and the tremendous loss of life that there was all over.'[31] Whatever Stalin's role, he reaped the benefits of the Red Army's success and his reputation among communists was enhanced during this period. As Isaac Deutscher accurately states, 'The nation was willing to forgive Stalin even his misdeeds and to retain in its memory only his better efforts.'[32] From 1945 there was a marked increase in the number of countries that now had socialist economies and internationally, for the Soviet Union, there was a reversal from the physical isolation of the 1930s. Seemingly, Stalin represented the invincibility of socialism by contrast with the demise of Hitler and his transient rule. The Soviet economy appeared to be strengthened with as much capital invested from 1946 to 1950 as there had been in the 13 years preceding the war.[33] From 1947, with credit agreements and in some cases the writing off of reparations, there was a greater economic link with the new socialist economies and this was confirmed through the Council of Mutual Economic Assistance (COMECON) set up in 1949.

Opportunities to visit the Soviet Union increased after the war and in Scotland there were regular visits and tours, the latter often arranged through the Scottish–USSR Friendship Society based in Glasgow. To combat the cold war and consolidate support for the international communist movement and its drive for peace, more international gatherings were encouraged and delegations were regularly welcomed. The Women's International Democratic Federation, to which the women's assembly in Britain was affiliated, held conferences. One was held in Romania in 1950:

> Some of the women who were organizing the women's conference … had suffered very severely under the Nazis during the period of the war and you could see it. They were very stoic women, there was no getting away from it, none more than Anna Pauker. … All along the road, when we were going to the congress, going to Bucharest first, every station we stopped at there was women there to meet us and to get to know us and give us wee posies of flowers and wee knick-knacks.[34]

7. Marion Robertson in the centre with the British delegates, Romania, 1950.

Pauker, from a Jewish family, was arrested and imprisoned in 1936 and exchanged for Romanian detainees after the Soviet invasion of Bessarabia in 1940. Stalin welcomed her to Moscow and she stayed there until 1944. After the war she was secretary of the Romanian CP and, in government, minister of foreign affairs and deputy prime minister.[35] The conference brought together European delegates and the Romanian authorities accorded it great importance by fêting its guests and taking them around various collective farms and factories. Though conditions were primitive, one could not, at this time, blame failed socialist policies because the country was only just recovering from the war. An element of doubt about the level of socialist democracy in operation could come through the often quick and inexplicable political changes that occurred in the early 1950s.

The press had carried reports from Romania of a purge of '192,000 members of the Romanian Workers' Party'[36] in July 1950. As it turned out, a couple of years after the WIDF conference, Pauker was purged politically and ostracized to the wilderness. She was expelled from the Romanian Workers' Party and lost her government post. She died in 1960.[37]

Biannual world youth festivals, usually held in a socialist country, were the biggest international gatherings. They promoted national independence from colonialism and Soviet-supported peace measures. The first festival was held in Prague in 1948 and the second in Budapest in August 1949, with students from 63 countries representing 57 million youths.[38] Visitors' children were given nursery school places and factory profits paid for the subsidized meals. Mines were nationalized in 1946 and, by 1948, so too was any industrial plant that employed more than 100 people.[39] When the festival ended, 250,000 Hungarian youths from various organizations took part in the closing ceremony.[40]

The World Federation of Democratic Youth and the International Union of Students organized these festivals. Although CPs in all countries obviously encouraged them, they were not meant just for YCL members. The British Youth Peace Committee, which organized the British contingent, was a separate body, but with CP support. It aimed to encourage youths from varied backgrounds to meet and promote peace in their respective countries, thus lessening tension between the East and West.

There is hardly a better example of the Western authorities' attitude to these events and their attempts to disrupt the festival than that suffered by youths travelling to the World Youth Festival in Berlin in 1951. The slogan for the festival was 'Youth Unite in the Fight for Peace against the Danger of the New War'. The *Glasgow Herald* held that: 'It is a foregone conclusion that they will return with glowing accounts of lavish hospitality, stirring demonstrations and magnificent artistic and athletic achievements.'[41] This reporter was obviously unaware of the Western authorities' proposed tactics. West Germany banned delegates from flying over its territory, so the only routes were by sea or across Europe by ferry, rail and road. It was only two years since the 'Berlin Airlift', which occurred amid Soviet calls to prevent the formation of a West German state.[42] Half the British delegation went on the Polish ship *Batory* and got to the festival in time, but the other half were thwarted from the moment they arrived in France:

> when we crossed the Channel and landed at Calais, the police on the French side had all our names. They let us all through except the leadership of the delegation and they were all sent back; they were eventually flown to Berlin but they were turned back at the Channel. So we then got onto a train which took us through France and Switzerland into Austria and when we got to Innsbruck, again we got word through the grapevine that there was trouble ahead.[43]

Overall, 100 people were turned back from French and Belgian ports, much like hundreds of foreign delegates travelling to the International Peace Conference in England the previous year .[44] In Austria the US army deliberately intervened to stop the train carrying the youth delegation. With rifles and fixed bayonets at Saalfelden they ejected those going to the festival on the grounds that they required 'grey passes', which they had been told previously they did not need to obtain. First stopped from leaving the train, the youths were then transported between Innsbruck and Saalfelden. Having been taken back and forth between stations, some wandered off near Saalfelden:

> We had walked up just past this farm when lorries in fields switched on their headlamps and blinded us and they came down. In fact, there was a lorry parked on the road and it had a machine gun trained on us. … One of our people … was knocked over by an American jeep. In fact, if they had known, he was an American who was with us and he was bruised from head to foot. Another chap was butted in the head with a rifle butt and was taken into the station at Saalfelden, and stitched up without any anaesthetic. He was later diagnosed as having concussion … his name was Colin Sweet.[45]

A young woman had been hit by a train and was badly injured. Colin Sweet and the other youths were forced back on the train. The harassment continued and it was clear that the authorities, under the guise of needing a grey pass, were intent on stopping the young people from getting to Berlin and wanted them to accept a train that would take them back from where they had come. Stranded at a woodyard and without basic facilities, women had to get fellow youths to stand round and make a 'screen' while they took turns to relieve themselves. They were humiliated in front of the American soldiers who stood by and made lewd comments:

> By this time we were all a bit desperate to go to the toilet, the chaps with us could go behind a hut or whatever but the girls couldn't very well do this, so some of the boys had found some breeze blocks and they built a shelter for us, but the Americans wouldn't let us go on our own so we always went in pairs and the American soldiers went with us and stood watching whatever we were doing, it was most embarrassing if nothing else.[46]

When railway workers told them they were to be taken to a displaced persons' camp, the students pulled the communication cords on a train to Innsbruck and, after a scuffle with police, they stayed there. A delegation, headed by a Scottish pipe band playing (rather bizarrely) *Rule Britannia* and *Jerusalem*, went to see the British consulate there who proved unhelpful.[47] The Austrian Youth Movement helped the delegates avoid the Western troops detailed to stop them at Bruck. Trade unionists helped them with money and food:

> Bruck-ad-Mur reminded me very much of our border towns, and we walked down and through the square and out one of the side streets and disappeared. We had been taken into a communal hall and from there groups of us were taken to public baths, and for a meal; they really looked after us very well and we discovered it was the Communist Party of this particular town that had come to look after us and that was the first time *I felt* confident we would see Berlin.[48]

Sympathy from some Austrians who fed them and helped find a way round the cordon meant that most of them managed to reach east Berlin and the Russian zone. They missed most of the festival and a national Scottish performance was cancelled because not enough delegates had reached Berlin in time.[49] Needless to say, any illusions young communists may have had about the the American presence in Europe was shattered when experiencing such treatment:

> I felt sorry for these young conscripts, I mean they were standing at night and all they could read were *stupid comics* and I thought, 'God, what kind of mentality have these men?' … I mean they were *men* not boys, and they were reading comics that said *Pow! Wow!* that sort of thing.[50]

The delegation had been at the centre of an international incident that typified relations between East and West at that time. When 900 delegates returned to Britain on the *Batory* they made it plain that they would be complaining about their treatment.[51]

Questions were raised in the House of Commons and the National Council of Civil Liberties conducted an inquiry into the affair. Despite claims that the youths were brainwashed and used by the Russian authorities (which was why Herbert Morrison had asked the Bonn government to stop them),[52] not all who attended were enamoured by socialism – 'our party had many differing impressions of what they saw.'[53] And those who did not sympathize with what they saw said so. It was the obvious cost of having a genuine delegation and not one full of sympathizers. Young Conservatives, two schoolmasters and some grammar school pupils were among those on the trip to Berlin and were thrown off the train along with the others.[54] Fortunately, the incident did not discourage female party members from going to future youth festivals. After Berlin the next festival was in Romania in 1953:

> Well, we were in Bucharest and we didn't really travel outwith Bucharest very much. It was a very young city in relation to socialism, I would imagine. And things were moving quite quickly and there was a lovely air of youthfulness about the place, and rebuilding and regrowth and all that, and I felt there was a wonderful atmosphere no matter where you went.[55]

The first idea the authorities wanted to dispel was that communist countries were aggressors and intent on international domination. Young communists may have expected to see positive aspects to these new societies, but at this early stage it was understood that some still depended on agriculture and visitors were not going to see wealthy socialism:[56]

> They weren't as well dressed as people in this country but I don't think you would expect that anyway. There seemed to be a lot of sports facilities for young people, behind buildings and places where there was just a small piece of area. If it wasn't a wee garden then it would maybe be a wee volleyball court or something of that kind, which was very impressive really.[57]

Public ownership of utilities was considered important. Women could see the recent advances in Britain, limited nationalization with noticeable results, as a partial advance on what was really needed – full public ownership. It was not the standard of living (which was rising in western Europe) that was compared, but who actually controlled the economy.

To communists visiting the Eastern Bloc it seemed as if the workers' parties were in control. Willie Gallacher, visiting the 1953 festival, marvelled at the palace in Bucharest because 'instead of a family of parasites occupying that great building it has now become a special kind of cultural and educational institution for the children of the workers'.[58] He was obviously making a comparison with the Russian Revolution and assuming that socialism was advancing in the same way in these countries. By 1955 Romania could in fact boast that 3.5 million of the four million people who were illiterate after the war could now read and write,[59] which was seen as further proof of the CPSU's beneficial influence since 1945.

Some, however, admitted to having seen a more repressive side at the 1955 World Youth Festival in Poland. Janey and Norman Buchan had been shocked by the level of deprivation and the shortage of food:

> This woman was cutting our hair. … And all that this woman said was 'have you anything for sale?' And that was absolute … and this was five years after the war and you were always getting this 'the war, the war, the war'. And I met up with some young American communists there, they were *absolutely* shattered.[60]

The less than wholesome support the socialist administration had in the populace was noticeable and security was tight at the delegates' hotel. While YCL members could see advances being made with the reconstruction of Warsaw after its wartime devastation,[61] there obviously was not quite the same enthusiasm compared with the Bucharest festival a couple of years before.

1956

In his New Year's message Harry Pollitt declared that '1956 will be a great year of action'.[62] He was clearly unaware of how true these words would prove both nationally and internationally for the communist movement.

When the CPSU met for its twentieth congress in February, Khrushchev, giving the central committee's report, was confident for the future and the congress reports to British party members said that 'by 1960 the Soviet Union will produce more steel, power, cement and fuel than is now produced by Britain, France and West Germany put together.'[63] With 7,215,505 members, the CPSU was three times as large as at the eighteenth congress,[64] and its leading role was deeply entrenched in Soviet society. Lenin was given continual credit for his great political leadership and principle of 'collective leadership'.[65] The failings of party members were acknowledged and the report contained recommendations for changes to the party structure, but on the whole its reform proposals were constructive.[66] Stalin's name was noticeable for its brief mention rather than usual omnipresence. Some delegates had learnt of Khrushchev's criticisms of Stalin's rule at a closed session of the congress, from where it leaked out to the world's press. In May the British party expressed its shock[67] and the speech was published in the *Observer* in June. In Poland, where party reformers had waged a successful struggle for autonomy, 15,000 copies of the speech were unofficially printed and distributed.[68] Until the revelations in 1956 there appears to have been no real questioning of Stalin's rule from those interviewed who were active at the time. For instance, none thought the criticisms they heard about his authority had any validity:

> Well, of course, during the war Joe was a great man and it wasn't until the twentieth congress of the Communist Party that it all came out. Up until then, Joe Stalin was a great person. When people talked about the Gulag and all the terrible things that were happening, you thought it was just capitalist propaganda, you didn't believe it. It was pretty devastating to find out later on that it was all true.[69]

Articles had consistently emphasized economic achievements since the end of the war, for example by 1949 industrial production was at twice its prewar level.[70] Progress was compared favourably with the countries under the Marshall Plan whose industrial production was said to have exceeded their 1937 rate by 4 per cent compared with 44 per cent for the popular democracies and 100 per cent for the Soviet Union.[71]

The announcement of Stalin's death in 1953 saddened many party members and a loyal tribute by Harry Pollitt echoed many of their sentiments.[72] It is difficult to convey the shock that greeted Khrushchev's secret speech in 1956 and the subsequent confirmation by CP leaders in Britain that mistakes had been made because of Stalin's personality. Dissenters demanding fundamental changes were greater in numbers than ever before.

Once members accepted that the accusations levelled against Stalin were true, those who had been involved at the highest level with him were criticized for having done nothing to stop him and failing to admit to the mistakes earlier. Indeed, there was a certain amount of anger at the party leaders in the Soviet Union who had watched the degeneration occurring:

> And then you came to know that there were others in the party who *had* known that this was happening and I had no doubt that they felt it was for the good of the international movement to keep it quiet, but that isn't how I felt about it. I felt very angry, very upset as well but very angry that it had all been hidden because had it not been hidden it might not have happened to the extent that it did happen. And as we know … thousands of good communists and communist families … were just eliminated and that, as well, was very upsetting.[73]

Dissent and unease accompanied the revelation that Jews had been persecuted in the Soviet Union, especially given that they had been recognized as a nationality in the Soviet Union since the Russian Revolution. The CPGB had many Jewish members and Glasgow had a strong Jewish community, mainly in the Gorbals area, many of whom had been left-wing refugees fleeing persecution in Europe at the start of the century.[74] The CP in Britain had a Jewish cultural committee and in Scotland the party had a Jewish advisory committee. In 1956 a meeting of Jewish CP members took place in Manchester. At this meeting Hyman Levy, a prominent scientist (and brilliant mathematician) originally from Edinburgh, raised crucial questions about the purges:

> In Manchester he addressed the conference and he said, 'we were asking questions.' He said, 'Ilya Erenberg came to my house in London, and comrade to comrade, of many many years, speaking Yiddish, I said to him, 'Ilya whatever happened to Mikhoels and Izik Feffer?' They came to Britain during the war to appeal for money, they came to Glasgow, there were huge meetings we had here for them, and he [Levy] said 'we never hear of them'. And to the conference Levy turns and says that 'Erenberg said to me "they are very well, I saw Izik in his dacha outside Moscow only a fortnight ago", when he said that to me comrades Izik Feffer was five years in his grave.' He said 'who the hell am I to be lied to about the Soviet Union?' … Apparently at that point friends of mine who were there said 'Jesus Christ, to think that they could have done that.'[75]

The implications here were enormous. Erenberg was a respected writer and was active in the peace movement, having been an inaugural bureau member of the World Peace Council in 1950/1.[76] Ironically, he was credited with helping to bring in a more liberal climate after Stalin's death and for reviving an interest in aspects of culture that had been neglected.[77] Mikhoels and Feffer had come to the West at Stalin's behest during the war as part of the Jewish Anti-Fascist Front to raise money for the Soviet war effort. They travelled to Canada, the USA and Mexico and also came to Britain, holding the said meeting in Glasgow. The party's National Jewish Committee had only recently been formed and it helped organize their visit.[78] Feffer was a respected playwright. Mikhoels was considered the greatest Yiddish actor of his day and he helped preserve the Jewish theatrical tradition. He was artistic head of the Moscow Jewish theatre from 1928 and in 1939 was granted the title of 'people's artist of the Soviet Union'. He was also awarded the order of Lenin.[79]

The late 1940s saw a dramatic change in the official attitude to Jewish culture; anti-Semitic persecution occurred on such a scale that it was only relinquished on Stalin's death and later admitted to by the party. It was during this period that both Feffer and Mikhoels perished. For those who believed the allegations at the time, such base prejudices were repulsive coming from the Bolshevik tradition, for since the revolution 'Yiddish literature, theatre, schools and press blossomed in a land where Jews had been ghettoized and oppressed for centuries.'[80] Hyman Levy came to Scotland to discuss matters with others worried about what they had heard:

> Levy came to Glasgow to give a report back and I'll never forget it … At one point, one of the women just had to get up and go out.[81] And I said to him, 'Hyman, you're saying to me that things like the savagery of the army, the savagery of the secret police, the brutality to people, you mean that?' He said, 'Look I'm not going to go into it Janey, for God's sake, let me just say this to you … the Soviet secret police had nothing to learn from the fascists.'[82]

Having heard these accounts many people left the party. An opposition group in the CPGB, calling for more open debate and a full discussion of past failures, launched a magazine to allow party members to air their grievances and comment on points raised in its articles:

> I supported the *New Reasoner*[83] group, Edward Thompson and John Saville who were producing this little journal, which I thought was

> wonderful. And we all agreed … that we weren't going to leave the party until we could see whether we could change it so that's what I mean by being a dissident, that we were part of a group that was demanding that the party *change* that year. I had big rows with my family that year, *big* rows.[84]

The Reasoner was highly critical of the party. It said political controversy was 'barely discernible at most times and … unrelieved dullness has repelled many who are otherwise sympathetic to Marxism'.[85] The majority of the party in Scotland disagreed with the extent of this fault finding. The yearning for a new style of politics and call for fundamental changes to the party's structure made some members uneasy (or just overwhelmed). For others it was the only way to develop the CP into a mass party similar to some of its sister parties in Europe.

There could have been no better time to contrast the indecisiveness of the CPGB with the PCI, the Italian CP that had developed new programmes to take it towards elected power and eventually a transition to socialism. With a membership of 2.5 million in 1955 and with 9586 sections and 1578 party groups,[86] it was the strongest CP in the Western world and its influence on its working-class was unmatched by any other CP. Developing a strategy that took it away from the orthodox line of the Soviet Union, the PCI saw advances being made by progressive elements in all organizations and stated:

> The move to the left cannot today be the aim of the struggle of Socialists or Communists alone, or even of the Socialists and Communists together. It is the aim of all forces of the people: Communist and Socialist, Social Democrat and Republican, Christian Democrat and Catholic, each of which must work in its own sphere.[87]

Togliatti believed that with such a strategy socialism in Italy could be won through parliament: 'Today the situation is that socialist ideas have deeply penetrated the minds of the people.'[88] For those increasingly critical of the CPGB, here was an alternative that seemed to be heading in the opposite direction of forming alliances with various groups and interests to influence more people. It was a strategy that was to develop in the 1960s and 1970s and would find both enthusiastic support and hostility in the CPGB.

One should not underestimate the sympathy people still felt for Stalin. If there had been major faults then others were thought complicit as well: 'If he did what they said he did, why did they let him? They were equally guilty if that were the case.'[89] The extremes to which Stalin went were criticized, not the policies the party had applied. This point was pivotal in that members could still believe that socialism had been retained and that the faults were attributable to personal failings and not structural degeneration. *The Reasoner*'s attack on the CPGB for seeing working-class interests tied up with the Soviet Union's foreign policy[90] could not be better illustrated than by a major international event.

Hungary

In late October 1956 large demonstrations in Hungary against the government were put down with the help of Soviet troops, which then withdrew. A bigger wave of opposition then rose up in Budapest and the city was in revolt. Soviet troops re-entered and there was heavy fighting until the uprising was finally crushed. Many CP members saw it as a counter-revolution on the grounds that communist officials and party members were killed on the streets of the capital. Graphic details of the crimes were published[91] and party members were reminded of the Hungarian Horthy state before the war and the menace of fascism. In addition, the last ten years had seen relentless opposition to the international communist movement and communists hounded in the West, so many CP members doubted the validity of nearly everything the press said against the Soviet Union. It was barely seven years since the arrest,[92] trial and imprisonment of Cardinal Mindzenty who symbolized, especially for communists, the reactionary nature of the opposition in the new people's democracies. He was charged with trying to overthrow the republic and with treason.[93] That the capitalist countries continually called for his release and touted him as a potential leader in Hungary[94] was seen as proof of their duplicity with right-wing elements that were said to have taken the 1956 revolt further:

> We lost quite a number of our comrades then, they just couldn't agree. My brother is very friendly with Charlie Coutts who was actually there, on the streets of Hungary when it was going on. He ... saw the party members being butchered in the street, it wasn't all one sided. ... I just thought that the counter-revolutionaries were at work and they were destroying Hungary and that the Soviet tanks were quite right to be there and as I say when you saw Hun-

> garian communists hanging from lampposts it was a fellow feeling, that these were your comrades that they were doing this to.[95]

Peter Fryer, the *Daily Worker* correspondent in Hungary, left the CP when his reports were either censored or not published. Though admitting that counter-revolutionaries existed,[96] Fryer believed that this was a genuine workers' revolt against an oppressive and corrupt CP. Proof of socialist and communist elements in the uprising were evident in the *Observer*'s extensive coverage,[97] though this did not necessarily mean that the uprising was leading to a consciously directed and democratic form of socialism. For communists loyal to the Soviet Union it was quite the opposite. In *Eye Witness in Hungary*, published in 1957, Coutts tried to balance criticism of the Hungarian Workers' Party – the target of 'the greatest upsurge of national feeling in Hungarian history'[98] and a particularly repressive socialist model – against an argument that Soviet troop intervention had been necessary. Future publications justified the fate of Imre Nagy,[99] whom Janos Kadar had replaced, on the grounds that Nagy and his supporters had 'degenerated from opportunists to revisionists, to renegades, to traitors and then to counter-revolutionaries'.[100] Nagy was later secretly executed. Many members thought that an invasion was all the Soviet Union could do to save socialism. Others had doubts:

> I wasn't terribly happy about that and of course the Communist Party convinced everybody that if they hadn't done that the reactionary forces would have stepped in, Hungary would have been overthrown and we would have gone back to the old right-wing … leadership. But I still was never too happy about the Soviet troops especially [with] … people being killed. … I know the Communist Party had to … defend it, those sort of policies, but I'm sure that there [were] people who were maybe making statements but within their self … not truly believing them, that's how sometimes I felt.[101]

At this point in Scotland many notable people left the CP. Rhoda Fraser, deeply distressed by Khrushchev's revelations, had already decided to go (as had her husband). Some branches in Glasgow, like Pollokshaws and central ones, lost members as did some in Edinburgh, which lost area official and former International Brigader Donald Renton.[102] Jack Ashton was brought in as an area official to try and hold the party together.[103]

Renton[104] recommended Ashton, who had been working for the Soviet press department, mainly to distribute *Soviet Weekly* and *Soviet News*.[105] In Fife, where the CP influence was strong, the split went right into the most dedicated communist families like the Moffats. A senior family member, Alex Moffat, an area official of the Scottish NUM and on the EC,[106] left the party, whereas a junior family member joined it in solidarity:

> My Uncle Alex left the party and that was a shock to me as I think it was my father who believed that if you had concerns or doubts about anything that went on in the party or in the socialist world you should stay in the party and fight for what you believed in – you should wait on a full report about what was taking place in Hungary – and I thought Uncle Alex should have done that.[107]

Hugh MacDiarmid, the greatest living Scots poet, also joined the party over the issue of Hungary. Always politically sympathetic to the CP and to Scottish nationalism, he later stood as the CP candidate in the 1964 general election against the then prime minister Alec Douglas-Home.

To supporters of *The Reasoner* group, Hungary was a further reason to transform the CPGB through internal changes. It had also occurred at a time when Anthony Eden, the British prime minister, had shown his contempt for President Nasser and Egyptian sovereignty by concocting, with France and Israel, a plan to invade Egypt and take control of the Suez Canal. Had it not been for the events in Budapest, it was felt that the left in Britain, with active groups like the CP-supported Movement for Colonial Freedom,[108] might have been in better position to oppose the Eden government. Those around *The Reasoner*, while strongly condemning the British government's attack on Egypt, blamed the communist authorities for the events in Hungary:[109]

> I remember going home and saying to my stepmother and father 'I just can't bear this, this is obscene how the party's behaving over Hungary. Why can't we just cut our connections with the Soviet Union and Moscow who obviously don't have the interests of any other working class at heart except their own and maybe not even that and have an independent party that can come out with its own analysis and won't be so isolated from the rest of the British political public?'[110]

Suez was a perfect example of the colonial powers' traditional approach to developing countries. As a countermeasure, Khrushchev voiced his support for the Egyptian people. With condemnation from the USA, Suez was a graphic illustration of the end of British imperial strength and, after 1956, British-ruled colonies raced towards independence. What was seen as the hypocrisy of the establishment made an indelible impression on young people who did not identify with Britain's past role in the world and identified with left-wing arguments. There was obvious frustration in the party that more could have been done had they not had to defend the actions of the socialist bloc at the same time.

Party members who supported the Soviet Union's actions believed that socialism was being preserved and the invasion had been essential and had the support of a large section of the Hungarian population:

> I personally thought there was a need for the Hungarian government, as they did, to invite their allies the Soviets to support them against all the subversive stuff that was going on. … I honestly believed it was the West, mainly the USA, that was doing their damnedest to undermine any progress that was going on in the socialist countries and I was prepared to defend socialism and our comrades in Eastern Europe.[111]

The events of 1956 affected members of the British CP dramatically. It questioned both the invincibility of the Soviet Union's political leadership and an unswerving acceptance of the dictates of the party leadership in Britain. The party's Scottish district exemplified this because it had always acted as a unified and solid political force. It still did, but a highly articulate and respected array of people who were a properly organized opposition in the CPGB had set a precedent. This precedent would make it easier for people to criticize the Soviet Union's actions in the future and allow them room to develop alternative political theories. There was more open criticism even from those who had been active in the 1930s and had been in the party for nearly twenty years:

> I never was terribly happy I think after the Stalin thing, the Stalin revelations. One was a bit careful in accepting just willy-nilly anything that was done. … I, myself, at the Khrushchev period, started to question anything … and did it in meetings. In fact I think I was kind of ostracized for a wee while. Another comrade and myself

> had the same opinion but I didnae care, people thought we had no right to be talking like that but I didnae care. We were at a women's advisory and I'd got up and spoke about something and I said I thought it was rather sad that this sort of thing should happen … especially the Hungarian intervention … people argued with me but I didnae agree with it at all.[112]

The Reasoner opposition was seen, denounced even, as intellectual. While in composition this was untrue, it posed a problem in Scotland. Party membership was so working-class that those who acted on Khrushchev's speech and opposed the Hungarian invasion were often worker intellectuals, the type of member the Scottish party had nurtured. Lawrence Daly of the Scottish NUM was one such figure, though he denied the tag of intellectual. Highly intelligent and articulate, the party leadership saw him as a future leader. He had left before the invasion of Hungary. Those who fought the leadership sought to try and change things round at the special conference that took place in April 1957. They felt the commission on inner party democracy provided the opportunity to change the whole nature of how the party was run, especially democratic centralism. When they lost out on this they published a minority report, which was rejected, and this is when many left. Some who left the CP set up a network of the left and for a time there were national conferences and discussions about regrouping and presenting a socialist alternative.

In two issues of *The Reasoner*, Ron Meek had written letters suggesting that the dissidents were not united in their alternative route. Lawrence Daly led the Fife Secular League (FSL) and at first it was successful in winning some council seats and existing as a new political entity. In the 1959 general election it beat the CP into fourth place in West Fife, though the party still had five councillors in the constituency.[113] The Marxist tradition lived on in that there was no rush to the Labour Party, but rather an attempt to build something more radical. That it failed, despite its initial success, and Daly and the league dissolved into the Labour Party, is an illustration of the kind of problem CP dissidents faced.

There was no room in British politics for an organized political alternative to fit between the Labour Party's social democracy and the CP's radical Marxism. In Scotland the loss in membership did not alter the party's character. As we shall see in the 1960s, no area of the Scottish district was irreparably damaged by the events of 1956 (two of the interviewees left at this time, one in Glasgow and one at St Andrew's) and for a number of years no alternative grew outside the CP. Still, the beginnings of new movements and ideas would grow and later become recognized. Simone de Beauvoir's *The Second Sex* had first been published in 1949 and Betty Friedan's later work had come out in 1963, but it would be a little while longer before feminist ideas began to take root in the CP.

Those who left the CP, especially the younger members, may have felt they had more political life ahead of them, and many did. People like John Saville, Edward Thompson, Doris Lessing and Raphael Samuel in England, and Lawrence Daly, Janey and Norman Buchan, and teenager Jean McCrindle in Scotland, who was the sole party member at St Andrew's University, all proved their worth in different fields as notable academics, writers and politicians. Yet, the experience of life in the CP, of its demands, level of debate and one's absolute commitment to its cause was seldom equalled or exceeded:

> We were exceptional I suspect in thinking it was worth going on trying because the party was *our life*, it really was. I've never experienced politics like that ever again except the women's movement actually, when it becomes your life again. But as a political party I've never had that again.[114]

Distribution of the *New Left Review* was not extensive in Scotland and at the *NLR* conference the FSL had been the only Scottish organization present.[115] Leaving the CP had only strengthened the resolve of those who remained and after 1957 there was less obvious criticism of the Soviet Union, at least from within the Scottish district, although there were changes that Pollitt could not have envisaged. John Gollan replaced him when he relinquished the post of general secretary in 1956. Ten of the 42 people on the party's EC were Scottish and had been brought up in Scottish branches, though some were now national officials. Agnes McLean was one of only five women on the EC. Over the next 30 years the CP would have a Scottish leader and this was important in keeping the continued strong level of loyalty to the policy direction of the EC from the Scottish district in the future.

The USSR in the early 1960s

By the turn of the decade there was a more optimistic air in the Soviet

Union and for communists elsewhere a strong belief that socialism had renewed itself. The launch of Sputnik in 1957, which the British CP saw as a 'great inspiration to the party and the working class',[116] and Khrushchev's confident manner, evident in his speeches at the time, mirrored the leadership's newfound conviction. The liberalization that occurred after 1956 allowed greater artistic expression and there was less arbitrary punishment of political opponents. Despite great economic growth and advance in the socialist countries, their living standards were still lower than those of western Europe, which was now entering its most prosperous postwar phase, and there were cultural differences that illustrated this in the early 1960s:

> I says to the women, I says 'it's like turning the clock back 50 years from the level we're at and the level they were at.' So it was … And then it was the factories. It was a big engineering factory we were taken [to] and they were very proud of the fact that some of the women were turners. I thought the conditions were awful.[117]

The quality of consumer goods for the Soviet people was also a problem (often pointed to as an endemic fault). Because such emphasis was placed on industrial production, the population's basic needs were catered for, but there was not the choice or quality that existed in the West. It was recognized as a problem, but not successfully remedied. Demand often outstripped the supply of goods and there were regular shortages:

> I was shocked at the poor quality of their goods when I went there. I remember one day I said to the person who was in charge of our party, could I see a typical Moscow store, so he took me to a Moscow co-op and first of all it was very poor. The building itself was very unprepossessing and there was great queues for things, and when I saw what they were queuing for, it was so shoddy and the goods were so awful, I wouldn't have thanked you if you'd given me them for nothing, let alone queue for them. And that really shocked me because I thought they ought to have been much, much beyond that stage and nae producing shoddy goods for the people.[118]

One might see these faults as either economic incompetence or as having to concentrate more on labour-intensive skilled factory work such as machine tool production. That there were communally owned facilities for workers such as meals for the end of the day shift and crèche facilities perhaps meant that consumer goods were less highly prioritized. Communist women visitors saw that there were good social services available for all and this was regarded as essential. It was important in influencing how they saw this form of socialism:

> when I was in the Donbass we saw … crèches for children and all the schools. … There were so many different languages in a vast country like the Soviet Union but they spoke their own mother tongue, but they had to learn Russian as a second language and every one of them spoke Russian and almost every one of them, wee things this size, could speak English or French. Their education system was great.[119]

This view was by no means exceptional among the women interviewed, whether visiting before or after 1964. It is an area where Khrushchev's reforms were quite successful. The number of pupils in higher and secondary technical education had increased noticeably since the late 1950s; numbers quadrupled between 1940 and 1964.[120] In Britain women party members were used to a poor level of social provision for children and women workers, and many working-class people felt the tiered welfare state worked against them. The high standard of education and priority it was given in the Soviet Union was something to which they could relate. That the schools seemed well run and ordered suggested that there was little alienation overall. At the English-speaking school in Leningrad:

> the headmistress gave us a little talk and we were handed over to two … pupils to take us round and show us the classrooms. And I remember going into one classroom and they could speak to us, I said 'Little girl what are you studying?' and she said 'We are doing a study on Robin Hood just now' and I mind that, I remember that. Then they put on impromptu concerts for us; a little boy recited Burns and they sang songs and gave one act of *Pygmalion*, it was on the spur of the moment, arranged in their concert hall for us.[121]

Visitors were still seeing advances in socialism and many who went to socialist countries in this decade were pleased with what they saw. If they were lucky, as were some Scottish CP women,[122] they might meet internationally known figures like Yuri Gagarin and Valentina Tereshokova, the first man and woman in space. Because Tereshokova was from a working-class family, was the first ever woman astronaut and was politically active, she embodied chances for women under socialism. She became 'chairman' of the Soviet committee on women in 1968 and was later a member of the party's central committee.[123] The space programme at the time was seen as an extension of superpower conflict in that the two opposing political systems were determined to outdo their opponents. However, the cost and technology needed, along with that of the arms race, demanded a lot from the Soviet economy's resources. Few criticized this because pressure to maintain a high level of expenditure in advanced technological areas came from the danger of the USA gaining an advantage:

> The most serious [criticism] that I had was the most unpopular. All that money had been spent on the space programme when they were supposed to be working towards a socialist society where people would have enough consumer goods; ... that money could have been spent on consumer goods for people.[124]

Those from a British party delegation or a trade union delegation also had the chance to meet high ranking party officials, and were accorded the best hospitality with guided tours and official gatherings:

> We met Khrushchev and his wife; we were introduced to them at this glittering reception. It was glittering in ... that the surroundings were glittering. It was the Kremlin and the chandeliers and everything, but the people that were there were just ordinary, they werenae all dressed up or anything like that.[125]

Until 1968 there was very little disillusionment about the Soviet Union, and few of those interviewed believed it was not basically socialist:

> There wasnae any unemployment at that time and I had been living in Manchester in the early 1960s at a time of very very high youth unemployment. And I just remembered all the young lads coming into the jail on remand, picked up 'loitering with intent' and I remember thinking the fact that everybody was given the dignity of

> having a job was very important. Also that there was health care and there was care for the aged; that there was never any insecurity and you werenae really aware of dire poverty.[126]

The events of 1956 could not be swept away and members of the younger generation were less likely than their predecessors to accept the integrity and political invincibility of the Soviet leadership. However, one should not underestimate their loyalty and genuine confidence that the Soviet system would continue its economic growth and eventually catch up technologically with the West. Khrushchev as a leader had a human persona and had shown that, despite admitting to horrendous crimes, the CPSU had been regenerated under his rule. Communists still saw it as a progressive socialist force in the world.

Cuba

While socialism in eastern Europe may have seemed uninspiring, the Cuban revolution of 1959 was quite different. It inspired communists because it obviously had mass popular support and was so near to the centre of the world's strongest capitalist economy. With the Bay of Pigs invasion in April 1961, the USA under Kennedy failed to overthrow the new government in Cuba, and the administration under Fidel Castro strengthened its support:

> Cuba meant an example of a country, and a less developed country, trying to be free to develop in its own way and the US had been so vile there. Everything you read about Cuba and of Batista was just disgusting. And when you're young I guess you over-simplify as well and it was very romantic all of this, the liberation of Cuba from Santiago northwards and all and it was important. And then Fidel's speech from the dock, you know 'History will absolve me'. That was published as a pamphlet and that was one of the first pamphlets I ever read.[127]

Except for one incident that threatened *any* future political permutation, communists could feel optimistic about the 1960s if this, along with the burgeoning anti-colonial movements, was to be the trend. The Cuban missile crisis was a moment when the cold war seemed to be near to reaching an apocalyptic conclusion. On 22 October 1962[128] President Kennedy announced that the USA was ready to stop at all costs the delivery of nuclear warheads to Cuba where nuclear bases had been built and which was only 90 miles from its shores. The US navy implemented a blockade of the island. It is hard to convey the feeling of gloom and real fear that a nuclear war seemed likely:

> One thing I remember about it is how close we were to a third world war and how you felt about that and as I say I had a young family at the time so I was concerned we were going to be thrown into this holocaust. I also remember that it was American imperialism that was threatening the independence of Cuba.[129]

Party members felt they should do something. A 'Hands off Cuba' campaign had already started in Edinburgh and during the crisis supporters organized a poster parade and marched in single file up the Bridges. They also organized petitions in Princes Street. Because there was so little anyone could do, party members like Isa Porte in Cambuslang felt impelled to do what they could to show solidarity when the worst seemed imminent:

> When it came over the television about *the* crisis day when it looked as if nothing could stop it being a war … my husband and I made a poster, went down to the local shops and stood there for a few hours and all it said was 'No War Over Cuba'. Just to let the people think about it. And the next night there were big meetings in Glasgow about it which all the local people joined in.[130]

The USA was seen as the prime imperialist country and socialism's main enemy. In the 1960s and early 1970s much energy and emotion would centre on solidarity with Vietnam against US government policies. For many young women members it was the first major international issue and, unlike the Cuban missile crisis, it was not a brief incident but became an integral part of their lives and political commitment.

Khrushchev was replaced in 1964 amid heavy criticism of his agricultural policies, yet in the 1960s world socialism regained its idealism of previous generations. One may attribute this to a change of climate in the Khrushchev years and to the fact that for remaining communists, however traumatized, belief in the Soviet Union was not altogether shattered. Trips to the socialist countries were still enthusiastically undertaken:

> I went to east Germany just after I had joined the YCL, I went on a ditch-digging working party, which was great fun, just cos' you were there with a crowd, and I was making a lot of new friends. The food was terrible, it was hard work but what was entertaining about it was just meeting people.[131]

This attitude was typical of the new wave of YCL members who came into the party and in the next chapter I attempt to convey the views and influences of this new generation and compare them with those covered in the preceding chapters.

Conclusion

In this chapter I have discussed why party members believed in the Soviet Union, believed that Stalin's policies were helping in building socialism and why many members supported the intervention of 1956. Having the luxury of hindsight it is easy to condemn CP members.

Communists saw the capitalist world's hostility as proof of the Soviet Union's socialist character. They saw the actions against the kulaks and coercion of the peasantry as offensives against exploiters and reactionary elements who deserved to be punished. Party members in Britain were getting at the ruling class by believing that they were being comprehensively defeated and taught a lesson in the Soviet Union.

Stalin was believed to have inherited Lenin's qualities, but those with knowledge of party infighting and tactics against the opposition knew better. For obvious reasons now, there was little real opposition to Stalin, which only confirmed that his rule was genuine, democratic and popular. After all, communists might well ask, who were the capitalist class to preach about democracy? They offered nothing but mass unemployment and reactionary regimes in countries where labour movements had been well organized and were now disabled or smashed. Also, these countries' imperial power was putting down independence movements. Surely the Soviet Union personified the opposite of all this? It was seen to be the friend of workers and fascism's only real opponent. To criticize socialist countries was to crack the surface and thus allow things to disintegrate.

That the CPGB was critical of the CPSU and of Stalin's policies was evident from the change of line in 1939. Rather than meekly accept the new theory from Moscow, three CP leaders questioned it in a stunning series of central committee meetings. Recent evidence has shown there was 'give and take' between Soviet and British party leaders in the early stages of the war after Pollitt's displacement.[132] Undoubtedly, few if any ordinary party members knew of these discreet contacts, but it is obvious that the new line was discussed and members certainly expressed their views. We now know, from what members *did know*, that they aired their unease. Crucially, before 1956, here is an example of dissent in the party that counters the often perpetrated picture of an obsequious membership.

After the war CP members were able to look at various ultra-left groups that seemed eternally anti-Soviet and whose undistinguished impact suggested the CP must be doing *something* right, for it remained the largest party to the left of the Labour Party. That most party members did not go into the minutiae of detail of what was going on in the Soviet Union is not surprising, for it was enough to be active in the party. Reports were received in glowing terms about the progress being made. Most members, men or women, had no desire to delve further than what they were told. Who could believe that at its first historical test, after having been the aim of so many workers since the nineteenth century and with such a momentous revolution, things could go so drastically wrong? The CP, especially in Scotland, was a party of action and if matters seemed all right in the USSR then there was practical work to get on with. This was a trait, perhaps a crucial fault, of the Scottish district but it also explains a cohesiveness that gave the party a vigorous campaigning character second to none.

How did women experience the USSR and allied countries? Many party members saw a healthy socialism. First, the collective ownership of property meant that the people they met seemed to have some say in running their lives. Social provision was given high priority, whereas in Britain women were repressed economically and socially and often left to deal with child rearing and schooling. They could see that the Soviet Union's greater resources reduced women's domestic burden and brought them freedom and benefits. That women still played a subordinate role was not disputed, but there seemed to have been progress. Members found evidence of socialism and, in this period (1929–64), no interviewee was disillusioned by her visit to the Soviet Union. Far from it, they were excited by what they saw, though not uncritical. The interviews show a more balanced assessment of conditions in the socialist countries than party reporting of visits, which seem wholly eulogistic.[133]

The events of 1956 marked a crucial time for many of the women. It was a shock to find that the accusations they had seen as a distortion of the truth now had to be reassessed. Stalin had embodied living socialism (he may well have been idolized more than the interviewees revealed) but now the new authoritative voice of the CPSU was stating that he had endangered many aspects of it. It is ironic that *The Reasoner* opposition in the British party came from the very body it now wanted to reject, the CPSU, whose actions had caused wide dissent in the CPGB. Impressive and articulate though its publication was, it is difficult to believe that those around *The Reasoner* did not realize that their actions would lead to expulsion or resignation. They wanted to replace Marxism-Leninism with a more humanist Marxism and seemed to blame democratic centralism for everything; some opponents saw them as intellectuals. In the first issue of *The Reasoner* it was stated that: 'A political movement which places stress on authority and in which political argument and decision are circumscribed lacks appeal to a working class which is amongst the most politically conscious, and experienced in the capitalist world.'[134]

Far from British workers being naturally inclined to socialism, as this suggests, any party loyalist might posit that the same working class had right-wing Labour leaders who contributed continually, and in Ernest Bevin's case, decisively to the cold war. They were far from being active anti-imperialists. Unlike Russian workers, British, especially English, workers had over a century's experience of working in industry, but that had not made them politically conscious, just better organized at the workplace. It is easy to see the growing economic power of trade unionism at this time nurturing an inherent romanticism and this idealist view was held not only by some intellectuals but also by trade unionists and workers in the party.[135] No one doubted the ability of the dissenters who left.

By the time of the commission on the IPD report, the differences were irreparable. There does, however, seem to be a lack of appreciation of the leadership's sudden adaptability. The majority report *was* critical,[136] as were the individual submissions of its signatories such as Bourne, Cheek and Halpin.[137] Also, citing the experience of the left in the early part of the century, the report justified democratic centralism as it had been 'adopted by our Party as a result of our experience'[138] citing the problems of left-wing parties in Britain. It was thought that unless centralism were retained the party would disintegrate, especially if factions were allowed.[139] The mistakes of the past were not attributed to the method of organization but to its interpretation; also recognized was the way district secretariats 'often made decisions' that should have been the remit of the district committee.[140] Further points were made about the domination of the many by the few in the party. That such criticisms were forwarded shows that it was not only the CPSU that was attempting self reform. The CPGB was by no means finished, certainly not in Scotland, where women were to increase their influence continually in the coming decades.

Women who supported the Soviet intervention in Hungary did so because reactionary elements were involved in the uprising and execution of people who were associated with the government. Later admissions to Scottish CP members about the degenerate state of the Hungarian Workers' Party showed that a reaction against the regime was inevitable.[141] These events did not signal the end of the CPGB or CPs elsewhere. Khrushchev's reforms and the confident tone of the world's CPs were evident at the start of the 1960s. Commenting on developments since 1957 representatives of communist and workers' parties' in Moscow in 1960 declared:

> *The chief result is the rapid growth of the might and international influence of the world socialist system, the vigorous process of disintegration of the colonial system under the impact of the national liberation movement, the intensification of class struggles in the capitalist world, and the continued decline and decay of the world capitalist system. The superiority of the forces of socialism over those of imperialism, of the forces of peace over those of war, is becoming ever more marked in the world arena* [original italics].[142]

A new rank of women entered the CP in Scotland in the early 1960s believing they could contribute to changing the future. Party membership had not declined irreversibly after Hungary, despite 7000 members lost in Britain. In Scotland the next decade appeared to offer greater opportunities than ever before and a new generation fully believed it could transform the world in which it lived.

Chapter 6

Proud, Radical and Optimistic in a Changing World: The 1960s Generation, 1960–76

> It was a huge change from these party members who had been in the party in the 1950s. For us in the 1960s it was about asserting our culture and part of that was about asserting the autonomy of the YCL and we talked about that quite a lot, and trying to relate, belatedly, to the burgeoning youth culture in Britain.[1]

A new era

The events of 1956 did not signal the end of the CP and, in Scotland, at the turn of the decade it began to take on a new lease of life. British membership had increased from 24,900 in 1958 to 33,008 by 1963 with a noticeable advance since 1961 of 5700 members.[2] Near full employment had given the British working class a better standard of living than before and a more confident mood was evident in their workplace organization. There was also a more independent youth with more confidence in asserting itself than previous generations.

In this chapter I rely mainly on testimony from those who grew up in the 1960s, were active in the YCL, then progressed to the party branch. In Scotland women were still a minority in the party and in 1966 made up only 29 per cent of the membership – 1500 over 1334 in 1964.[3] John Gollan claimed that over one-third of the members at the British level were women,[4] suggesting a lower level in Scotland, but in these years women were involved in more aspects of the party than ever before and became more prominent and central to its work.

Peace

The peace issue had always been central to the CP, which put pressure on British governments to take a less militaristic stance and tried to highlight their subservience to US foreign policy through NATO.[5] Since 1958, 40,000 US troops and 18 bomber bases had been established in Britain.[6] There were annual marches to Aldermaston, which introduced women to the CND in the late 1950s and engaged party women's energy.[7] The history of anti-militarism dated back to early in the century and preceded the CPGB. It had been an essential element in Scotland of the ILP and the Socialist Sunday School. Women were genuinely concerned about the arms race.

> I think the fear of war is stronger in women maybe than it is in men or maybe it's just the macho image of men who maybe don't show how concerned they might be, but I think women are really very, very conscious of just what it means to get involved in war.[8]

When it was announced in 1960 that submarines carrying Polaris missiles were to be sited at Holy Loch on the Clyde there was an immediate reaction from party members both in the YCL and on the executive of the Glasgow Trades Council. A campaign was launched to protest against the new US base. In 1961 there were mass arrests as activists, many of them women, some of whom were in the CP, staged a mass sit-down at Ardnadam Pier near Dunoon. Surrounded by police and their Alsatian dogs the protesters were read the Riot Act:

> So they came and carried us off and … took us to a makeshift police station that was a garage and there we were charged and they searched us. … There was ministers, doctors, all sorts of people, students, working women and men, and the women were taken to Dunoon and there was about eight of us all put in a big cell and locked up. … Well I wanted to plead 'Not Guilty' to 'Breach of the Peace' but I was advised to accept that because I was working as a home help and I would have had to return to Dunoon and lost more work and I was advised to plead 'Guilty' which I hated to do and they asked if I worked and because I worked, a working wife, I was fined £10, but when my husband was taken up on Monday … he was only fined £7 because he was a labourer and I was fined £10 because I was a working wife.[9]

Of the women interviewed, May Annan[10] and Mary Park[11] were arrested that day, as were other party women. In some cases collections were taken for the participants, as at Rolls Royce when Agnes McLean and other protesters who worked there were fined. The fines were considered high compared with the usual amount imposed for a similar civil offence. The protests had been good humoured with participants singing peace songs, including the recently penned *Ding Dong Dollar* by John Mack about the US presence at Dunoon sung to the tune of *Ye Canny Shove Yuir Granny Aff a Bus*. Other well known songs on the subject were *Boomerang* by Matt McGinn and Thurso Bewick's *Ye'll No Sit Here* to commemorate the sit-down.[12] The first US battleship to arrive with missiles was the USS *Proteus*, which came on 3 March 1961 and was met by a few peace canoeists.[13] The captain is alleged to have said 'Who are these damned Eskimos?'

The peace issue brought women from different generations together for a single purpose. Unlike the CP in Scotland, CND went into rapid decline in the 1960s. That the CP and YCL did not follow the same fate had much to do with a new generation of activists who came into the party and carried on its organizational work while allying it to new causes.

Postwar influences and the YCL

While the YCL kept to party traditions, it also tried to adapt to the youth of the 1960s. Arguably, this mix gave the YCL youngsters from families in the Labour movement as well as new members attracted by the dedication of CP members. This new postwar generation, with its enhanced economic strength and greater sense of independence, was sceptical of some traditional values, particularly the role of the churches, for religion was still strong in Scotland.

The Irish-Catholics' strong antipathy to the British empire and identification with socialist politics allowed the Catholic Church to exercise some influence in the Labour Party in the post-1945 period.[14] However, Catholic support for Labour did not mean an endorsement of left-wing politics, and involvement with communists met with outright condemnation. The Catholic Church was a highly conservative institution and hostile to communists and its influence was arguably one reason for the clear delineation between Labour and communist politics in Scotland. This had been less apparent before the battle with the ILP.

Just as religion had strong roots, so too did communist families. Their parents and often grandparents had been involved in Red Clydeside, the rent strikes and the first actions in support of the Russian Revolution. Children from an early age were aware of their parents' values and activities:

8. Mary Park on the cover of the Dutch youth movement magazine with Dutch youth admiring her kilt.

> Well you could say I was born into a communist family, my father had already been a well established communist in the area. My earliest recollections are from approximately 1945. As a three year-old I was aware that my dad was campaigning for the homeless people in the area who at that time had been housed in the old Nissen huts which had been occupied by the soldiers until the end of the war.[15]

Although there was a gap between the experiences of the previous three decades and the optimistic and advancing 1960s, there was an appreciation of past sacrifice. There was the legacy of the Spanish Civil War and much admiration for those who had fought, and died, for the cause:

> My father's youngest brother at the age of 21 volunteered to fight in the International Brigade and he was one of the first people from Scotland to go out there. He went out in 1936 and he was in the Thaelman Battalion and he was killed at the Battle of Aldere Del Monte. He was in the same battalion as Esmond Rommely, Jessica Mitford's husband, and he was killed. He had only been in Spain for about two and a half months and he was killed and I think that also influenced my father again in the sort of feeling that his main preoccupation was his family.[16]

The welfare state and seemingly permanent safety net it promised the population meant that working-class families now had an opportunity, albeit limited, to receive an education, health resources and a higher standard of living. In parts of Scotland the statutory schooling and better employment prospects for women revealed continuing social inequalities:

> When I went to school there was some really kind of raggy kids and I can always remember feeling quite sorry for them and *not* despising them but thinking 'What a shame'. ... And I remember the first job I had was in a builder's office, James Crawfurd & Sons, and it was still ha'pennies, ... I worked in the wages department and they always rounded the figure down for the wages and I remember thinking 'That's not fair.'[17]

The wider the sphere of employment for women the greater the scope they had to become involved in trade unions and to join the party. In this respect the 1960s' generation of party women would have a greater breadth of influences. From the early 1960s the YCL began to grow noticeably and its British membership target of 4500 was reached by 1962. This was its highest figure since 1945.[18] In Scotland membership rose from 712 in 1962 to 1334 in 1964.[19] Likewise, there was an increase in adult membership and overall an increase in members of 19 per cent.[20] The Labour Party Young Socialists were recently established and became markedly more active in the early 1960s:[21]

> It was quite a revelation to find young people who were politically active. I knew there were people like my father who were involved in the trade unions, but to find a group of young people who were very well informed and could argue their corner was quite inspiring.[22]

By the early 1960s Young Socialists were continuing a tradition of opposing the leadership that went back to the Labour League of Youth in the 1930s. There was a difference between the confident radical idealism of the party's youth and the more cautious social democracy of the mainstream Labour Party. With more experience, women in the CP at this time had no doubts about the limitations of the Labour Party:

> Well, even Labour at its best is always going to be reformist. It's never going to change the system. I joined the Communist Party because you believed so much that you were going to change the world, you were going to change the system. But the Labour Party never, ever, they never even pretended to do that, they just want to make things a bit … nicer, a bit fairer.[23]

In 1962 Neil Carmichael was the Labour candidate for a parliamentary by-election in Glasgow. At this time a group of young left-wing activists came to Glasgow from the northeast of Scotland. They sought out the local Labour Party in the West End, encountered the various tendencies of the Young Socialists, got involved in the 1962 Woodside parliamentary by-election campaign, and then decided to join the CP:

> Neil Carmichael never once in his loudhailer mentioned socialism. We thought this was just a bloody nonsense. So we reckoned you

> couldn't be a socialist – we made very simplistic views about what socialism was and the way to get it – that you couldn't really be a socialist in the Labour Party. You could be a socialist in the Young Socialists but the Labour Party 'grown-ups' were going to clamp down as soon as you got out of line. … So we actually went up to the YCL and said 'Can we join?' – three able bodied young people, and this made their day![24]

This group saw the CP as the only left-wing alternative. The Labour Party had already excluded activists involved in the anti-Polaris demonstrations and Young Socialists who had heckled Hugh Gaitskell, the Labour leader, on May Day in Glasgow that year.[25] Neil Carmichael received nominations from Woodside ward and the Young Socialists and subsequently won the by-election. Future Labour governments did nothing to dispel the contempt for stale, right-wing politics that offered no strong alternative and for a party that was only seen at elections. To retain these young members and have a future the CP had to show it was serious. There were no clever tactics to be used here, but the party's short heritage and the influence of its most senior members was still inspiring. Katy Campbell recalls a meeting at which Willie Gallacher spoke: 'I don't remember *everything* that Willie Gallacher said, but one thing I do remember him talking about was meeting Lenin and this has been something which is a memory that I have always treasured; to have heard a comrade who met and spoke with Lenin.'[26]

At this time the YCL was the dominant political youth body in Scotland and, among other things, it highlighted the rise in unemployment, which was increasingly affecting youth[27] and was noticeably worse in Scotland than elsewhere in Britain.[28] Membership was always a problem for the YCL and in this respect it was always weaker than the CP. Yet, there was growth in this decade with a trebling of British membership in the early 1960s[29] and an updating of its image:

> I joined and went into the YCL and they were the happiest days of my life, *I loved the YCL, oh I loved it* … it was the sort of heydays of the 1960s and we used to have some great times, we had a lot in our YCL branch, our YCL branch just swung, it was *swinging*, it was a great branch.[30]

A new influx of young YCL members identified as much with the new trends of youth behaviour as they did with the political values of the party and this must be seen as one of the reasons for it not becoming an archaic and outdated institution. Socializing together was as much a part of YCL life as formal branch meetings and education and there was an attempt to bring the two together and so attract more youth to the cause:

> We set up a YCL club in Glasgow, we called it the Mandela Club and I was very involved in that. It was a basement over in the south side just across the river and that was our attempt to involve the youth in a much broader way in politics and we had an expresso machine and we played pop music and we thought we were the bee's knees. We'd got this club going and one or two people did turn up just out of curiosity. It was a horrible dump of a place but we tried to get them dancing. ... I remember when the local gang came in with their chains and hatchets, they were after one of the guys in the YCL who was Asian ... it was terrifying, just terrifying. They went away without doing too much damage in the end, but they smashed the place up a bit and I think we lost our bottle after that about the club.[31]

There was little enthusiasm for the club after that incident,[32] but one can hardly fault the YCL for not having had a policy to combat youth violence, which was sadly endemic in Glasgow at that time. The YCL also had regular meetings and rallies in Renfield Street in Glasgow where there would be a small stage where members would sing and speakers would address crowds in the city centre while the party's youth paper *Challenge* was sold. Sales would also take place outside dance halls like the Locarno at Charing Cross[33] and this carried on a tradition from the past as well as visiting housing schemes and areas throughout Scotland. The CP was at one time bigger than the Labour Party in Glasgow[34] and there was undoubted confidence when the YCL went campaigning:

> Jane McKay was Scottish secretary of the Young Communist League at that time and I can clearly remember going to visit Jane to have the discussion about how I would carry out my function as *Challenge* organizer. I was extremely overawed by this responsibility I might add and took it very very seriously indeed. And I went to

> this meeting with Jane in her house … where I produced all kinds of targets and such like for *Challenge*.[35]

There seemed to be greater equality for women in the YCL. There was an attempt to involve married couples in YCL branch activity and campaigning. The YCL undermined the party's old socializing conventions, for pop music, unconventional lifestyles and better career prospects made for regular relaxed socials where there was less emphasis on the formality of sandwiches and the folk song culture of previous decades:

> It was a time when we were trying to change the kind of model of the YCL and we were trying to become less staid and we were getting into pop music and we hired this miners' holiday camp in Skegness and we had a whole range of debates about music and youth culture and it was a time when the YCL was trying to incorporate youth culture and I remember the night of the big dance we had. The Kinks playing, oh yes I remember dancing to the Kinks that night.[36] So, really I would have said almost 1970 when we moved into being party activists rather than YCL activists. We were in our late twenties.[37]

I do not wish to demote the folk circuit that was going through an important revival with communists like Ewan McColl and Peggy Seeger writing and recording songs about industrial and social life in Britain. The Glaswegian folk singer Matt McGinn put his pertinent humour to song and was heavily involved in party cultural activities. The YCL identified with the confident assertive drive of the young and tried to make it a characteristic of the party's youth. With the issuing of 400,000 leaflets of *The Trend-Communism* in 1967 and the setting up of 53 new branches[38] the YCL was regarded as a modern entity. This did not mean there was any distancing of political belief; it was a way of renewing the party's politics and making them fashionable. People felt confident that conditions were more advantageous for the left than ever before in Britain:

> We were going to reach a higher stage of civilization and it would just be so [much] more challenging. Certainly there was a huge camaraderie as well and this was very important. … Another thing

> that we found about the Communist Party 'grown-ups', as opposed to the 'grown-ups' in the Labour Party whom we did not hold much for, the party members were by and large very, very fine people. Very fair, very able, highly moral, extremely, very, very supportive of us who had just joined, so we got a very, very good response, very supportive and were very, very nice, by and large. That was another good influence, the fact that the whole party we saw as being very good hard-working, worthwhile people.[39]

This cohesiveness and the integrated nature of the party earned its younger members' respect. There were limits to the effectiveness of the YCL's campaigns and the target of 1000 members in Scotland, from looking possible in the early 1960s seemed unlikely by the end of the decade. Attempts were still being made to influence more Scottish youth in the branch localities. With its myriad of gangs, youth violence was particularly bad in Glasgow in the 1960s and suggested a bleak future.[40] The YCL attempted some kind of contact and influence:

> we ran an education school out in the youth hostel out in Loch Lomond, it was Maryhill branch, and we invited a whole lot of these youngsters that we knew in Maryhill and they were all in a gang, Maryhill Tongs I remember but we thought 'Well that's okay, you have to go to the grass roots, youth culture' and we invited them all up. That night we'd done a block booking in the youth hostel and we got the use of a seminar room and we were doing Marxist education during the day and at night the warden came out in a kilt and he was trying to get us to do Highland dancing and these guys from Maryhill, and we were just sweating but they behaved themselves really well until he suddenly said 'Right now, it's bed time.' Ten o'clock the lights out and they were looking around for what you do now. There was a whole carry on in the dorms … I remember at six o'clock in the morning Doug having to get up and let them out because they thought 'Oh no, we're no' having anymore, we're away back to Glasgow' and they went off into the dawn to hitch a lift back to civilization.[41]

As YCL membership began to fall[42] and the enthusiasm of the early 1960s became diffused into different areas of activity, the incentive to keep up the youth work waned. Although the YCL remained active, those involved throughout the 1960s were part of its most coherent period as a youth organization and the one that nurtured and educated the party's future leadership.

Despite its lower membership, there was a tradition in CP politics in Edinburgh for young women from the university branch to progress to an area branch. At the university branch in Edinburgh, party members mixed with students from various countries. New party members who entered this branch got a more international perspective. The presence of more foreign students meant that the 1960s' generation could identify more tangibly with struggles abroad as they made contact with, and heard speakers from, Africa, the Middle East and Asia. Another influence that was part of the make-up of Edinburgh with its strong professional and white-collar working population was the intellectual input of established writers such as Honor Arundel who was on the Scottish committee:

> Well Honor had the lot, she was an intellectual, she was a woman, she was middle class and also she was an extremely nervous woman. Speaking caused her such a physical effort but it never stopped her doing it and she was so full of conviction. Very gently spoken she wasn't strident at all talking about culture and it was the time that George Lukacs was writing and Arnold Kettle was writing … and for students I suppose it was a big deal. … She had already published her books for teenagers, which were selling well, and she was writing a book on Marxist culture and then, a year or two after I got to know her, she got sick, she got cancer. And so they left Edinburgh and I lost touch with her then.[43]

Arundel was a successful children's novelist and one-time critic for the *Daily Worker*. She had married Alex MacCrindle, an actor and fellow party member. In 1965 she wrote *The Freedom of Art* in response to Ernest Fischer's *The Necessity of Art*, which had been published in 1963.[44] She died of cancer in 1973. Jack Ashton, a party industrial organizer, and actor Iain Cuthbertson took her funeral oration.

Some women may have felt more confident about applying themselves in the party because of their work and trade union experience, which made them less inhibited when serving on party committees. The Scottish committee endorsed its speakers and as education was a central part of branch life there were now more tutors to teach a wider range of topics.[45]

In the late 1960s the differences between factory and area branches were greater. The latter often had no more than a paper membership, but because factory branches were integrated with shop-floor work, their membership was high, class-conscious and active. 'Trade union communism' advanced in the late 1960s as organized labour in Britain became more militant and the CP operated strongly in this area.[46] There were white-collar and less traditional party branches in the West End of Glasgow and in Edinburgh City where party education could allow more time for reading and discussion:

> The way that they ran it was we would choose a Marxist text like Engels's *Origin of the Family* or *Wages Prices and Profit* or whatever and we would be told in advance what chapters we would deal with. We would be expected to have read them and to come and be fully participatory, which I think is great. ... But there would always be somebody who would come who wasn't a theoretician who'd just come from a trade dispute or had had a hard time at his work place. That was of course important but in our branch the majority of people were brain workers.[47]

The EC was the most important committee in the CP at British level with delegates elected at congress through the recommended list representing factory and area branches and usually most districts of the party. Delegates to the national executive expected a high level of debate at the meetings where crucial national and international issues were discussed:

> You always went to a national executive with a sense of anticipation because the quality of the preparation that was put into the papers that led the discussion was always very high. ... I always ... felt that you'd get a new insight somehow and just a very good quality of argument always.[48]

International issues: Vietnam

The campaign to support the national liberation movement in Vietnam took up a great amount of the party's campaigning time, especially the YCL's. The CP had aired its opposition to US intervention in Vietnam in the early 1960s and by 1966 it was becoming a major issue. Some 1000 people a week were being 'murdered' and, along with the bombing of Hanoi, ugly new weaponry such as chemicals, napalm bombs, poison gas and lazy-dog bombs was increasingly being used.[49] By early 1968 the Tet Offensive, which was organized in the south, had shattered any doubts about the National Liberation Front's commitment and strength. *Challenge* reported mass support for the liberation movement, rampages by US troops and links between industry and the military.[50] The party was quick to get support from unions and Medical Aid for Vietnam. In Scotland, as elsewhere in Britain, the armoury of new hideous devices thrown into battle and the blanket bombing of whole areas of the country caused genuine disgust. Lobbies were arranged because the Wilson government supported the US actions.[51] Party women involved in the peace committee in Aberdeen lobbied the local Labour MP:

> we went to see Donald Dewar on the same issue and he was very unsympathetic to us and he told me I was emotional. I went on aboot people being killed and aboot Agent Orange, how they were destroying their crops and their vegetation and maybe creating abortive pregnancies and deformed children and we didnae get a bit o' sympathy or support fae Donald Dewar, he was very much the solicitor on that occasion. He's very clever and good wi' his tongue, so he didna gi' us any support and nae any straight answers either and I felt very angry wi' him.[52]

Margaret Rose reported to the Scottish committee that 'Dewar was arrogant last time the peace committee visited him but when evidence established that a majority of his constituency were against the war he became a bit more cagey'.[53] Labour's whole policy was seen as subservient to US foreign policy. This subservience encouraged youth to join the CP or other new left groups and reminded older members of the British government's attitude to the Spanish republic 30 years before.

Having asked the NLF what practical support it could give, the YCL organized a bus to travel through Britain collecting bikes to be sent to Vietnam. Supporting the national liberation movement was a continuous part of YCL campaigning. *Challenge* carried pictures of hideously disfigured young children along with its headline *Hey! Hey! LBJ. How Many Kids Did You Kill Today?*[54] The subsequent revelations of US army offensives against the civilian population such as the My Lai massacre, which occurred in 1968 but only became known a year later, only enraged YCL members more, as did the secret bombing of Cambodia in 1970:

> We were so incensed, we were so emotional. Young people … become extremely emotional about situations and of course it's like every generation – you can see the inexperience, the wisdom has not set in. … I wrote to Nixon, I told him what a *turd* he was. It was so angry; it was so emotional; it was charged.[55]

To understand the genuine outrage of party members and others, one example of the horrors of the war should suffice. *Challenge* reported the testimony of a US ex-serviceman who described a female NLF suspect taken prisoner who had a signal flare thrust up her sexual organs:

> She looked at them with an air of disbelief … and then as the flare went off, her whole body contorted like one of those cartoon figures you see and then they threw her corpse over the side. I know you'll be shocked about what I'm telling you, but after a few months out in Vietnam, nice guys start behaving lower than animals![56]

There were 500,000 US troops in South Vietnam. In the USA 750,000 demonstrated against the war on Moratorium Day in November 1969.[57] Vietnamese representatives graphically described the situation when they toured and spoke at CP meetings, including one in Edinburgh:

> They were so individual, they were so different. One of them was very *brusque* and one of them was very, very gentle. They had two different approaches and they were given to understatement rather than over-statement so that it was only after they had gone away I thought '*My God*,' he was describing napalm. One of them actually had napalm burns and I'd never seen what it was like before. … So whenever there was fund-raisers for Vietnam for ever after that the party was always involved because the personal thing is *so* important.[58]

Here it is apposite to consider why Vietnam was so important. The injustice of a small country fighting for independence against such odds was made more graphic with satellite pictures that made news immediate and digestible. A whole population was under siege and the contribution of children, youth and women was evident.[59] In Scotland there was practical activity that could make an important contribution and CP women's groups organized activities to raise support for the struggle:

> the women's assembly and women's movement, the communist women's movement, we did knitting, blankets and little vests for the children who had to shelter during the Americans' bombing raids and the wool had to be dyed navy blue or dark green so there was less chance of being seen from the air. And we collected wool, bought it and collected it from people and I had a big pot and dyed the wool dark blue and whatever and then knitted it up for the kids.[60]

Unlike Spain, the Soviet Union was not isolated in its support of this struggle, for with other socialist countries and the Non-Aligned Movement there was a sizeable force against US policy. And, unlike Spain, there was a hope for victory.

Czechoslovakia

Having replaced the repressive Novotný leadership of the Czechoslovakian CP in January 1968, the CCP, led by new first secretary Alexander Dubcek, embarked on a programme of major reforms. Publication of an action programme brought support from many quarters and the Prague spring quickly began to interest young communists in Britain. The Czechoslovak Union of Youth (CSM) invited a YCL delegation to visit in 1968.[61] With the invasion on 20 August of troops from five Warsaw Pact countries, the new political shift was short lived:[62]

> You felt 'Oh crikey'. ... Czechoslovakia was a turning point for me and the YCL. That day we decided we'd have to do something and we had contact with the national YCL and we agreed on a line despite the fact that the party had nae met and declared its line and that was unprecedented. And we went out into Glasgow and we got the soapbox and we had a public meeting, I mean there must have been half a dozen people heard us. Nevertheless, it was a momentous thing for us to do was to go public on attacking the, or defending Czechoslovakia when the party had nae come. It was like the YCL growing up as well.[63]

Barney Davis's counterblast in *Cogito*[64] to Palme Dutt's sympathetic explanation for Soviet action in the *Labour Monthly* of October 1968 marked a turning point for the YCL. The YCL had come of age in that it acted on its own initiative and gave scant respect to those it accused of 'political chicanery'.[65]

The CCP criticized the 'condemned bureaucratic police methods' of the past while the party still gave allegiance to Marxism-Leninism.[66] Open discussion had been encouraged, even from anti-socialist groups, and this had been used as a pretext for the armed action. Now the unique developments of the last few months were over. As over Hungary, some, but this time a minority, supported the invasion. The five powers whose forces went in said there was a threat from NATO and West German revanchists who were helping this 'peaceful counter-revolution'.[67] There was disagreement at the highest level in Scotland:

> Jimmy Reid nearly jumped down my throat, he was the Scottish secretary and the Scottish committee met on a Sunday and I was the first person there apart from Reid. He was in himself and big mouth I said to him, 'You know I read the *Morning Star* yesterday and I didnae know whether I was reading the *Morning Star* or the *Daily Express*,' 'What do you mean?' he said and I said 'In the Czechoslovakian situation' and, oh, he *gutted* me. I said 'I think the Soviet Union was quite right to go in there because there was a counter-revolution taking place stirred up by the American CIA and the Catholic Church and goodness knows who else.' I wasn't flavour of the month but that didnae bother me over much where Jimmy Reid was concerned.[68]

The Czechoslovak youth movement (the CSM) had started to lose members by the mid-1960s and there were student protests in 1967. Part of the reform movement had been a renewal of youth organizations and they supported the Dubcek leadership. The opposition to the intervention had been unanimous from the Czech CP though there was a deliberate policy of non-violent opposition in the wake of the invasion. Internationally, 25 CPs were critical of the Warsaw Pact, including wholesale condemnation from the British party. This appeared to echo the feelings of the majority of party members:

> Johnny Gollan ... very forcibly put the case to the secretariat that how he would react if somebody, the Soviet government, waded in against his wishes as a leader of the party. He was very opposed to that; so was I. The thing is that Joe my husband didn't swallow it and neither did Robert. They wouldn't accept that it was necessary, it

> was necessary not to intervene. We were against intervention and Johnny Gollan was very much for that line.[69]

For Gollan it was critical to keep the party united and to avoid a split or desertions, as in 1956. The Scottish CP was gaining members at this time, having increased from 7300 in 1966 to 7605 in 1968[70] and a non-critical stance may well have meant losses and a blow to the advances in the 1960s. Ironically, the YCL, the most critical of the Soviet action, had suffered a decline in Scotland from 1500 to 1200 members[71] and arresting this became harder, though for numerous reasons.

There was no agreement among the younger party members even though the YCL had been sympathetic to and excited by Dubcek and the reformers' policies. What is clear is that those who supported the actions against the Czechoslovak party leadership thought that the reforms were going too far and were undermining the socialist system there. There was still a fierce loyalty for the explanations given by the Soviet Union at the time:

> [This was] because of the need to preserve socialism, in terms of the Soviet's own position. I really did have a problem with that, I accepted the party's, one has to do that, but I had a problem. … I know it was condemned, and in a sense that's the problem. I can't say now that it was right. … There were differences of opinion. … I remember Willie Thompson speaking … very vehemently for the party's position on that.[72]

The events of this period engendered passionate debate. Most members would hear about the party's policy at their branch meetings or directly from the leadership at an aggregate meeting. Gollan, the party's general secretary, was not known for showing his feelings, yet he was greatly affected by the events of 1968:

> I can remember John Gollan speaking. I think it was over in the old Kingston Hall but that would be just after Czechoslovakia I think, and I remember him making a *very, very* passionate speech. Again, he was replying to the discussion on quite a few very bad statements that I would have thought were made, very much so, about Stalin and how wonderful he was, very much from that political standpoint. And I remember Johnny, who was always

> quite a nervous speaker, putting his notes aside and sort of making the point that some of the finest sons and daughters of the CPSU had been liquidated wrongly, trumped up charges and we weren't ever going to let that happen again.[73]

Gollan voiced the CPGB's opposition at an international conference of CPs in 1969. The British party refused to accept a 'general ideological line' or need for a 'new international centre'.[74] Though the YCL still supported the socialist countries and even said it believed the Soviet Union was 'motivated by concern for the best interests of socialism',[75] there was less support for the socialist countries than there had been and this was most notable in the YCL. Its sense of betrayal was summed up as follows: 'The Czechoslovak revolt against bureaucracy raised hopes on the left that at last we were going to see the successful combination of socialism and democratic freedoms in a traditionally developed industrial society.'[76] What stands out is the crucial part that international politics played in party members' lives in this period. Next, events in Scotland were to occupy most of the YCL and party's energy into the 1970s.

Trade unionism triumphs

The CP had been critical of the complacency towards equal pay for women and stated in 1963 that 'We must say, and say bluntly, that the attitude of trade unions to working women has been one of organized hypocrisy.'[77] J. R. Campbell pointed out that resolutions were passed at the TUC but when negotiations took place on the shop floor differentials were negotiated that increased the wage disparity between the sexes.[78] In the late 1960s the campaign for equal pay for women reached its zenith before the enabling legislation of the 1970s. The party had set up campaign committees on equal pay as well as other issues like the need for more nursery schools.[79] In 1968 local trades councils in Scotland held a series of meetings on equal pay with Agnes McLean, who as early as 1952 had negotiated an agreement on equal pay at Rolls Royce in Glasgow,[80] and Kay Carmichael (Labour MP Neil Carmichael's partner) often putting the case. At the Scottish congress the same year, Scottish secretary Jimmy Reid said:

> Women communists in Scotland like Agnes McLean and Mamie McConnell have played an outstanding part in the developing movement of women workers. The left must pledge its support for

> any and every action taken by the women workers in Scotland for the immediate application of the principle of equal pay.[81]

Party women on the shop floor were unequivocal in their support for the Ford women workers who went on strike over equal pay in 1968. When minister of employment Barbara Castle addressed the STUC in 1969 she met a lobby of women over the issue of equal pay and a small group of women with placards stood outside the hall where the congress met. Castle had come to Scotland to defend *In Place of Strife*, the Labour government's proposals for industrial relations reform. Party members with industrial experience were less than enamoured with these measures, which would have severely restricted free collective bargaining:

> I really think that Barbara Castle, with all her brightness and all the rest o' it, was forced, by her prime minister, no' to take the thing too far, you can only go so far and no further. I felt, 'very bright woman and good speaker' and that, but that does nae get you places and she certainly didnae win the favour of the trade unions at that time because workers can see through. The holes are as big as bloody mountains.[82]

The proposals were dropped after mass opposition.[83] Barbara Castle failed abysmally to win over the STUC congress at Rothesay where the government measures were decisively rejected.[84] By 1970, despite more unionization and 8,839,000 women employed (nearly half of all adult women in Britain),[85] there were still huge disparities. Two-thirds of all working women were married and three-quarters had 'domestic responsibilities in addition to their jobs'.[86] Women worked more hours, earned less than men and while their number in work was increasing the proportion in skilled, managerial and professional jobs was declining.[87] Some impetus was needed because by 1970 membership had fallen to 6934 from 7605 in 1968.[88] YCL numbers were worse, with only 503 members in 1970.[89]

Upper Clyde Shipbuilders, a consortium of yards on the Clyde, had faced the threat of closure for a while,[90] but this increased when the Conservative government was elected in 1970. By this time there were 100,000 unemployed people in Scotland.[91] The government's refusal to give the yards £6 million in working capital met with an organized response. Communist shop stewards, most notably Jimmy Reid, Jimmy

Airlie and Sammy Barr, were at the forefront of the shop stewards who coordinated what was to be known as the 'work-in' whereby the workforce ran the yards and continued to complete orders. Although support for the action seemed solid there was little complacency about the possibility of divisions:

> The Scottish committee was central to how that dispute unfolded. [There were] great arguments about ensuring that the momentum kept rolling because if you didn't maintain the momentum, if you stopped you would go back. And if they couldn't keep extending the support for this struggle then they were beaten and of course the big thing that worried them was that there would be the split, the Green/Orange split and very, very careful to try and in every way prevent that from happening because that could have split the whole movement. So that was very central and very important and great details discussed about this.[92]

As the coordinating committee's proposals were disseminated, the trade union movement showed the solidarity and enthusiasm for which the CP had always fought and for which it had always prepared itself for a leading role. If the yards closed then 8500 shipyard workers would be made redundant along with another 20,000 in supply industries.[93] As the leadership eloquently explained, this was a fight for the right to work and for the immediate survival of communities in Glasgow and Clydebank but whose outcome would affect the future of the whole movement. As activity increased during 1971, party members in all vicinities of work put their weight behind continuing the momentum:

> We pulled out the stops, all the branches pulled out the stops; that was the major issue and that was the UCS and the UCS work-in and everybody did it. Fund-raising, jumble sales, socials, bingo, you name it, all sorts of sponsors we had, you name it, we had it. It was marvellous and of course you can just imagine the demonstrations and rallies that we had – countless rallies, *mass demonstrations* – yes we all went to them.[94]

Party members were very aware of the importance of the UCS struggle and the role of some party leaders in it. There were mass rallies, one in June prior to the start of the work-in attracted over 50,000. Then, at an enormous day of action on 18 August 1971, 200,000 people at work took action, 20 per cent of the working population in Scotland, and over 80,000 attended a rally at Glasgow Green – the biggest seen since the Chartists.[95] 'I think it was *marvellous*, it was a *marvellous* demonstration that was taking place. … I think it gave you a feeling that you were really glad to have joined the Communist Party and to be a member of the Communist Party.'[96]

Donations from unions, workplaces, individuals and various organizations helped to keep the momentum going and ensured that the coordinating committee representing all the unions could be resolute in its basic demands. Women employed in industry for the first time learnt a dramatic lesson about the rapidity with which trade union militancy and a confident workforce can combat government measures, as they had in 1969 over trade union reform:

> Oh well, it was wonderful, that was a wonderful period. That was when you experienced the feeling that things could change, you could change things; it was wonderful. You will probably get other stories from the works and those who were involved in it, but I worked in Beatties, which was a women's industry and wasnae known for its militancy or anything like that … it was a biscuit factory. And it permeated in there tremendously and we stopped, the day of the UCS work-in we stopped work and went up. … Well it gave them the feeling that they could be organized and get somewhere, get things done. And I mean they did, they supported them, they sent money to them, which was a *big thing*, it may sound trite but it was a big thing for them to do, you know. And of course that march itself, it's the highlight of [?]; I've been on a few quite big [ones]; but the UCS work – it was something that we'll maybe never – maybe we will – but it really was, what a *day*, *what a feeling*.[97]

The unions that led the UCS work-in were long established, primarily skilled unions in engineering and shipbuilding. That there were many party members in the traditional industries of engineering and shipbuilding meant that they gained an important influence in Scottish trade union politics and through this, by pursuing CP policies for unity among the left, were able to bring together a broad movement. In one sense there was the continuing dominance of the male industrial trade unionist in the CP and the UCS issue inevitably strengthened this. Also, the success of the outcome for the workers, the government backing down and through reorganization retaining the yards in 1972, showed the strength of the trade union movement in Scotland and Britain.

The work-in leader, Jimmy Reid, was very popular in the CP. He was young, erudite and above all a brilliant orator. Reid's election as rector of Glasgow University in 1972 stemmed from the UCS success. He was also a councillor in Clydebank where the party had four councillors in 1970 (three by 1971) and had campaigned locally on many issues:[98]

> We went round the doors on a regular basis; we worked on questions like Medical Aid for Vietnam, but we also, on day-to-day issues there was lots of problems in Faifley then because we were in Scottish special houses: very, very basic, no great amenities, much needed done to them and we had a list of problems and we had a big rent strike and many, many meetings. The meetings were so big that you could hardly get into the school. So we were involved in all that and the Communist Party at one time had more than 100 members in their branch in Faifley alone, which was no mean feat. People came to the party and they trusted you, they came with their problems and you did what you could for them.[99]

Clydebank council was one of the few that were continually involved in practical defiance against the government's Housing Finance Act 1972. On Clydebank town council, with support from some Labour Party councillors, there was an attempt to defy the act. Similar action was being taken by other councils like Cowdenbeath where Willie Sharp had become the first communist provost in Britain. However, it was obvious that a few dissident councils were going to be isolated and would suffer surcharging.

The political committee in London debated an appropriate strategy. This was smaller than the EC. Members of the executive who did not sit on the political committee were invited to this meeting as were the Clydebank councillors. Reid was passionate about wanting to continue the opposition, along with Clay Cross council in Derbyshire.

> We talked to the Clay Cross people and told them that we were going to pull back and tried to get them to pull back with us and Jimmy was for keeping going and so there was a big meeting, an important meeting, there was about a dozen to fifteen people, and

> they were all just wading into Jimmy and it was a fantastic thing to sit and watch because the psychology of the whole thing had Jimmy holding on, tremendously powerful figure, tremendously powerful intellect, but these arguments were coming strong and he was arguing back because it was a fine line that divided; it was about tactics, about ways forward and it was an important powerful discussion. And then you just saw Jimmy just collapse, that was it, he couldn't win them and he admitted psychological defeat and while he didn't admit psychological defeat in the words that he used, you just knew there was a kind of change in the meeting and you knew there was a change in what had happened.[100]

The Court of Session[101] fined Clydebank council £5000 for non-implementation and a fund was set up to pay it.[102] By early 1973 it was clear that the campaign had lost its earlier momentum and the Scottish councils that had remained defiant, including Saltcoats[103] and Cumbernauld,[104] backed down. Clay Cross carried on and was surcharged. There were expectations that Jimmy Reid could become the first communist MP since Gallacher and such hopes were raised during his election campaign in Clydebank in 1974. However, Reid had a history of organizational incompetence and party members were aware of his shortfalls. Some were more than a little annoyed at his complacency and arrogance, for he firmly believed he was going to win:

> Well, Jimmy had a great gift of being able to express what the punters, that was his expression, 'What the punters were thinking', he really did. He was so often right but then in the course of the election they asked the women in the branch to try and organize house meetings to hear Jimmy as the candidate and I organized one in here for my neighbours and went round them all, invited them all to come and I got quite a turn out and Jimmy didn't come till about, och, about half past nine or something. The women were fed up waiting. In the first place they were fed up waiting for him and then he swept in like an entourage, swept in with big overcoats on and he talked down to the women. ... They werenae convinced they were going to vote for him ... and a lot expressed disappointment to me afterwards.[105]

Reid was convincingly beaten. In 1976 he left the party disillusioned by his failure to make a political breakthrough. Although some people voiced negative opinions of him, others like May Annan stressed the positive aspects of his role in the CP and his charismatic persona. Some communists held him up as an idol,[106] but he was by no means exceptional compared with those around him. The party produced many capable people, but Reid was the most publicly attractive of them.

In Scotland the party's influence was broader than ever before because of its success in trade unions and in community groups such as tenants' associations.[107] Union membership was increasing and young workers were encouraged to participate in trades councils in Scotland and in newly formed youth sections in the TUC. The denouement for the establishment must have been a fear of union militancy seeping through to young minds, which it did to the extent that even the CP was seen as slightly old hat.

The YCL at British level had been instrumental in the formation of the National Union of School Students (NUSS),[108] but the Scottish district of the YCL admitted it had been 'later than most'[109] in responding to this new eagerness among school students. The YCL in Scotland stalled its decline and grew to 455 in November 1972,[110] since March 1971 when it had 380 members; the benefits of the UCS and other trade union campaigns seem evident. The YCL now had 15 functioning branches in 1972 compared with only 7 in 1970.[111] By the end of 1972 there were four branches in Glasgow (the south was divided into southeast and southwest)[112] and an area committee. There were still branches in all four major cities and Scottish sales of *Challenge* had increased since its new format in 1971. Speaking at the YCL Scottish congress in 1972 Scottish district secretary Alex Murray said: 'It is an extremely exciting period for Communists to live and work in. A time of great pride for Communists at this moment, is being a young Communist.'[113] There was reason to believe that progressive changes would increase both at home and abroad. Once again it was the development of a socialist experiment abroad, this time in Latin America, that was to cause much interest.

Chile

Salvador Allende, elected Chile's new president in September 1970 with an alliance of parties supporting him, promised great change. The Popular Unity government was a progressive movement that included socialists, communists and liberals. This alliance won a near majority of parliamentary seats against its nearest rival, the Christian Democrats, but was a minority against the total opposition. As in Czechoslovakia, some party members placed great hope in this experiment, but, apart from the important role of the peasantry,[114] there was a major difference with which communists everywhere could identify. Popular Unity was an example of what could be done with political alliances and a mandate from the electorate in a country where democratic parliamentary elections were held. (Allende had got the single biggest vote in the presidential election.)

This was leaps and bounds ahead of the trade union advances to which the British CP, with its small political clout, was restricted. Allende held out hope of a slow but sure transition from a capitalist to a socialist society in the near future. People believed this and acted *en masse* in support of the government. The Nixon administration in the USA strongly opposed any left-wing influence, especially on its own continent. With support from right-wing parties and sections of the middle class, a military coup was mounted against Allende and the Popular Unity government in September 1973. Those who had hoped for great change saw instead the physical annihilation of the left in Chile.

Trade unions in Britain immediately condemned the action and tried to find out what had happened to people recently in contact with the Labour movement in Europe. Some of the largest political marches in Scotland were for Chile and they gathered a quick response, as in Edinburgh:

> Judith Hart spoke at the Mound on the very weekend it happened or something, it was a *rush* meeting within hours of the overthrow you know. Oh, oh, I mean, oh Chile was a real; a terrible, terrible setback; it was regarded as such and, oh, [there were] *real feelings*, strong emotional feelings about Chile.[115]

It was a double blow for those who had put energy into developing a strategy to get power through parliament in the belief that it could be turned round by constitutional means. Land was redistributed; there were wage increases and a fall in unemployment.[116] The nationalization of the copper industry, however, affected three US companies.[117] While advances had been made, movements near the USA challenged the economic system. 'I was horrified, I was really upset when it happened, obviously we all were and it was terrifying. I remember saying to Roger

'Well if that's your *British Road to Socialism* you can stuff it' and he got a bit agitated about that.'[118]

Allende's reforms also included ending discrimination against single mothers and the formation of a national secretariat for women. There was a better health service for women and free milk was distributed daily. The coup reversed these measures and by 1976 it was estimated that 50 per cent of children suffered from malnutrition.[119] Women had suffered much physical torture at the hands of the junta. From late 1973 refugees began to arrive in Europe and some families came to Scotland where they settled in Glasgow, Falkirk, Edinburgh and villages such as Lochgelly in Fife:

> And some of them went to mining villages in West Lothian and the kindness that people showed them, they were overwhelmed. They would arrive and often the party branch in the village would organize the house being furnished and getting furniture together, getting a cooker. The local council would give them a house but the party branch would organize food for them being in the house.[120]

People began to meet and help those who had come over to escape persecution. Women learnt about Chilean politics and the political divisions even among the refugees. Not all refugees were on the left, for many sections of the population were persecuted, and those who were on the left were not always in the same party. Despite having fled their country and being in exile thousands of miles away, the Chileans impressed party members by their ability to entertain their hosts and maintain their culture despite their moderate means:

> I think initially we thought that all the refugees were revolutionaries who'd been out fighting on the streets and obviously this wasn't the case because very many of them were out by association with somebody else, but it was very interesting to see how they managed to pull themselves together, maintain their identity and their music was terrific, that had a big impact on me.[121]

The Pinochet regime was not going to be replaced in the foreseeable future, though attempts were made to isolate it internationally with unions in Britain boycotting some exports. The Chile Solidarity Campaign was formed[122] and was active in Scotland among trades councils. It encouraged people to send cards to prisoners to ensure they knew they had not been forgotten and that the authorities were aware of international support. It was also successful in persuading the Labour government in Britain to refuse the postponement of debt payments by the Chilean junta.[123]

Cuba

In December 1973, soon after the military coup in Chile, John Gollan, Jack Woddis and Irene Swan from the CPGB national executive went on the first party delegation to Cuba at the invitation of the Cuban CP. Swan had been elected first woman chairperson of the party in 1972. They were well received because they came from a country with a strong trade union movement in which the party had a disproportionate influence. Once there they met the leaders of the revolution:

> Johnny was seeking to keep the end of the British party up because there was no way Castro was going to ride, he was a leader of *state*, he was a head of state, we met many heads of state and here are we just a piddling little Communist Party and it was about Johnny keeping his end up and keeping the British party's end up and the authority of the politics of the British party. And our general view was that we had made an impression on Castro, he had respected our politics; that was the assessment we made, whether we were kidding ourselves or not I don't know but that was the assessment that we had made. And he was very *warm*, very warm indeed. I mean we could have been much more significant in some ways to him, but very warm and very welcoming. And I can remember inviting him to Britain, I said he should come, and Europe as well, because he could have an effect, I thought, on the youth because he was such a striking figure and the quality of his charisma because of what had happened in Cuba and that.[124]

By the late 1960s Cuba's education system had advanced enormously. Nursery and primary school education were more widely available than ever before. From 717,000 pupils in primary schools in 1959, by 1969 there were 1,460,000.[125] Adult education had also improved with 25,000 university students in 1959 and 34,000 ten years later; and there were also 170,000 scholarships in school, university and adult education.[126] The youth organized as Pioneers and in a Secondary School Students' Union, which was not linked to the Cuban YCL.

When the 'year of education' was declared in 1961, 28 per cent of

9. Young British Pioneers. Frieda Park is third from the left in the front row. Her cousin Ann Park is third from the right, back row.

the population was illiterate.[127] By 1971, 28 per cent was engaged in full-time study.[128] Youths worked voluntarily for a few hours a day, usually gaining farm experience. Some were critical of the influence of the Soviet CP and possible bureaucratization, but the delegation was supportive of the changes the revolution had brought and it remained the one revolutionary socialist outpost in the Americas. President Allende of Chile had visited the year before to much acclaim; now all his reforms were being dismantled and economic and diplomatic ties with Cuba were broken. In January 1974 a new maternity law was introduced in Cuba based on previous legislation. Women were given time off for prenatal medical care and six weeks off prior to childbirth and three months afterwards. Time off was also given for paediatric treatment.[129]

The Cuban revolution was recognized as having had a broad base of support yet its fortunes contrasted with those of Popular Unity in Chile. Traditionalists in the party could point to the true nature of capitalism and the folly of parliamentary politics. However, there was no clear-cut division over the Chilean strategy. For its brief period of power, Popular Unity was a great inspiration to CP members. Few would be critical of a president and government that had given so much hope of a new path to socialism in the Western world, whose efforts had been continuously undermined and were finally crushed.

Developing criticisms in the party

The 1972 election of Irene Swan as the CP's first woman chairperson had been a major breakthrough. She had progressed from the Scottish committee to the NEC. This was only the second time in Britain that a woman had chaired a political party.[130] If this showed what was attainable given the right support and circumstances it was still an exception. Whereas single women could commit more to regular party meetings and union activity, this was not so for married women.[131] There was gender inequality because mainly males were involved in party meetings and activity. In the 1970s this was a deficiency that certain women brought to the fore.

One example of the traditional subservient role women were expected to play, irrespective of age, was at weekend schools. These often took place in remote venues, sometimes way out in the country, and the women at times were expected to carry out the menial tasks involved in getting things up and running for the event:

> there was also a kind of expectation that the women would do the cooking, which I happened to be quite good at and didn't mind. I'd far rather do it and eat decent food than let somebody else cook a load of crap and then have to eat it. But some of the other girls thought, and I think they had an *absolute* point, 'Well bugger me, we've come on this course, we don't want to be left going into the shops five miles down the road and organizing food for 14' and this kind of thing and that was a bone of contention.[132]

Personal relationships were, however, re-evaluated. Some young couples, because there was more choice over when or if to get married, tried to be more democratic in their political and domestic lives. Among them there was more chance that political duties and the women's secondary political role might be less rigidly applied than before and so a balanced commitment from both partners could continue.

The party recognized that women did the housework, were often also in paid work and then could not get to branch meetings because the husband took priority.[133] Attempts had been made to rectify this, but without questioning the premise of the party's structure.[134] Now there was stronger criticism of accepting the status quo until the shift to socialism had been achieved, which until now had been the party's attitude.[135] Questions were also raised about party education and the fundamental basis of Marxism:

> I couldn't put this in a sequence in time, but I remember there being quite fierce discussion and debate about Marxist classes and women needing to have these Marxist classes whereas certainly myself and a group of women were much more interested in dealing with women's lives and issues affecting them *here and now*. And in fact some of these debates became quite vigorous and we were in the group that wanted to get ahead and discuss issues affecting women, whereas another group felt that we had to have the grounding in Marxism before we could be doing that, so.[136]

Outsiders saw the party's response to the Women's Liberation Movement (WLM) as belated and insincere. In November 1970 the party held a conference on the implications of the WLM.[137] Three important campaigns were highlighted: abortion and contraception, nursery schools, and equal opportunity in education. Also, while equal pay was an essential demand it would not automatically change domestic oppression. Beatrix Campbell had already started to introduce feminist ideas into mainstream party discussion.[138] In November 1971 at the party's 32nd national congress the EC presented its draft resolution on 'Women in Society'.[139] From the branches and districts there were 252 amendments ranging from incidental one-liners to extensive reworkings of the statement.[140] There were brief amendments from Scotland, the nature of which show that feminism had not really permeated the district or branches. There were calls to see women as a separate and more repressed group and women in the party would soon bring up rape and domestic violence as central debates. *Marxism Today* discussed this from January 1973 to February 1974, one article stating: 'The emergence of an autonomous Women's Liberation Movement has been the stimulus for questioning and challenging the existing Marxist theory, or absence of it.'[141] It had also discussed marriage as a repressive institution where women had no rights and their individual sexuality was subordinate to the role of the family unit in society and was controlled by men.

Young couples, especially when the party employed one on a small income, made great sacrifices trying to build up membership and get campaigns off the ground: an initial confidence had overridden many emerging problems that would need to be resolved:

> I suppose the other effect was that Doug was out all the time, being a YCL organizer meant you were out every evening as well as during the day. We were *both* dedicated to the cause, wrapped up in the YCL activities, which meant that we didnae pay attention to our own personal lives very much, things were subsumed.[142]

Women were still restricted and the male orientation of labour movement politics – by design or circumstance – was raised in the 1970s as a contentious point. Women could end up in the same conventional roles despite having entered employment, gone to university, or perhaps establishing a career.

Feminism was introduced into the CP in the early-1970s, with its proponents pointing to complacency and deficiencies in the party's approach to the 'women's question'. On what might be termed the traditionalists' side, there were those who thought this was a distraction and a middle-class one at that. What seems evident from the material the party was now producing and publications generally was that a section of party women strongly identified with, and recognized the validity of, a gender-based analysis. For some party women feminism replaced the enthusiasm and belief in vanguard class politics as providing answers to fundamental questions and this was a major revelation:

> It had a tremendous impact on me personally, the women's movement, and I began to read *Spare Rib* and *Red Rag* came out at that time as well, all the periodicals and I began to read a lot of novels as well. And I suppose I see in my latter time in the party as being part of the project to feminize the party and taking part in that project.[143]

By the early 1970s[144] the SWAC was meeting irregularly and barely functioning at all; at the 1974 Scottish Congress, resolutions called for its re-establishment, for the establishment of women's groups in areas and branches and for positive discrimination towards women.[145] There was criticism of the few questions given to women in the party[146] and of their limited number on the Scottish committee.

From the mid-1970s the SWAC was meeting quarterly and there were now area advisory committees in Glasgow (with women's groups in Yoker, Kelvin, Drumchapel, Central/Camlachie, Maryhill and Govanhill) and Fife, and women's groups in Glenrothes, Paisley, East Kilbride and Edinburgh.[147] A bulletin was produced and it seemed as if there was some regeneration of the SWAC: 'All in all, progress has been made but much more remains to be done.'[148] A few major issues and demands now took precedence in the work of the SWAC and were brought to the Glasgow and Scottish committees for discussion: 'There were a whole number of issues coming up at that point. There were domestic issues like abortion, women's control of their fertility, child-care – that was a huge issue that we campaigned on, there was a closure of a nursery and we had a big campaign in Glasgow.'[149] Not all communists supported abortion on demand, and women forwarding support for the National Abortion Campaign[150] found that there were men (and some party women)[151] who found it hard to come to terms with these demands and this often reflected the influences of religious backgrounds and a social conservatism. A strong case had to be put before the leadership:

> For example the abortion issue in the 1970s was one that I took up within the party. When I say I took up I don't mean to sound individualistic about it but it was an issue I felt very strongly about it and I fought within the Glasgow party and the Scottish party for the issue to be taken up by the party, abortion rights, and by the trade union movement … lip service was paid if you understand. No, it wasn't taken up automatically because I remember being invited into an executive meeting to put the case for it.[152]

Women seeking internal changes pointedly worked within the party structure shaping the role of the SWAC in relation to the Scottish committee rather than the other way around. Another crucial turn was a new view towards the Soviet Union and challenging the traditional belief that the position of women there had fundamentally changed:[153]

> There was an element in the party that thought that feminism was a diversion and that it didnae relate to the class struggle and that once we got the revolution then all of these problems would be sorted out. And they would point to the position of women in the communist countries and say that it all improves once you've got a revolution. The counter blast to that for us was that in fact there

> was research coming out that women were still doing the double shift in the Soviet Union, ... they still didnae have power, they were still going home and doing the housework.[154]

Some agreed that there were deficiencies in the party and that important issues had not been addressed, but they did not embrace a wholesale change. Members still believed that as a campaigning body and as a left-wing force no other organization could touch the CP when it put its weight behind issues. From this stemmed an apprehension about changing the party out of all recognition. It was the beginning of many shocks to the system for those who feared the fundamental implications.

There were women who did not accept the politics of feminism. They accepted some of the criticisms but still believed in the traditional Marxist-Leninist approach rather than discussing how present inequalities could be tackled *before* advance could be made. Some party women in the Edinburgh women's group felt that feminism could have negative features:

> Some of us who went to the group had become very sceptical of ultra-feminism because we had gone to women's liberation workshop meetings at various times, I did and several others did, and couldn't handle the anti-men strand, not all the women but a very persistent tendency to be down on men, and that just struck us as irrational and not very Marxist.[155]

The party, while increasingly recognizing the need to address the many inherent inequalities in the movement, still sought a unitary approach. However, it seemed to be swinging behind those eager to recognize there was a serious deficiency in policy. One publication stated: 'But it is also important to recognize the class basis of oppression. Women can be brought to realize that they are a specially oppressed group (the 'slave of a slave' as it has been put) – but that the oppressors are not all men but capitalist society.'[156] In Scotland, such topics for debate were starting to emerge in the mid-1970s but did not reach open confrontation until the debate over the new draft of *The British Road to Socialism* in 1977.

Changes: the Edinburgh women's advisory group

One way women asserted themselves in the party and helped develop their confidence was to have separate meetings for women only. The Edinburgh women's advisory group developed from women who put on a play for the United Nations International Women's Year in 1975.[157] The play, commemorating the fight for women's suffrage, dealt with problems women had faced, such as being treated for pregnancy and working in a Dundee jute mill. The play was rehearsed over six months – a process that brought party women together in this way for the first time – and put on in Edinburgh at the trades council and at a large party rally in Glasgow. The response was so positive that it was decided to keep on meeting. The group seemed to encompass women from all sides of the party and was neither distinctly for the dissemination of feminist ideas nor initiated by them. What it did provide was an environment for women only to meet and discuss issues either specifically relating to their gender or to discuss literature as a group without any male presence. This opportunity had very positive results despite some CP men feeling left out and powerless:

> We didn't always have a text because as we became a group, you know how a group builds, we just came together to be together and my marriage broke up, several other ... marriages broke up so it was a support group as well, it wasn't just a brain thing at all. It became very much a solidarity and support group as well, and interesting how in the women's group, supposing we were six or ten or three ... *everybody* spoke but *everybody*, I mean people you never heard open their mouths at party meetings. So interesting and so much of it very reflective, I mean years of reflection coming out about life in general in the world that the party men would never hear.[158]

Interestingly, the group lasted from the mid-1970s to the early 1980s with its activities purposefully announced at branch and area meetings. It deliberately met away from the party's premises and on a rota basis. One reason it began to fall apart was that division emerged over the suggested texts, but while the group lasted it was seen as a very positive venture.

The political differences that would culminate in distinct ideological groups in the party had their roots in the early 1970s. These developed with the influence of the Italian and Spanish CPs and what was to be called Eurocommunism. The Scottish district did not formally embrace any of these terms as it had never led any ideological offensive or introduced any new political ideas into the CPGB, hence its loyal image. It could criticize itself: 'In terms of theory, the Left in Scotland has a record that leaves a lot to be desired.'[159] New ideas were raised in other domains:

> I went to the Communist University of London in 1974 I think. That was the first time I'd come across people who said 'I prefer Gramsci to Lenin' and I thought 'That's a very strange thing to say', that was when all that was just beginning to happen and they were off in another kind of world that I hadn't made contact with before. So it was a funny mix that Communist University of London between that group of folk, it was Judy Bloomfield I remember, but also equally quite a lot of people who were much more traditional Marxists, James Klugmann was speaking at it and folk like that so it was quite a funny mix.[160]

The changes that became apparent in the CP in the late 1970s began to appear at the start of the decade in certain districts such as London. That they were not yet predominant in Scotland may have been because of the achievements of the trade union movement and an ongoing united approach. Also there was still one triumph that all members celebrated.

On May Day 1975 the *Morning Star* carried the headline 'Victory'. The Vietnam War was over; a final offensive codenamed 'Campaign Ho Chi Minh' had defeated the US-backed government in the south. Launched on 26 April, over by 30 April, a new provisional revolutionary government was in power.[161] As well as elation there was a need to rebuild the country:

> Well, when I … went to Vietnam, it was like being high the whole time because everyone was liberated and they had their own country to themselves and although they were in want most of them, very skinny and starving, it was indescribable the feeling, the sort of lift of everyone.[162]

In Scotland, Medical Aid for Vietnam had been well supported by the Scottish NUM, which levied its members at one stage, and by the STUC, at whose congresses it took collections. There were women who had been involved from the inception of these campaigns in Scotland and who had raised money. The Vietnamese government presented Mary Cowan of Dalkeith with an award for the fund-raising and voluntary work she had done in Vietnam, such as translating written works (from the original French) in a state publishing house:

> I was given the medal of friendship and the first one that they gave because I happened to be handy. I was on the spot of course and I was an old person and I was coming back to Britain and so they had a little ceremony and gave me the medal of friendship, which I've since lost, it was pinched on Berwick station. … Oh, I felt furious and upset, very upset and I got in touch with the police at once and the policeman said 'Oh it's not so much the little things you lose, it's your faith in human nature', nice remark from the police [*laughs*]. Anyway that was that, I've never had it back.[163]

Conclusion

In this chapter I have focused on the younger women in the YCL and later their participation in the party. Many of the issues in which they were involved, Vietnam, Czechoslovakia and UCS, were not exclusively youth ones. They were part of the CP's whole political struggle. Accordingly, the place for young communists was in the party branches as much as in the YCL and so there was less reason not to go straight into branch activity.[164]

The party had survived the events of 1956 surprisingly well and its members accepted, either through experience or through having a CP family background, the politics and nature of the CP as it now stood. The CP in Scotland was basically homogenous and efficiently run, particularly the YCL branches, which seemed better balanced than the CP branches, where there was some disparity between the intense and active trade union communist politics of the industrial branches and the less dynamic and less influential area branches.[165] Women in the 1960s who were predominantly in the area branches may have partially offset some deficiencies, first by their aforementioned YCL involvement in greater numbers and second by the conscious changes that were brought about by some of them in the party branches and committees in the 1970s.

Czechoslovakia marked a critical turning point because it signalled the end of united support for the Soviet Union, which had been a characteristic of the Scottish district and had seen them through the losses of 1956. Thereafter, there was more open criticism of the socialist countries and John Gollan's article in *Marxism Today* in January 1976 was more the opening of a debate than its denouement. The party came to terms with the 1956 events only 20 years after they had occurred and at a time when feminist politics was becoming more influential in it. There now started an even greater debate over whether the party should go further with its reforms, as the Italian CP appeared to be doing, or if it had gone too far down the road of reformism and non-communist policies.

Until Czechoslovakia, members still believed in the party's leading role and in the progressive nature of world socialism. After 1968 major questions arose about the role of the party and its attitude to women, though the politics of the WLM came into the party in Scotland somewhat later. While critics faulted party women for embracing gender issues so late, they did in fact survive longer in the CP than elsewhere. This must be seen against the success of trade union matters from the late 1960s and the advances in membership and shop-floor activity. By 1968 the Scottish district was noticeably the strongest in the CPGB with 7617 of its 32,054 members (24 per cent).[166] The party in Scotland was helping to play a leading role in uniting the left and producing political leaders. All seemed to be coming to fruition at about the time of UCS; that it never came to more and lethargy set in is surely one reason why permanent divisions occurred later.

The party did try to merge the aspirations of women's liberation with its socialist politics, but the demands of the WLM were seen as challenging certain fundamental structures in society when the party was for overall change to socialism.[167] Trying to come to terms with this influx of ideas, the party then posited: 'Will not the women's movement be a very powerful force in carrying forward the struggle to realize liberation fully?'[168] The validity of feminist politics in the CP was that it illustrated to many women (and men) the party's complacency towards inequalities in the party. Party women were not unanimous in support of feminist policies and by no means was this because of age difference, yet gender, gay politics,[169] race[170] and class were to be greatly debated in the CP and continually reassessed until the party's demise.

Party membership revived in the 1970s and there was an increase from 7116 to 7585 between 1972 and 1973;[171] it then began to fall slowly until in 1976 it stood at 6580. Towards the close of the decade there were 178 branches in 14 areas of which 137 were area branches, 38 factory/industrial branches and 7 student branches.[172] Curiously, there was an increase of factory/industrial branches and a decrease of student branches suggesting that the workplace was proportionally increasing as the recession began to take hold. From 1972 to 1973 there had been an increase in YCL membership to 609[173] in Scotland but by 1976 it was down to 440.[174] Related to this, sales of *Challenge* had risen to over 1160 per issue but fell after 1974; the change of format had proved successful for a while.

The world seemed to be advancing towards socialism with national independence and socialist movements making more impact than ever before. The immediacy of events, related through words and images often gleaned through radio and film, made for an exciting political apprenticeship and this at a time when career and economic prospects were better than ever.

Thus, if the internal politics of the CP seemed to take precedence over what was going on outside, this would be an exaggeration when addressing women's activities from 1960 to 1975. All the positive advances for working people in Scotland and Britain – social reform, greater union density, successful industrial action, the defeat of the Heath government, more national awareness in Scotland expectantly leading to the 1979 referendum – could be allied to events abroad by communists: the victory of socialist forces in Vietnam, Angola[175] and Mozambique, revolution in Portugal, the death of Franco in Spain. Despite the defeats (for example Chile, Ireland,[176] the militaristic actions of the US government), and even though there were now over 162,000 unemployed[177] in Scotland, it had been a very positive time to have been involved in the CP:

> Because it was optimistic, because it was forward looking, we were going somewhere, we were building and even at the beginning of the 1970s the setbacks were small, we were winning, we were going to get there. I wasn't under any illusions that socialism was round the corner, it wasn't. When we were young I think perhaps there was that element there but as I got older it wasn't like that but it was still very, very positive, and winnable above all.[178]

Chapter 7

Open Discord, Internal Division and Permanent Decline, 1977–91

> I was very sad that it had come to that. Some of them I felt thought that they didn't want the party to change *at all*, which I thought was being awfully selfish. You couldn't have a Communist Party that only catered for the hungry thirties and the anti-fascist forties and the cold war fifties and the Peacenik sixties and the Women's Lib seventies. You had to have a Communist Party that could respond to and be passed on to younger, if you like, revolutionary people. You can't have one generation that says 'It's my party and you will not change it.'[1]

The British Road to Socialism debate

In this chapter I discuss the opinions of the opposing sides in the disputes that emerged during and after the debate of the new draft of *The British Road to Socialism* in 1977. Also, I recount the widening areas of disagreement that came to a head over the *Morning Star* and the People's Press Printing Society (PPPS).

Nationally and internationally there were many political changes, including the election of a Conservative government in 1979 and the emergence of Gorbachev as general secretary of the CPSU in 1985. Towards the end of the 1970s CP membership had begun to fall again and the party's earlier successes began to wane.[2] Members were disappointed at another right-wing Labour government and the party's failure to make more of the UCS dispute and its role in the trade unions, particularly in Scotland where mass union activity and one-day strikes had continued.[3]

The party still had a high profile, especially in Glasgow where it boasted a membership of 2400 in 40 branches.[4] In Glasgow, one of the most deprived cities in Europe, 45 per cent of women went out to work,[5] more than in any other city in Britain, and youth unemployment had reached 200,000.[6] Some 10,000 of the population were of Asian origin and the party had recently been fighting a growing number of fascist groups in the city.[7] Several members were still confident that the party could become a major force, but as industry declined, unions lost members and unemployment increased, most realized that this was more a hope than a probability. Supporting new social forces was seen as a way of winning new members; the party could diversify and embrace causes it had hitherto seen as supplementary to the class struggle. It was here that the new draft of *The British Road* played a vital part in redirecting the party's campaigning.

The opposition to the 1968 draft of *The British Road to Socialism* was insignificant compared with that to the new draft in the run-up to the 1977 congress. John Gollan's article *Socialist Democracy: Some Problems* had prepared the ground for a qualitative break with the past and the party's exclusive role in the fight for socialism.[8] There now emerged severe and permanent divisions, with two opposing sides representing incompatible ideologies – some wanted the party to work with the working class and its industrial base in the trade unions, while others, now increasingly to the fore, wanted to emphasize alliances with the women's movement and other interest groups, and to embrace more causes than the party had hitherto addressed. The major difference in the new draft of *The British Road* was the definition of a broad democratic alliance.[9] This was to replace the 'broad popular alliance around the leadership of the working class'[10] of the previous edition. The new draft emphasized achieving socialism through alliances with other sections and groups in British society. A parliamentary majority and changes to the state apparatus would be central to class struggle.[11] The vanguard role of the party was now noticeably diminished, though Marxism-Leninism was mentioned.[12] 'I was in support of it. I felt that it took account of changes in the world, and also changes within Britain and I very, very much subscribed to the idea of a broad democratic alliance.'[13]

The difference was obvious to all party activists involved in the debates on policy. The new concept of a broad democratic alliance suggested joining forces with groups the party had previously ignored, sometimes deliberately. The traditionalists saw the changes as scaling down the party's 'leading role' as the principal force for socialism:

> The formulation which preceded the broad democratic alliance was the anti-monopoly alliance which seemed to me to have a much clearer class content and it wasn't only about the working class it was about everyone whose interests were not served by monopoly capitalism. The broad democratic alliance has no *focus*. What is it aimed at? It's a nice idea but how do you forge it? What are the terms in which it would be created? It didn't have any political bite really.[14]

The continuing strength of trade unionism at this time and the lack of socialist policies from the Labour government, which introduced monetarism from 1976, convinced the traditionalists that the leading role of the working class should remain primary. Whatever one thought of the new draft, members detected a new vigour to the debate about the programme and its importance in changing the party's direction; in fact, it received more attention outside and inside the party than all the drafts since 1950. The democratic traditions in Britain were emphasized:

> Every country has its own identity, its own way which is the only Marxist view of it because different countries have got different traditions and different ways and they are bound to be different. I didn't see any problem with *The British Road* ... in theory it was parliamentary because we were going to get members of parliament, we were going to shoot to power, but I think in our heart of hearts we knew that it was just a theoretical position because we couldn't even get a councillor never mind an MP.[15]

In Scotland the debates became heated, but the party draft carried the day in terms of support from the Scottish district. At aggregate meetings and in the branches[16] there were more definite splits. Those opposed to the changes claimed they had support in a number of branches – in Glasgow, Fife, Clydebank, the Vale of Leven, Stirling, Falkirk and, to a lesser extent, Edinburgh and Dundee.[17] The latter is a good example of an area with a strong industrial base, an active and lively YCL and deep loyalty to the party leadership.[18] There were to be more bitter, heartfelt and passionately argued meetings over the *BRS* than over any issue since the internal changes of 1956 and Czechoslovakia in 1968:

> It wasn't exactly bloodshed but it was horrendous ... meetings were packed if there was a controversial issue coming up;

> everybody, different sides, would get their troops out and going into a meeting you would glance round and think 'Oh God, there's something coming up, now what are they doing here? What's brought them out? You know we'll have to watch our step here.' And it really was horrible; it was really *bitter*, *nasty*, very nasty.[19]

Such an atmosphere was not conducive to a party seeking renewal, but there seemed so much at stake, a political heritage that all those in the debate sought to uphold. At the 1977 British congress the changes were voted in despite a noticeable minority against them. There was a small split with the emergence of the New Communist Party led by Sid French from the Surrey district. The NCP had only a handful of members in Scotland, including a few women.[20] The disagreements and splits at British congress shocked younger Scottish delegates, especially from outside Glasgow, who were unused to the deeply expressed differences they saw at British level.[21]

In a July 1977 circular the Glasgow secretary Ian McKay predicted growing disagreements over policy. He noticed a 'lack of conviction'[22] towards *The British Road to Socialism* and broad democratic alliance, and saw the anti-leadership tendency in the Glasgow party as 'a new and serious feature of the present situation'.[23] Some of this emerging opposition still believed in the party's leading role and the dictatorship of the proletariat, and opposed the 'historic compromise' made in Italy between the Italian CP and Christian Democrats in agreeing to pass certain legislation. Citing the Gollan article, McKay noted that differences existed before the new *British Road to Socialism* was published but that an anti-leadership tendency was evident at the Glasgow conference on 28 May 1977 where an estimated 45–55 delegates voted against the party leaders.[24] This opposition was said to have come from non-industrial comrades.[25] Hence, from the beginning the hierarchy recognized and condemned the opposition to the leadership and the new policies. In contrast with the 1977 British congress, those who wanted to take the party in a new direction as mapped out by *The British Road* acquired a new confidence.

An opportunity for more changes came with a new commission on inner party democracy (IPD), which was to report back to the 1979 congress. Since not all those who upheld the changes to the party programme supported the constitutional shift for which one section of the party now fought, a realignment of forces began. For the reformers there now seemed an opportunity to try to change the CP structurally after years of disaffection at area and Scottish level:

> I used to have a problem with all the committees in that I used to describe it as 'the tyranny of the contribution'. That you didnae really have a debate, the scene was set by whoever was there from the political committee, the political statement was the scene setting and then the chair controlled the debate in that the tradition was that you got up when you had a contribution to make and you didnae interrupt that contribution and you didnae just say something if something came into your head; you had to wait until a contribution had somehow worked itself up or you had prepared it.[26]

The phrase 'the tyranny of the contribution' described the tradition at Scottish or area meetings of giving detailed stage-managed reports that allowed no room for spontaneous or impromptu inputs. The political committee would hand down a political statement and then committee members would make their own rehearsed offerings while the meeting was strongly controlled from the chair. These criticisms went deep into the party psyche, and in the debates about party democracy the reformers saw the same procedure stifling them at committee level:

> There was a growing cynicism about how the eastern European countries were operating and the whole notion of democracy, and that was what prompted our IPD proposals as well. This notion that we were very good at the centralist bit but ... hopeless at the democracy and a lot of the stuff about the women's movement fitted into that because I remember doing meetings about feminism in the socialist countries and what the implications were and realizing that they didnae tolerate autonomous movements within their countries.[27]

Among the dedicated activists the contentions over IPD were no less earnest than *The British Road* debate, though there were noticeably fewer contributions from branches and committees.[28] The fear of change going too far came not only from the traditionalist wing but also from the party hierarchy and party members who had supported recent changes. This opposition to the more radical IPD proposals[29] was a strong characteristic of the Scottish party in that its potent industrial

10. Glasgow communists celebrate 60 years of struggle, 1980. Pat Milligan front row on the left, Marion and Joe Henery third row right. Bill Cowe, former Scottish industrial organizer is in right-hand corner.

base and working-class membership still strongly identified with a centralized structure. Despite being defeated on their more radical proposals for IPD,[30] the reformers still had the momentum on their side. They increased their numbers on the Scottish committee by being put on the recommended list that the elections preparation committee put to congress:

> Jimmy Airlie had proposed a trade union convenor from Dundee, I think, and he was on the list but it was the point at which feminists were beginning to make some kind of impact on the committee and we were making this strong argument that there was hardly any women on and that women didnae play an equal part in the party and so on. So the EPC was moved to, probably for all kinds of reasons I can't remember, put me on instead.[31]

Some women made a pointed contribution at the sixtieth birthday celebrations for the party in Glasgow City Halls in 1980. Several of them marched and criticized male communists who left their wives at home while they did all the politicking in the pub. It was a night to celebrate the party's history as well as to endorse its most recent policies.

As these new ideas began to become more focused at Scottish level there was an even greater input from a section seeking to try and inject enthusiasm for change and a new perspective associated with the Spanish and Italian CPs, not that there was a wholesale identification with the term 'Eurocommunism'. Most party members did not use the term and is it not evident in Scottish party publications of the time. The new social forces were identified with this trend and the party leadership in Scotland accepted and encouraged them in the hope that there would be growth through their adoption, but not all members were so sure. 'What we seemed to be doing was saying 'Eurocommunism, that's great' whereas our situation was really totally different, we were a real minority party.'[32]

Party districts in England, especially London and the northwest, were openly divided over the political issues. However, the specific nature and homogeneity of the Scottish party prevented such a visible break, for no camp wanted to be seen as detrimental to the party. Indeed, this was a vital and important characteristic of the Scottish district, whose members were still on the whole unified and still worked together when the need arose. It is this that accounts for the continuing support given to the leadership as much as any in-depth knowledge and agreement with the new policies in *The British Road to Socialism*.

Feminism from the late 1970s

In the last chapter I showed how some party women converted to feminist politics in the early to mid-1970s. The late 1970s saw the implementation of feminist policies once the party had adopted them. The dedicated work of party women in the SWAC and women's groups ensured that the party accommodated many aspects of feminism and the politics of the women's movement became increasingly accepted. More women understood the pertinence and relevance of the measures for which they now fought:

> When the women's movement was starting to become more active, I identified with it right away because I had always felt the suppression even within my own home, I always felt subservient and it really annoyed me that because the men were the wage earners they took upon themselves this authority over women, and while I mean my husband wasn't the worst of many, he was as good as most, at

> the same time he was affected by it as well, so obviously so was I. When the feminist movement began to grow I was right with it and while I felt that the Communist Party wasn't exactly a feminist party but at least they were trying ... to develop a feminist approach, not always successfully, I mean we had as many male chauvinists in the Communist Party as there were in any other sector of society but at least they were aware that they had to try and embrace this new idea.[33]

Reconstituted, the SWAC fought for abortion rights (against the Corrie Bill for example[34]) and for more awareness of rape and domestic violence in society. Male brutality towards women extended to child abuse and some startling statistics were used to illustrate this: 97 per cent of adults who abused children were male and in 92 per cent of cases the children they abused were female.[35] Violence was not just seen as a product of capitalism but of patriarchy, the imbalance of power between men and women. Feminists believed that the left had woefully neglected these areas. There was a difference between feminists who sought more separation from men socially and sexually and the socialist and Marxist feminists who saw the problem being resolved at some stage under socialism. Central to the feminism in the party was the criticism that class power alone as an explanation denied the reality of women's oppression.[36] A beginning was a commitment to changing the role of women in the party:

> I mean we were the group of women that really took issue with being expected to run the bazaars and stuff. ... I can remember an incident even at Scottish committee where this old male comrade told ... a very sexist joke and I remember thinking 'I wonder if I should take it up?' and being a bit scared because he was old, he had done a lot but I remember at the next committee, once I had plucked up courage and thought about it, I thought 'No I am going to take that up.' In my book it wasn't on but it was hard to raise it without appearing to be critical of this old comrade.[37]

Having changed the perspective of women in the party, feminist politics was now changing the manner in which the party operated and the role of women in its structures. A qualitative leap was made from the first half of the 1970s, with people being won over to feminism, to feminism making an impact structurally in the latter half of that decade. Still, establishing women's groups and area advisories could meet with opposition from party members who saw it as irrelevant and had no grasp of the new role some women were attempting to establish. In this respect there was as much opposition through ignorance as through ideological hostility:

> We had a women's group and I can remember our branch secretary telling us we couldn't have a women's group, even to the stage of coming to somebody's house, aye! We arranged to have this group of us in Clouston Street and this was a debate about whether we should – I remember the secretary saying 'Look we're not a women's magazine.'[38]

The positive role of women's groups was seen in their freer atmosphere and greater scope for the personal development of women than the party branch allowed. The Edinburgh women's group was open to non-party women[39] and, until disagreements in the early 1980s, was very successful in this sphere. Women's groups could also provide a stepping stone for women returning to party activity after an absence:

> because men dominate within society, within the family, within any situation men will dominate and they will dominate the speeches and the speaking and the conversation, so therefore women *do* have to assert themselves and it can be quite difficult. That was why the women's groups were useful, I personally got reinvolved with the party through a women's group in Govanhill but it was education classes they were running.[40]

Gay rights were raised in the party in Scotland and a gay rights advisory committee met for the first time in the late 1970s in Edinburgh and Glasgow. There was also a YCL gay committee.[41] The party worked with the Gay Activist Alliance and it was argued that the gay movement must be seen as 'an integral part of the left and progressive movement'.[42] The importance of 'coming out' was showing pride in personal sexuality and in opposing accepted norms about the role of the family in society.[43] The left was criticized for having treated homosexuality as a bourgeois deviance; it was treated thus in socialist countries, including Cuba.[44] The 1967 legislation decriminalizing homosexuality excluded Scotland and Northern Ireland. Lesbianism was still unrecognized because, according to feminists, it was not accepted that women could have their own sexuality. That the CP in Scotland now discussed these issues and that feminism was being accommodated in the party was seen as a major advance for the reformers. Many traditional attitudes survived in the labour movement and, on one occasion, party women rose to the challenge of organizing and presenting their case to a group of Scottish miners:

> It was a weekend education school and the pits sent various delegates to the school. I don't know how the party managed to have that kind of hegemony but I guess it did in the pits, and we were to run this weekend school with these miners on women's issues and the women's movement. … We were talking about how women serviced their families and clearly a lot of them had never thought of that and had just always taken it for granted. And we talked about the roles that women had in the house and listed them and this young guy said he'd lived with his mother and he still lived with his mother and he said 'Right enough, I come in and she sets my dinner on the table. She does nae just set my dinner doon she sauts it for me'; she put salt on for him [*laughs*] and it was the way he said it was like a sudden realization of the extent to which she was servicing him … the weekend was *fantastic*,[45] it was just wonderful.[46]

The customary role accorded to mothers in capitalist societies was questioned, as was the party's previous view on it. The Glasgow Women's Advisory, reconstituted in 1977,[47] argued for more child-care facilities and pointed to research that disputed that children would become dysfunctional unless their mother looked after them.[48] Research now showed that several adults of either sex could form relationships that would benefit the child in the same way.[49] The SWAC stated that women were restricted to their domestic role because of the lack of child-care facilities. In Glasgow this meant that only 31.7 per cent of three to four year-olds attended nursery schools, and only one in eight of these did so full time.[50] More workplace crèches, child minders and nursery school facilities[51] were needed to free women from their imposed role. The Glasgow advisory's document was distributed widely to party branches and groups such as Gingerbread and the Child Poverty Action Group.[52] In 1980 the SWAC held a successful day school on 'Women's Right to Work', presented by

Sue Slipman. This was followed by a 'Reclaim the Night' march,[53] which became an annual event.[54]

While more party members recognized women's oppression this did not mean that all party women automatically accepted the feminist agenda. The Edinburgh women's group appears to have worked because it brought women from all sides of the party together and, although proving the need for women's organization and the very positive effects of meeting together, it was not ideologically committed to any camp:

> I think when we met as women we met to supply something we felt lacking in the Communist Party, that's for sure, but we hoped that we could have it all taken on board and we were, most of us, active in the party as well so we were trying to cover the spectrum. The way the feminist issues began to be addressed in the party became like, it was a single issue, they were neglecting the other issues I thought and I thought it was counter-productive because it antagonized people. It was confrontational.[55]

There was criticism that single issues like gender, race and sexual politics were becoming prime focuses for party work rather than being integrated into the overall struggle for socialism. The rejoinder to this was that these inequalities needed immediate recognition and specific policies to win more people over to the CP and socialism. Those who opposed single issue politics pointed to the limited resonance of feminist politics to many sections of women:

> because of the divorce of the trade union struggles from political struggles that took place there failed to be a focus on working-class women and again that's where, when the more middle-class sections, which were typified in the Eurocommunist element, began to gain ground; they had discussion groups on sexuality and stuff like that, which has some importance but was perhaps not key to the reality of life that faced women at that time and still faces them today when you're really struggling to get by. I'm not saying that we should neglect the mechanisms of oppression but I don't think it had a resonance with working-class women. [56]

By the early 1980s the party leadership in Scotland was criticizing women on the Scottish committee for neither attending SWAC meetings nor becoming 'involved in any aspect of the fight to take forward in Scotland, party policy on women as agreed at National Congress'.[57] This comment alluded to an episode in Edinburgh when the women's advisory group successfully moved a resolution to the City committee in October 1981 against a proposed nominee from the Scottish committee, also an Edinburgh woman activist, to the NEC at the November Congress.[58] The reformers were critical of the woman in question and she, not surprisingly, was disillusioned by the episode. It was a sign of traumatic battles ahead and it upset some women who supported radical changes. On the other hand, there were party members – namely 'pro-feminist' men – who supported the resolution. The ideological divide would be compounded by a government against which the party could neither come to terms nor unify.

Conflict

The failed 'yes' campaign for a Scottish parliament in the 1979 referendum and the Labour government's subsequent election defeat signalled the end of CP advances. The Thatcher government's monetarist policies reduced the capacity of much traditional industry and, with 30,000 jobs lost in the west of Scotland in a year, unemployment increased dramatically.[59] The Thatcher government's first term was its hardest, but after the Falklands War in 1982[60] and the overwhelming defeat of the Labour Party in the 1983 general election there was a definite retreat for left-wing politics. Some in the CP attributed this to the lack of socialist direction and timidity of the labour and trade union hierarchy to meet the challenge and show leadership. For the reformers this was the era of 'Thatcherism', a new defining period in British politics and a total break with the past:

> I would go along with the notion that *Marxism Today* tried to put across, that in fact Thatcherism was the revolutionary force, that it won hearts and minds, that there were major shifts in traditional values and that the way society was developing anyway meant there was huge shifts in work patterns … there was such a huge upheaval that Thatcher won hegemony.[61]

There was a rapid decline in employment in the engineering, shipbuilding and mining industries, which were all closely associated with militant trade unionism. The growth of the service sector and white-collar employment meant there was a change in the composition of the workforce. While trade unionism was numerically large it no longer had a natural allegiance to the Labour Party.[62] This was more apparent in England than in Scotland. The creation of the SDP was also seen as a realignment of political forces unfavourable to the left.[63] From this viewpoint the party needed to eschew its traditionally militant industrial character or die. Membership of the party in Scotland was 5216 in October 1980 and, while it had stabilized, in ten years it had lost 33 per cent of its members.[64]

A debate about the future of trade unionism had opened even before the 1979 election. In *The Forward March of Labour Halted?* Eric Hobsbawm suggested that postwar advances were over. Inequality in unions and the absence of women from positions on executives and as full-time officers was now being openly addressed.[65] The return to free collective bargaining was thought to increase differentials between men and women and to uphold patriarchal values.[66] Traditionalists saw these as excuses to support right-wing methods such as wage restraint and the last Labour government's failed social contract. The base of the party's strength was its industrial membership in well organized unions. An article by Tony Lane attacking the shop stewards movement, which appeared in *Marxism Today*, now edited by Martin Jacques, angered some party members:

> I saw it as being very critical. I mean I spoke against the Tony Lane article and said it was a hotch-potch, and it was so provocative, and it was timed for a TUC from what I remember, and I can remember saying that 'how irresponsible'. … I worked in a secretarial capacity for a trade union; I knew all the loyal comrades that had always worked there but I also knew that the trade union movement was changing and you couldn't *not say* that it was changing and that the basis of the shop stewards movement was shifting altogether.[67]

Marxism Today was strongly identified with Eurocommunism. Desiring a change in the party's internal structure and in the way it approached issues, the magazine became the theoretical house for ideas that were not always to party members' tastes. To those used to the magazine's old style under James Klugmann, the articles seemed inaccessible and incomprehensible compared with the digestible contents of *Comment* or *Labour Monthly*. Yet, this new style was also attracting a new readership:

> I went along with the new ideas to a certain extent but *Marxism Today* was a magazine I stopped buying because first of all the language, I mean I would start to read an article in *Marxism Today* and I would get to three or four paragraphs and I would need to go back to the beginning again and say 'what are they talking about?' I found that the language that was being used in *Marxism Today* was alien to me, but over and above that there were certain discussions and certain people who, I mean I didn't approve of them interviewing right-wing members of the Tory party for instance, I didn't think that was relevant and there were certain things about *Marxism Today* that I didn't like but mainly the reason I stopped buying it was because I couldn't understand it half the time.[68]

This was from a supporter of the new social forces in the party. Not surprisingly, opponents of the changes were even more scathing:

> I was a bit dismayed by it really. When I first joined the party I took out a subscription to *Marxism Today* and I used to struggle through all the articles by Martin Jacques and Stuart Hall and try to understand them. Their ideas never used to make sense to me and I thought it was because I didn't know very much but I came to the view that it was because they were just wrong, their whole analysis of power and the state, and the nature of the working class. They just bore no relation to the reality that we all know about, the nature of capitalist society and power within it, it was just nonsense. I still think it is *nonsense.*[69]

Like so many issues, interviewing a Tory MP divided the membership between those who saw it as bold and breaking new ground and those who saw it as accommodating the enemy. The reformers who identified with *Marxism Today* and who emphasized the importance of Gramsci did not have counterparts in Scotland. There was no organized bloc of distinct Eurocommunists. Most members still supported (or reluctantly accepted) the changes and so there was no divide between middle-class elements and industrial workers, or 'Euros' and 'Tankies'. In Scotland one could not associate the politics of either with any one side or trend in the party. Branches, areas and committees had a mix of both. In contrast to this was the management committee of the PPPS, which oversaw the running of the *Morning Star* and met in London. Although controlled by its shareholders, the CP still strongly influenced the paper and forwarded nominees to this committee. By the early 1980s differences were becoming increasingly bitter and the atmosphere at meetings contrasted with the experience of committee members from Scotland:

> I never felt ostracized from our politics, I never felt as though people were vindictive about my politics. I felt I could move around in Scotland in an open way and also in the Scottish party, even though you didn't agree with one another. I never experienced sectarianism in Scotland but by golly when I went down to work in London, the London party was just so riven with sectarian politics, it was horrible, absolutely horrible. I couldn't understand; sectarianism is one of the most horrible things in the world and I used to think that it belonged to other than the Communist Party, to other groupings on the left because I'd never experienced sectarianism as I did when I went to London, I thought it was just dreadful.[70]

A major dispute broke out in the PPPS management committee between the party's EC and the *Morning Star* editor, Tony Chater. The party EC accused Chater of not following party policy and adopting procedures the party congress had rejected. Congress also criticized the paper and its editor. A section of party activists allied with some PPPS shareholders feared that new proposals for the paper would conclude with it becoming a weekly and so ending its role as the only daily paper produced for the labour movement. They were also convinced that it would eventually be wound up if these changes were implemented and so they supported the editor. This opposition argued that the paper was accountable to the shareholders directly and not to the party. The opposing sides in this practical dispute on the whole mirrored the political differences over *The British Road to Socialism*. Consequently, there was mounting antagonism on the PPPS management committee:

> The party never talked about the working class, always talked about the working people and time and time again Tony Chater would bring an editorial to us which talked about the working class and I would always have to say 'Can I just have the wording changed please, we don't use the term working class we talk about the working people' and he would accept it but that was it. And I was sitting in among a whole lot of people who were actually opposed to the

line of the party executive but I hadn't the wit and sense to see it because I just did not see their sectarianism.[71]

Those who opposed the CP executive's plans for the *Morning Star* were labelled sectarian and the split was obvious elsewhere. In some districts in England the division between members supporting or opposing the party's EC was the same as on the paper's management committee. In the northwest district, which covered Manchester and Liverpool, this was the first major political conflict experienced by the last new recruits to the YCL:

When I joined the YCL the people who were involved in starting the YCL came from pro-*Morning Star* trade unionist backgrounds and Manchester was split between the Euros and the Marxist–Leninists, very much along class lines. Euros were professional, middle-class, academic, that kind of group in the party and everybody else, they were the trade union communists and the working class. It wasn't my fault that those were the people that had been running the YCL but those were the people I kept in contact with, so I was therefore seen as part of this grouping and I'm quite happy to have been in that grouping but it wasn't something which I'd actively chosen at the time, it was accidental I'd come into the party that way. When I came up to Scotland obviously the political divisions within the party were quite different, there wasn't that kind of class basis to the position. I think it was much more complex in Scotland and in Glasgow. You had the phenomena of the party loyalists, large sections of the party who were working class and they just didn't accept the political developments there had been in the party and they saw that it was important to be loyal to the executive committee and that was their view and for a long, long time, even when there was expulsions and everything, they stuck to that position.[72]

From 1983 the PPPS meetings were packed. Opposing the party EC's list of candidates for the PPPS management committee were dissenting party members who stood by the editor of the paper, a section of the existing management committee and other shareholders. Those supporting the EC believed that the editor, who had been on the party EC, should have been disciplined and removed:

> I was sick, I was disgusted with the behaviour of the people who had been manipulating for years obviously to take over this paper and we were blithely ignorant that anybody within the Communist Party could manipulate to the extent that they were going to take this paper away from this new idea, it was because of the new ideas in the Communist Party and these people were determined that if there was a split they were going to have the paper, I think that was it. When it came to the bit, we were quite helpless to protect the paper from these people, they won the arguments, well they didn't win the arguments but they were able to win the support of people who were like-minded but I never understood how we could have lost that paper.[73]

Scottish members supporting the party executive, many of whom had sold the *Morning Star* for years,[74] believed the paper would be given a new lease of life if the current incumbents were removed. Many ordinary members did not realize that distrust had turned to open feud until they were urged to attend the PPPS AGM in Glasgow. The opposition feared the paper would be put into the hands of people with no intention of trying to make it work. Seeing subsidies being given to *Marxism Today* and its new priority in the party's strategy, it was felt that the *Morning Star* would be quietly disposed of:

> When the split came about the *Morning Star*, I was 199 per cent on the side of the people who were supporting the *Morning Star*, I was agin the executive because I firmly believed, by that time, that they were trying to destroy the *Morning Star*, that if they got their hands on the *Morning Star* it would no longer be on the street and in my opinion by the end of this period I saw the party crumbling and I wasn't sure that we would be able to save the party as I wanted to see it but I was damned determined that I would do everything in my power to save that paper.[75]

In Scotland, those opposing the EC's recommendations argued that the paper belonged to the labour movement and was accountable to its shareholders through a management committee and not directly to the party. Countering this was the riposte that the party had been the major influence in the paper and that EC nominations had always been accepted in the past. Both sides could technically prove their case. There were also supporters of *Straight Left*, a paper started in 1979,[76] but its history of factionalism made them (to the party hierarchy and unsympathetic members) the anti-party group *par excellence*. Although on the left and strong traditionalists, they operated separately from those around the *Morning Star*. An AGM of the PPPS took place on 3 June 1984 at the Woodside Halls in Glasgow. The hostile atmosphere and antagonistic behaviour of the participants augured badly for any future unity:

> A young woman gave me my papers and she said 'Right, you go into the hall and sit down' and I said 'Just a minute I'll do that when my husband's been dealt with, I'm waiting on my husband, I'm going into the hall along with him' and I felt it wasn't a very friendly attitude for a start, and we went in and sat down. And that was a very troubled meeting. Nothing went right as far as I was concerned. Mick Mcgahey got up to pass a resolution and was refused permission and it got quite heated and there were very angry exchanges within the meeting and after it and tempers were very frayed. … And we withdrew our shares and gave our money to charity but continued to purchase the paper. It's a very unhappy episode in my political life.[77]

In 1984 the AGMs met in seven cities in Britain. In Glasgow those supporting the party executive tried unsuccessfully to move a resolution against the paper's management committee. Countering this it was argued that the business for all AGMs had to be the same and that no motions could be taken on the day from the floor. The meeting broke up without a vote being taken, a vote that would have been vital in determining who would control the paper. The altercations continued:

> It was like rent-a-mob up the stairs – I don't know where they got them, stamping their feet and howling. *It was absolutely horrendous.* We were stuck right in the centre, we couldnae even get out and finally when it finished up we all went out, Eric Park's son got punched.[78] He was doing his steward and he got punched. When I got home I phoned Monty Berkeley [and] said 'What did you think of that?' He said, 'Cath, I went home,' he said, 'and I looked at my party card and I tore it in two. I've been 50 years in this party, if that's what it's come to I don't want to know.' It was absolutely awful.[79]

With no vote taken and the rest of the votes in Britain going against the reformers, the party lost its influence on the PPPS management committee and control of the *Morning Star*. The Glasgow AGM only confirmed the state of affairs in the Scottish CP – the party membership was irrevocably split. Symbolically, and it was a traumatic event for many members, the Glasgow meeting effectively marked the end of the CP in Scotland.[80] Though most party members still supported the leadership it appears that there was some pragmatic voting going on as subsequent AGM votes were decisive for the opposition despite the party trying to mobilize to reverse the decisions. There was definite support for the opposition from left-wing elements outside the CP but tactical voting must have been exercised by members on whom the party leadership thought it could rely. Active CP supporters of the *Morning Star* faced disciplining by the party hierarchy:

> It was seen as a crime, it was quite criminal. The *Morning Star* was 'anti-party', that was the phrase, 'anti-party'. For someone who spent their whole life working for the party and supporting it, I took that very badly. ... I was removed from the chair of the Glasgow party and although the reason for it was a vote of no confidence due to my conduct in the chairing of a meeting, it was basically they didn't want me up there any more. To an extent I had been put there with the approval obviously of the hierarchy, so I was to be removed when I didn't play the game.[81]

Coming at the twilight of the party's history, the divisions over the *Morning Star* caused animosity and anger among people who had been close friends or were in party families. The bitterness was deep and patently obvious in the interviews. The anger of both sides over their feelings of mistreatment and betrayal suggested that some relationships would never be the same again. It was an alarming time and, unlike events in 1956, these were disagreements over indigenous issues:

> It was very bad. We were called Trotskyites, we were also told that we had hijacked the paper, it was a disgrace – the letters that had been written in the paper, and I had written one myself about the previous *Morning Star* meetings. These were the actual annual general meetings and this was crucial votes for the editorial board at the time and we were just considered as traitors and it was just

> really dreadful and the thing is I was seen as being a renegade within my family. I was a rank bad yun.[82]

It was hard to find someone who did not have a strong word to say on this issue, on their opponents and on the resultant suspensions and expulsions.[83] In Scotland these began with the suspension of some members in 1985, then from 1986 expulsions. These included some well-known figures in the party such as John Foster, an established academic and selfless activist, and Andrew Clark, from a mining family and a *Morning Star* journalist. Instead of being formally expelled some members were not 'recarded', which meant they were effectively excluded from party activity and so were no longer members.[84] The party leadership justified this measure as certain members still supported the *Morning Star* and thus its stand against party policy.[85] Members on the receiving end of these measures saw the irony of the increasing use of democratic centralism to implement discipline by those who supposedly abhorred the mechanism.[86] Not all members supported any one side in the dispute and a fall in membership to 2900 by 1986[87] suggests many had quietly left:

> It was all this fighting, all this aggro and people not talking to each other and folk who had been friends, comrades, work associates, whatever for years and you suddenly *have to* make a definitive statement about things that (a) you don't think are that relevant when it really comes down to it, (b) there are positive things on both sides and you're being asked to make up your mind and stick to a position and I just felt I couldn't do it.[88]

The dramatic fall in membership, however, was possibly largely attributable to the 'colossal problems with deindustrialization and unemployment'.[89] Due to the government's rationalization programme and restriction of established trade union practices, the party was losing its most important base in the traditional industries.[90]

Breaking the back of trade union militancy 1983–85

From a communist perspective the splits and acrimony could not have come at a worse time. Although trade union organization was still evident despite the falling membership, in 1982 the minister for employment Norman Tebbit introduced new legislation restricting trade union rights and immunity from the law. Towards the end of 1983 there was a major dispute over union recognition in Warrington at the *Stockport Messenger* paper run by Eddie Shah. Mass pickets supported the reinstatement of sacked print workers. Here, local YCL members experienced an important dispute, which set a precedent for industrial conflict in the 1980s:

> It was not just the police, there were riot police but there were also the special patrol group, which Anderton, the chief constable in Manchester, had just set up and they were basically paramilitary police and they were brought out in force to counter the pickets. The whole experience that night was just horrific; it's the most horrific thing I'd ever seen in my life. You can read *State and Revolution* but when you actually see all the forces of the state out to physically smash people, it had a major effect on my political development at that time. It had a big effect personally because my sister was arrested that night. She was only 15, we stayed the whole night and, it must have been about five or six in the morning, most people were leaving and the police just went mad and attacked everybody. The police had this guy on the floor and they were just kicking his head in, the whole group of them, we were all screaming and my sister went in and tried to drag them off. She was only a wee girl and they just dragged her off, the police had all these cabin things. It was just horrifying and it just happened in minutes and she was arrested for obstructing the police and we all had to go along to the police station and try and find out where she'd be taken to. Loads of people had all been dragged off and we spent the morning at Warrington police station.[91]

If this confrontation with the authorities showed a hardened approach to trade unionists, it was mild compared with the next major dispute, which became the longest and most bitter industrial conflict since the 1926 miners' lockout and general strike. The forerunner to the miners' strike of 1984–85 was the fight to save the Kinneil and Cardowan collieries and strike action over Monktonhall, all pits being in Scotland. There was also a national overtime ban in opposition to redundancies.[92] What distinguished this strike from all others in the postwar era was that it was British wide and was for the retention of jobs in mining communities. The strike was purely for survival and the party recognized its importance. 'The miners' heroic struggle dominates the struggle and rightly so. It is one of the greatest and most fundamental struggles this century.'[93]

At the start of the strike the STUC's SWAC organized a women's demonstration in Edinburgh on the theme of 'Victorian values'. Women dressed up in Victorian outfits and some women from the coal fields also got involved.[94] An important turning point was a meeting in Lochgelly, at which women from mining families expressed their support for the strike:

> It was as a result of a decision taken in the party. Jean Miller had been at a party meeting for the whole of Britain and women were becoming involved in Barnsley and in Yorkshire. It was decided in Scotland that there should be a women's meeting in Lochgelly and that for me was the start of my personal involvement. We then set up a Scottish area women's support group and two women from each of the support groups in the various areas in Scotland were on the group. Fife, Lanarkshire, Ayrshire and Lothians and we came together and discussed many things. Again, too, women from the support groups were addressing meetings and playing a vital role in the situation. No matter what level the meeting was held a women speaker was always included. The women were also involved in the strike committee meetings that were being held in the districts.[95]

This did not mean a sudden transformation of the NUM with women now accepted in the front line of the struggle. Many prejudices remained among miners and women were often fighting on two fronts – against established family values and the government. By their perseverance they broke some prejudices down. They became actively involved in picketing and in organizing the kitchens. They also learnt to address meetings and so became more politically aware:

> I think it was the exact nature of the women's involvement in the Miners' Strike that was so important. They realized that the strike was for the future of their husbands, their brothers, their uncles, their fathers, but it was also for the future of their children and their communities. And on this occasion the media couldn't get women, as they normally had been able to do, to condemn their men for taking strike action and urging them to go back to work.

> They didn't get that. Women were in fact arguing for and were supportive of the strike action that was being taken by the miners.[96]

Although many in the Labour and trade union establishment, as well as the leadership of the CP, criticized the miners' leader Arthur Scargill, in Scotland the party membership united to give practical help to the strike. There were different views on who influenced women in the mining communities. Some party feminists gave credit to the women's movement,[97] while others argued that it was no more than straightforward support from working-class women for traditional class-based industrial action and that the women's movement had been negligible in the coal fields prior to the strike.[98] The CP women's advisory assisted women's support and action groups, while trades councils, trade union and party branches often adopted pit communities and raised funds for them. Groups and political parties in Dundee supported mining villages in Fife where there had been equally strong support for the miners in the 1972–74 dispute. In the west there were support groups in Glasgow and surrounding towns:

> The Paisley Trades Council organized collections every Friday and we had a good Labour controlled district council then and they gave us permission to [use] part of the Town Hall where we could take the collections and that, gave us the cans to do it and collect in the streets. We collected in this area I think it was about £85,000 in money and thousands of pounds in food because we used to stand down there outside the co-op when the people were coming out on a Friday with their groceries and all the big stores and *never had anybody* saying they wouldnae give you anything and we did it in Johnstone and Barrhead and Renfrew as well and the miners came up from Ayr, so many of them every week.[99]

Despite assistance from the public, many unionized workers were now cautious and reluctant to take industrial action in support of other disputes; they feared the sequestration of union assets. In Scotland, the STUC gave support and women's support groups were determined to show their solidarity with the strike and to join men on the picket line. They received the same physical and verbal abuse from the police[100] and were resolved to organize themselves:

> We also organized a rally at Polkemmet on 14 February, St Valentine's Day, and it was to be a women's rally to stop the pit from being closed but miners also came along although the majority were women and their children. There was a huge police force at the pit and I remember one incident where a young woman with two children was trying to get through the police cordon and this policeman told her to 'Get back in the f______ kitchen.' I said to him, 'Let her through, she's only trying to get through,' and he repeated what he had said. So she had to walk all the way round the police cordon. There was, however, a tremendous feeling amongst the women and they tended not to let an incident like this get the better of them.[101]

Unfortunately for the mining communities and labour movement, the dispute ended in defeat for the strike and the wholesale rundown of the mining industry. It had been an exhilarating 12 months and a fundamental turning point in British industrial relations. There was some disappointment that the politicization of the women did not continue and many dropped out. The rejection of associate membership of the women's support groups to the British NUM was also disappointing. At British level the women were organized as women against pit closures and a national committee coordinated their work. Here there seems to have been a split between what the CP termed the 'ultra' and 'hard-left' elements and themselves in the organization.[102] Strong differences among members of the national committee became obvious after the strike. The CP was aware of the criticisms directed at it[103] and one party organizer, Pete Carter, commented on 'the general hostility between the NUM and the party resulting from our analysis of the strike'.[104] Despite these differences, the strike had been enormously liberating. Having travelled throughout Britain, sometimes addressing meetings, the women involved felt proud:

> I mean it was a great time. I was involved in the strike and particularly with the women, I'll never regret that, that I was involved with them. ... My son worked in the mining industry and he was on strike for the whole year and I remember the day he went back into Monktonhall after the strike ended. Everybody was in tears, the men that were going back to work, the women who were there, the victimized miners who couldn't go back to their work – it was a

> very emotional day. But I think they had to go back at that stage, it couldn't have gone on any longer.[105]

Dramatic changes in the socialist countries

If there were changes in Britain in the 1980s, there were even more fundamental changes in international relations between the superpowers. The Brezhnev leadership, effective from 1964, brought in a stricter social regime than the brief spell of liberalization under Khrushchev. Fractures in communist unity had become permanent from 1968 after events in Czechoslovakia and were reinforced in 1969 at an international meeting of CPs in Moscow, which was called to try and placate differences. By the late 1970s there was less of an allegiance from CPs in Europe and more open criticism of Soviet rule. Official party delegations from Britain were still well treated but disapproval of their criticisms was noticeable:

> I went with Gordon to the celebrations for the revolution, that would be in 1977, the big one, and Gordon spoke to the central committee of the Soviet Communist Party and nobody clapped; they all to a man and woman sat on their hands because he was saying things. They could read the 'in' words, they knew the 'in' words and they knew when to clap and when not to clap and the British party's position was such that they didn't approve of us.[106]

Soviet intervention in Afghanistan in 1979 caused another point of disagreement in the CPGB. The traditionalists at the 1981 congress argued that the action was in defence of an infant socialist country surrounded by hostile regimes – 'And it was this thing of the Soviet Union invades "again", "This is what the Soviet Union is like" and the other side was supposed to be saving the Afghani people from this poverty and it was a *total* travesty of the facts.'[107] However, there was cynicism about the *coup d'état* between rival forces in the Afghan government and a fear of similar practices by other socialist regimes. Alongside the almost universal condemnation of the Soviet action, there was increasing hostility from the British and US governments and a reawakening of cold war politics. Once more CND became an active campaigning body protesting against the new arms race and the situating of Cruise missiles in Britain. Women ran a peace camp at Greenham Common and the CP supported moves towards arms reduction. Despite much activity, socialist politics seemed to have less resonance domestically and internationally than in the 1960s.

Communists had admired the socialist countries for having rebuilt their economies after the war and for a time believed that they were advancing towards socialism. The Romanian CP, which had been dominated by a few individuals since the war, had taken a separate foreign policy line from the Soviet Union in more recent years. The Romanian party congress in November 1984 made few positive impressions on Pat Milligan, a member of the CP's national executive who met the Romanian prime minister Nicolai Ceausescu and his wife Elena:

> Oh dear, how can you say it? I mean apart from all the portraits it was quite bizarre, you were driven around in all these big limousines and there was posters at every available lamp post of the man himself with the dark hair, darker than mine was at the time and you meet the person and he doesn't look anything like that. It's a bit like Saddam Hussein really. What I do remember about his wife there was a particular reception, she was so warming and she spoke a bit of English and was admiring my dress and I said it was my mother's and she said something to me like 'Oh mother's', I'd sort of said something to her 'Oh this is my mother's' and she went 'Mmm' and I said 'Oh my mother is much more fashionable than me' and she laughed at that and all of the time she was holding my hand.[108]

Visiting Western delegates were less enthusiastic about the socialism they saw in Romania; official rallies with their regimentation and discipline were unnerving. However, visitors were given the opportunity to hear and speak about developments in their respective countries, such as the miners' strike in Britain, which was now into its ninth month:

> Just the whole conduct of the congress, but also a demonstration that I took part in, that when I looked round at the people it was nothing like people you saw in demonstrations in Britain and particularly in Scotland. … They were just chanting, they were just like robots they really were, it was a family business really. I should say at that congress probably the most worthwhile thing in a lot of ways for me was that it was during the British miners' strike and I spoke at a few meetings and said things that now I wonder where I

> got that optimism from. That the role of women in particular in the miners' strike in Britain meant they would never ever go back to the position they had before. I didn't realize of course that we wouldn't have a coal field for men and women to try and get their proper place in. But I remember I spoke at a good few meetings and in the course of that I met comrades from Australia, New Zealand, from America, from the Caribbean. I think that was probably the most worthwhile aspect of that congress that [I was] there representing the British party as a Scots woman.[109]

A report of the visit to Bucharest, drafted for the national executive of the British CP, was rejected and never presented. It was felt to be too critical, especially given that the Romanian ambassador in Britain would usually be sent a copy.[110] Living socialism was failing to inspire many party members. Not surprisingly, those in the CPGB defending or attacking the socialist countries were pointed in entirely different political directions.

A change in the CPSU leadership brought brief hope to most quarters. In March 1985 Mikhail Gorbachev became general secretary of the CPSU. Noticeably younger than Yuri Andropov and Konstantin Chernenko who preceded him, Gorbachev brought in a period of brief optimism for most communists. An air of change and the new terminology of *Glasnost* and *Perestroika* promised to open up Soviet society to greater scrutiny and new economic reforms. It was not immediately apparent where Gorbachev was leading the Soviet Union but his young appearance and the vigour of his new administration suggested several possibilities of reform:

> I think Gorbachev wasn't supported enough. I feel sorry for Gorbachev because I could understand what he was trying to do. I felt as if he was trying to bring democracy to the Soviet Union but still have a socialist, a *good strong socialist* government but do things in a gradual way but unfortunately it just did not happen that way and I think there was far too many influences fae' the West that put paid to that. I think the pressures also of the cold war had really got to the stage where, economically, they could not cope.[111]

Most of the women believed that Gorbachev was sincere and that opening up debate in the Soviet Union was a good thing, but some had reservations. Suspicions were fuelled by the less than cautious welcome from Margaret Thatcher that she 'could do business with Mr Gorbachev'.

Party women visiting the Soviet Union in the 1980s still liked what they saw, but, now used to being in a party that accepted the need for more equality between the sexes and the importance of gay rights, there was criticism of the Soviet women's committee on these matters:

> I thought it was awful. I really thought they were years and years behind any kind of democratic development that even we had reached in this country, and its far enough back here. That's one thing the Communist Party were very much ahead of than the average person in the street; we believed in women having the same rights as men; we believed that homosexuals shouldn't be discriminated against; and the same with coloured people. But there was nothing like that there, they hadn't developed their ideas at all to that level and I was really quite disappointed that after all these years of supposed socialism there was still this backward looking attitude to so many things. There was no fight for women's rights there at all, there was no women getting together to discuss how they could improve their lot.[112]

With growing internal problems, fewer practical attempts to solve them, and changes to the accords and strategic arms agreements of the 1970s, the Soviet Union faced the most hostile opposition in the West since the height of the cold war in the 1950s. Once again the escalation of the arms race was the key to the conflict. The new Conservative and Republican governments in Britain and the USA were the main protagonists of non-appeasement and made concerted efforts to counter so-called threatening communist influences in the world. They supported opposition forces against ruling socialist governments in Afghanistan and Nicaragua with arms and finance. Both governments would fall before the end of the decade. In many ways the Sandinistas represented the ideals of Czechoslovak and Chilean democratic socialism in that they had a left-wing programme with a popular base, the proof being their re-election in 1985.

The arms race put further pressure on the Soviet economy and from the mid-1980s socialism seemed noticeably unstable. Under Gorbachev there was open criticism of the past, especially the mistakes and injustices of the Stalin era as well as those of Brezhnev and Gromyko. A distinctly looser attitude was adopted towards other countries in the eastern bloc and this quickly saw the Hungarian government opening its borders to allow thousands of east Germans to cross. Events unthinkable to communists a few months before came to a climax in November 1989 when the most graphic symbol of the opposing political systems fell. Party members were unprepared for what they saw:

> Empty inside, really empty. We felt as if our whole life had been for nothing, absolutely nothing. We felt that when we saw that Berlin Wall coming down that capitalism had actually invaded the Soviet Union because it was like an invasion, an invasion, you know without the army but it was there you could tell. The writing was on the wall. I said 'If they don't consolidate soon, if they don't stop the rot' but the rot had already started and you could tell by that anyway because east Germany to us was even better than the Soviet Union because we felt as if the Soviet Union – although we didn't question it when we were young – we used to think that it was that wee bit *rigorous* there was a certain *de riguer* with the Soviet Union whereas with east Germany we felt as if it was more democratic, you know it was more accessible.[113]

The GDR had always boasted a better standard of living than most other socialist countries. Although much had been achieved in employment and social services it had the character of an economy still reliant on basic industries, some of which had done great harm to the environment in attempting to keep up production levels. Watching the report of the collapse of the Berlin Wall had shaken party members as it seemed those eager to embrace the West were expecting too much from capitalism:

> I felt very unhappy and very sad about the collapse. I felt that it would bring further misery to the people. I didn't think that what happened would improve their standard of living. I felt that their standard of living would go down although it wasn't as good as we'd been told it was but on the other hand I felt it was going to be a lot worse than what they had at the moment and I felt very unhappy. I felt distressed, very distressed about it.[114]

Older members were demoralized because for so long they had believed that some progress had been made and as communists they had naturally identified with the socialist countries:

> Oh shattered, shattered, absolutely shattered. People in the party for years who had given a lifetime, not me, my old friend that died last year, Monty Berkeley, been in the party all his life, was shattered. But then again, everything is in the process of change, and capitalism will never be the answer, so it's got to come back, and I mean it wasn't a communist country was it? It was socialism, we thought, working towards communism, but they were a long way from achieving it.[115]

In Romania the Ceausescus were overthrown and executed in a popular revolt against the Romanian Workers Party in December 1989. In 1991 a failed coup against Gorbachev fuelled the rise of nationalism and with it a new leader, former communist Boris Yeltsin. World socialism in its strongest sphere was now gone. At the last stage of Soviet socialism the historical arguments about the disinterest and non-involvement of the population in the Bolshevik revolution were now reversed:

> People's attitude was like they didn't care. I was actually there when the Soviet Union ended. It was really a *weird* experience. We arrived in the Soviet Union and left Russia the day before Gorbachev resigned. ... And that was quite a bizarre experience ... because there was this total lack of popular involvement either for or against what was happening. So there's in a sense counter-revolution taking place without a revolution, the peaceful gradual road back to capitalism, and people were relatively disinterested because they didn't feel they could make any difference.[116]

The end of the Communist Party of Great Britain

In 1989 the CP was adopting a new document, *Manifesto for the New Times*, and a new identity. This was a programme that broke with the politics of class confrontation. It had been drawn up by a commission appointed by the EC and had 13 members, one of whom, Mhairi Stewart, was on the Scottish executive of the CP as well as the British executive.

The age of postmodernist politics was arriving and reformers thought that transformation would prepare them as a distinct if not major force in this new era. After all the problems and traumas of the past, many were pleased to make a break and try a new approach:

> I never had any doubts that the new kind of principles that we were adopting were the right ones. The women in the party had always felt, well for a long, long time, that we were much too hard and fast, the way we acted, our method of work was way behind the times that we had to start developing new ways to work. The women in the party at that time were in the forefront of this pressure to have a more open way of working and less of this heavy discipline.[117]

Post-Fordism was the new catch-phrase and capitalism was said to be past its classical production-line, blue-collar worker stage.[118] At the 41st congress in 1989, the CPGB's penultimate congress, senior party members who had supported many of the recent changes wholeheartedly, or out of loyalty, were now confronted with changes they could not identify with and a denouncing of the past they could not accept: 'Joe Marshall actually got up on the platform and at one point *rubbished* Harry Pollitt, Willie Gallacher, Peter Kerrigan and Gordon McLennan. Now Gordon McLennan was sitting there as a visitor and how he could sit and not do anything about that, I'll never understand.'[119]

Nina Temple replaced Gordon McLennan as party leader. She was the first woman general secretary of the party and still only in her thirties. The opponents of those arguing for transformation accused them of supporting the wholesale dissolution of the party. With the adoption of *A Manifesto for the New Times* there was no doubt that the party was no longer committed to the same type of socialism as its founders:

> I was sick. I really felt *sick* listening to it because people like Harry Pollitt and Willie Gallacher had been my heroes. I know the kind of life they'd had to lead and Johnny Gollan, Johnny Gollan was another one who gave his health for the party because long hours of working and not eating properly because he had these jobs to do for the party, they ruined their lives. I really felt that these young people who had never known or had come up through university never really knowing what it was to work far less anything else to criticize these people was just out of order but I was a visitor so I couldn't do anything about it.[120]

The enthusiasm for this new concept in politics brought out a new opposition in the party in Scotland. Those opposed to the changes and the change of name to Democratic Left organized to try and reverse the whole process that was winding up the party. Having lost their influence in the *Morning Star* dispute it was not surprising that the party leaders made a concerted effort to win through with this new strategy. Inevitably, their tactics brought criticism and hostility. Douglas Chalmers had been Scottish secretary since 1985 and received both fulsome support and open resentment from party members, but he was unprepared for this new opposition.[121] He had fully supported the changes and had overseen the expulsion and exclusion of members, but he could not be blamed for the splits and decline of the party in Scotland.

That process had started before his leadership. Now there was even opposition from previously sympathetic members. Support for the changes came from Jack Ashton, until recently the Scottish secretary, and John Kay, a long serving Scottish organizer. They now came head to head with opponents of the same generation, if not a little older and more experienced, like Bob Horne and Bill Lauchlan. There were also those allied to *Straight Left*, a faction in the party that had organized clandestinely its own education schools and meetings for a couple of decades. They appear to have had some support in Scotland and were possibly stronger in the branches than the party leadership estimated. They were, paradoxically, very much more part of the party's makeup and character than they or their opponents would ever care to admit, though they were firmly entrenched against the reforms adopted in the 1970s and 1980s.

The Scottish delegation that went down to the CPGB's last congress was split as never before, and this reflected the state of the party in Scotland. This was a party district whose delegates at congresses customarily supported the party executive, usually unanimously, and were placed where all delegates could see them. There was one last emotional attempt to keep the name 'Communist Party', for it was a party many people in Scotland had known, that families had been associated with and for whose cause people had given their lives. The debate on whether to change the name of the party was one of the last debates at the last CP congress and a Scottish woman delegate moved the resolution to retain the name:

> We had a very short time in which to speak, a matter of three or five minutes, something like that. So I wanted to make a case because the party had been rubbished, the whole communist tradition had been rubbished in the lead up to the congress and through it, as though it had been akin to fascism and something as evil as that. I *knew* that was nonsense and it also angered me because some of the people purveying it had come from party families like myself and had inherited all the very positive traditions of communism. So unwittingly I'd included those elements in the speech and while I was making it a whole lot of images of what the positives of communism and the communist tradition in Britain began to flash through my head and you could *feel* the tension actually rising in the hall as people anticipated what I was going to say next and defended the traditions of working-class struggle, of communists having a tradition of self education, of great culture. The ludicrous caricature that had been painted of the Communist Party, nobody would have joined it if it had been as people said it had been.[122]

For all the effort and emotion of some party members the vote was to change to Democratic Left. The CPGB was no more. The party had been extinguished by what was seen as a need to discard any association with what had occurred in the now defunct Soviet Union and the revolutionary socialism of Red Clydeside. Not all the women interviewed had bothered to stay and see this formal change, though most had. Some had gone over to the Communist Party of Britain (CPB). Some had left because they were weary with the in-fighting or disillusioned because they thought that the party would never change; others had left because it had changed too much. In Scotland the strong characteristic of unity of purpose among party members had long since gone. There were advocates of the changes who were still aware of the positive aspects of the CP that they had been associated with and of which they would always be proud:

> Well of course I think that there was certain characteristics about the Scottish party, well it seems to me as a Scotswoman that it was special and I think the Scottish party was a kind of, can I say rounded? Until we had all the problems and all the differences we

all seemed to be going the same way and being active in the same projects and campaigns and it was good to feel that. You felt as if the party was important and that you were important: it was important to you that you were in it.[123]

Chapter 8

Integral to the Cause: A Woman's Place in the Communist Party in Scotland

> I don't think there was *any* comparison, I really don't. Whatever you did with that background or that knowledge or whatever it was, it provided you with something that you got from no other organization I think, CND or the Labour Party or anything. I'm very grateful that I was educated in that way or helped to educate myself in that way. They really were shit hot on things like self-education, I think that's great because I'm all for that.[1]

> I mean you could dwell on it forever and say 'If only this or if only that' but none of that will work so it's a bit pointless I think. I do find that in terms of relationships funnily enough, during the debates and the difficult times some really strong friendships and comradeship's crumbled and that was *dreadful*, that was painful, that was physically and emotionally quite a painful thing. But as time has gone on [*laughs*] one can meet these old comrades and friends now and look at each other and say '*What on earth* was that all about?' which is good, the healing.[2]

In this study I set out to show the areas in which women were involved in the CP in Scotland and their views on various political and social issues. What I have attempted to reveal and what became increasingly obvious during the interviews was that women were at the heart of CP activity. They were central to its campaigns, an essential element of its operating ability and were also its invisible backbone. Although women were a smaller part of the membership in Scotland and assumed the less prestigious roles by not, on the whole, being leaders, they were involved in all the important struggles. They were on the Scottish committee and on area and branch committees. They were involved with party advisory committees, local campaigns, peace groups, cooperative guilds and numerous other groups. But central to their activity was usually the party branch and all the activity that one associates with that level of party work. Certainly, the bazaars were important but it was not as if women who did these menial tasks were unaware of the political issues, less capable in party education, or less able in their contribution:

> I think the party was terrific in as much as it helped you develop a way of looking at things, it sharpened your wits in a way, it enabled you to look at the hidden agenda about what people were saying and about what's actually going on. That sounds like real paranoid stuff, I don't mean that at all but when you hear a politician standing up and saying something you think 'Ah ha, he really means something else', that kind of thing.[3]

Women were limited by specific restrictions as it is obvious that their intellectual and practical ability was highly developed if not underrated. The non-recognition of their role is all the more regrettable when one considers how politically developed and aware they were. The perceptiveness and maturity of women in the party does not seem to have gained its due respect. If these limitations reflected a typical aspect of capitalism then criticism could be made that more should have been done to redress them in the party instead of accepting the straitjacket of social conventions imposed by such an exploitative system. No one can discount the existing culture of the time and the impoverishment that both sexes suffered, yet it is evident that there was little room to manoeuvre for women, especially as often they were expected to carry on their traditional domestic role. Such attitudes seemed to permeate the entire Scottish labour movement. Though the CP consistently called for equal pay for equal work, the arrival of feminist politics made this demand seem limited and meagre when so much more was needed to begin to address gender inequality. Hence, the liberating effect of these politics for some party women.

Women involved up until the 1960s might be seen as stuck in a corner performing the most unenviable tasks for the party. The post-1960s generation tends to see previous generations as too submissive and ready to accept a secondary role. With the oral evidence this no longer seems the case. The vibrancy and rebelliousness of the YCL was always one of its characteristics and this emerged during the interviews. How else could a group of young people survive the despair of the 1930s, the intimidating experiences of the cold war and episodes like the 1951 journey to the World Youth Festival in Berlin? In Scotland, despite its small size, the YCL always had a high profile, was extremely active and so fulfilled the expectations of many women looking for regular and intense political activity. Only now do we see some of the cohesiveness and resilience of the YCL in Scotland and just how important a body it was in convincing women to become fully involved in the party.

The SWAC was a body that raised the profile of women and tried to encourage campaigning on many issues. Of all the advisory committees it was the most important, for women were still in the background in the party's leadership and it was attempting to bring more women to the fore. Also the SWAC mainly involved those who wanted to concentrate on issues specifically related to women. It would be well to remember those women who felt they were equal to other party members and purposefully avoided women's groups and the SWAC. They operated in the party believing that they were treated as such by fellow members.

Despite cultural changes and growing opportunities for women, the 1960s generation of women seemed as committed as their predecessors to party work. The YCL was very active in parts of Scotland and the SWAC organized campaigns on women's health and regular education classes. Many of the women had been converted to communism from a young age through family influences, the Socialist Sunday School, the Woodcraft Folk and the cooperative movement, so their conversion was political and social rather than confined to the shop floor where strong CP organization often failed to transcend economism.

From the 1960s it seemed as if concessions could be won from capitalism and this encouraged a small group of young communists. Young men and women, sometimes working as full-time officers, engaged in selfless and time-consuming work in the cause of peace, Vietnam and against youth unemployment. Often the link with older CP members, frequently family, was seen as too important and relevant to be broken. Many women had been destined to join the party without an ounce of regret. Women could not be forced or even 'expected' blindly to join but they *wanted* to join. The communist politics they heard, the explanations they received and the relevance of these ideas all seemed to make sense from when they were young. Until the late 1970s it seemed as if socialism was not only possible but probable in the decades ahead.

One reason for such optimism was the Soviet Union, which most CP women saw as living socialism. It is harder now, with the globalization of capitalism, to understand how pivotal the socialist countries were seen to be in determining a positive outcome in the class struggle. After 1945 there was reason to believe that the forces of change were on the side of the left, despite the apathy of much of the working class in Britain. Right-wing politics had been discredited, independence movements were moving towards their goal and there were more socialist countries in the world. Even during the cold war there was a revolution in China and the Non-Aligned Movement was formed to encourage poorer nations. Thus, many women felt that the immediate postwar period was a time when socialism was becoming stronger and more influential worldwide and that, as communists, they were part of this movement. Despite admiring the Soviet Union and still believing it was going in the right direction, many women raised unexpectedly pertinent and revealing criticisms of certain aspects of Soviet society. They saw its economic deficiencies and the shortcomings of its leaders, yet strongly defended the socialist countries in the international context against often identifiable Western aggression.

One should not underestimate the amount of soul searching that went on, or disquiet felt about aspects of Soviet rule, although admittedly many testimonies on this were only forthcoming after the collapse of the socialist countries. While some women were finding the Soviet Union increasingly unattractive and there was limited support for it in the labour movement in Scotland, they appreciated its peace initiatives and the support it gave to newly independent countries and to national liberation movements. We should remember that people living in countries in debt to the West, or under ultra right-wing regimes, often saw the Soviet Union in a very different light from their counterparts in the West:

> I went with Marka [Burns] in 1982, her and I went, and I saw a lot of things to impress me. We went to this hotel in Moscow and it hadn't occurred to me before that the Eastern countries like Vietnam, China and the Africans, the hotel was full of people like that, students, well that sort of age group, all there for various different things and it occurred to me that that was where the Soviet Union had such a big influence of power because of course they were

> helping out, they were in a position to, well, whether they were in a position or not they were doing it. They were helping the small African emerging countries and there was these Africans there and Vietnamese and Indians, you got the feeling that the Soviet Union was bigger in every sense than the USA, in a good sense.[4]

Soviet problems may have seemed minor to workers who had few or no economic, social or political rights in the world. Thus, aspects of Soviet society that may have seemed to restrict freedoms enjoyed in advanced capitalist countries were not necessarily freedoms that workers elsewhere had experienced. The under-developed and exploited Third World felt less hostility to the socialism of the Eastern Bloc and a strong identification with that of Cuba and Vietnam.

In the 1970s women became fully established in the party in Scotland. They were working in the labour market in greater numbers than before and were also becoming better organized. In Britain there were noticeable trade union victories, especially between 1969 and 1976, though increasing weaknesses from 1977 onwards. Dramatic changes after the 1979 Conservative victory affected unions, the strength and influence of the labour movement and consequently the CP's base. Two major changes permanently altered the party. First, there was industrial decline and a loss of party members, many of them men who had been in industry. Second, an ideological divide split the previously unified party. The party might have survived one; it could not survive both. The women were split over what direction the party should take and they reflected the deep divisions in the party from the late 1970s. Originally, it seemed that the new politics of feminism could be blamed for diverting the party, but in truth these politics gave it a new impetus for a brief period and were a response to the neglect of women's oppression and increasing disillusionment. This was not lost even to some opponents of those politics:

> Internationally, you can see that's where the seed of Eurocommunism lies and a reaction to Stalinism and I think most of the leading theoretical lights within British Eurocommunism emerged out of student politics of the 1960s and the time particularly for events in Czechoslovakia had a big influence on that generation within the party. So I don't think they were sort of 'plants' or people who were against the party, a lot of them had grown up in

> the party, came from party backgrounds, had a record of work but I think that their views were wrong; they were reformist, but I can understand how those views developed.[5]

Feminists won reforms that the CP would not have adopted but for the influences of the WLM, which had kept some women in the party:

> And I don't think pursuing that line brought about the demise of the party and you've got to think, things that we take for granted now, not take for granted but we don't think a lot of, they've come about because of the feminist debates and struggles. It is quite interesting; I think people forget twenty years ago how things were for women.[6]

However, there was a problem. The new ideas of the 1970s and 1980s did not attract enough people to the CP. What had given the CP its strength was a strong core of working-class activists committed to the class struggle. By identifying with feminist politics the party was merely redressing an imbalance towards a much neglected area. However, by the 1980s it seemed that one was either 'for' feminism and the broad democratic alliance or one was 'for' a more centralized or even Leninist type party. The two sides, among others in this troubled equation, seemed incompatible in the one party.

Eurocommunism had much in common with 1980s' Labour Party social democracy, which moved to the right after the formation of the SDP and defeat of 'Bennism'.[7] The traditionalists had more in common with the Labour Party left wing, but there was not much joint work until the split in Scotland over the *Morning Star*. Therefore, the role the CP played in the depression of the 1980s was quite different from that of the 1930s when many women who joined in Scotland saw it as a left-wing body that was against the national government and that fought for fundamental change in Britain or abroad. The party's intense activity over the decades attracted many women, who knew they were joining the most active political party on the left. There was a definite commitment when one joined the CP:

> It was the party that really went out campaigning, let's face it, the Labour Party is not a campaigning party and we were the party that got people out in the streets of Glasgow with leaflets, we were the

> party that could be relied on to get the area covered with leaflets etc., and getting them to London; organizing trains etc. I must give credit to the leadership in Scotland, John Kay, Jack Ashton and these people, they really did a tremendous job and now that there is no Communist Party of Great Britain in Scotland, it shows.[8]

It was this distinctive role that the women respondents most admired. The CP led the fight against closures,[9] legislation restricting union practices, and wage restraint, and so highlighted the inadequacies of Labour government policy and the right-wing views of its leaders. Had the CP *not* existed one might wonder how many reforms attributed to action by the labour movement would have been achieved. It was this that encouraged so many women to remain in the party; it always did more than any other body on the left in Scotland, even if it seems they were aware that there was little progress towards it becoming a mass party.

In its last decade members were unprepared for the devastating events of 1989–91, which wiped out decades of socialist advance and left communists in a different world environment in the subsequent years. 'They've not been easy, they've been very depressing and also we certainly underestimated the power of imperialism, capitalism and monopoly capitalism to hang on and find new ways of screwing people's lives, we did, we made a very faulty analysis there.'[10] It would be unusual were one not to find people disillusioned and unsure about the future. The period since 1979 and 18 years of Conservative rule changed many women's perspectives, some fundamentally:

> Because I now believe that the Marxist view, that it is the class struggle that moves society forward, I reject totally and utterly, absolutely. That is not the engine of change in society, the resolution of that contradiction is not the primary contradiction that has to be resolved and I now am not a Marxist at all.[11]

Most graphically, the women who were in the Socialist Sunday School and Woodcraft Folk were part of a socialist culture in which there was genuine equality from an early age, more equality than would be found in the family, trade unions or even the CP. They had become militant socialists in their childhood and, aware of the mass poverty and injustices they faced, they believed in a vision of a better world. As Margaret Hunter commented: 'When we sang "we are the young Red

Guardsmen of the proletariat" we really meant it because we experienced the brutal attacks of the capitalists in our lives and felt the need to strike back.'[12] In all decades there were young women who could not accept the inequalities of capitalism and sought an organization that was doing something to challenge the monstrous contradictions that confronted them. These young women were not to become transient left-wing socialists. They were not involved only when there was cause for optimism. They had been active from their childhood, proudly atheistic, a tiny minority who went to a 'different' Sunday school, then on to the YCL and the CP.

Given the opportunity, all the women interviewed were active communists and most were highly politicized. They were virtually born into socialism, as is shown by their continued activity or allegiances, and they want to die as such. They were always an essential and integral part of the CP in Scotland. Today many are still fighting for fundamental change. Still believing in their socialist politics they are also aware of the receding chances of seeing in their lifetime the society that appeared to be nearer, not so long ago:

> I do have in my mind that we used to have real ding dongs with comrades who were friends as well as comrades and then after the meeting that was it, we were friends again we were dealing with. We came to a decision about what would be happening and how we would go about the campaign or whatever we were discussing and that was it, real comradeship there was.[13]

Appendix A: Interview Dates and Interview Lengths

Interview

	Name	Date(s)	Word Count
1	May Annan	22 April 1994	23,065
2	Jack Ashton	18 December 1996	10,048
3	Ouaine Bain	26 June 1994/17 August 1994	28,490
4	Cathy Brown	29 May 1994	15,888
5	Janey Buchan	4 October 1994/21 January 1997	18,079
6	Katy Campbell	28 March 1994/11 February 1997	17,819
7	Douglas Chalmers	5 December 1996	18,619
8	Kathryn Chalmers	22 March 1994	18,489
9	Jessie Clark	4 April 1994	14,947
10	Mary Cowan	16 March 1994	13,901
11	Mary Docherty	14 May 1994/14 March 1995	22,067
12	Marion Easedale	23 March 1994/17 November 1996	17,169
13	Ella Egan	17 October 1996/7 November 1996	23,390
14	Edith Findlay	10 September 1995	13,653
15	John Foster	23 November 1994	14,017
16	Katherine Gallin	13 April 1994	9,956
17	Susan Galloway	11 October 1995/1 November 1995	24,094
18	Marion Henery	6 April 1994/17 November 1995	17,515
19	Bob Horne	8 September 1994 to 4 May 1995	75,494
20	Jimmy Hunter	18 July 1995	8,355
21	Rose Kerrigan	9 July 1995	6,379
22	Jean McCrindle	28 June 1995	12,956
23	Jean Mackay	25 February 1994	10,278
24	Gordon Maclennan	29 June 1995	10,833
25	Pat Milligan	15 March 1994/11 May 1994	23,639
26	Alice Milne	10 July 1994	18,835
27	Effie O'Hare	23 March 1994/20 March 1996	21,264
28	Frieda Park	7 November 1994	30,001
29	Mary Park	13 December 1994/14 Nov. 1996	26,970

30	Isa Porte	16 February 1994/12 Dec. 1996	11,170
31	Jenny Richardson	31 March 1994	13,815
32	Marion Robertson	19 April 1994/20 October 1995	28,219
33	Maureen Sanders	25 March 1994	11,048
34	Anna Sardesai	27 August 1994	21,966
35	Mabs Skinner	15 April 1994	19,155
36	Isobel Service	26 November 1998/28 January 1999	20,407
37	Jim Service	19 November 1998/3 February 1999	18,208
38	Christine Sloan	24 March 1994/26 April 1994	21,699
39	Irene Swan	23 September 1995/28 October 1995	41,202
40	Noreen Thompson	28 June 1994	9,464
41	Willie Thompson	13 June 1994	22,341
42	Barbara Thorpe	31 August 1995/14 September 1995	20,913

Total number of words = 825,817

Appendix B: Age Gradient

	Name	*Year of Birth*	*Joined YCL/CP*	*Left*
1.	Rose Kerrigan	1903	Foundation 1921	1991
2.	Effie O'Hare	1903	1936	1991
3.	Mary Docherty	1908	1926	1991
4.	Marion Henery	1910	1929	1991
5.	Isa Porte	1911	1930	1991
6.	Mabs Skinner	1912	1941	1986
7.	Marion Robertson	1913	1933/4	1991
8.	Mary Cowan	1914	1941–6 (rejoined 1965)	1991
9.	May Annan	1916	1938	1991
10.	Alice Milne	1922	1938	1991
11.	Katherine Gallin	1923	1943	1991
12.	Marion Easedale	1923	1944	1991
13.	Janey Buchan	1926	1942	1956
14.	Jenny Richardson	1926	1942	1991
15.	Jessie Clark	1927	1946	1987
16.	Mary Park	1930	1950	1987
17.	Jean Mackay	1930	1959/60	198?
18.	Irene Swan	1932	1955	1991
19.	Ella Egan	1933	1956	1991
20.	Jean McCrindle	1937	1955	1957
21.	Anna Sardesai	1940	1963	1991
22.	Noreen Thompson	1940	1962	1991
23.	Ouaine Bain	1940	1963	1989/90
24.	Barbara Thorpe	1940	1961	1985/86
25.	Maureen Sanders	1942	1968	1989
26.	Kathryn Chalmers	1942	1960/1	1988
27.	Katy Campbell	1942	1963	1987
28.	Pat Milligan	1942	1961	1991
29.	Christine Sloan	1947	1966	1985
30.	Frieda Park	1956	1974	1991
31.	Susan Galloway	1965	1982	1988
32.	Cathy Brown		1958	1987
33.	Isobel Service	1928	1944	1991

Eight of the women joined the YCL/CP before 1939. Eight joined from 1940–50, Five from 1951–60, nine from 1961–70 and two from 1971, – Mary Cowan's membership lapsed.

Appendix C: Communist Party of Great Britain in Scotland

Secretariat/Executive Committee (9–10)

Scottish Committee (40–45)

Elected at the Scottish Congress

Advisory Committees

Scottish Women's Advisory Committee

Economic | Local Government | Industrial | Cultural

AREA COMMITTEES

BRANCHES

Local Area Branches | Workplace (and Student) Branches

Both Equal Constitutionally

Areas Existing from the 1960s

Glasgow, Lanarkshire, Renfrewshire, Ayrshire, Dunbartonshire
West Lothian

South of Scotland, Edinburgh, Fife, Dundee,
Aberdeen and Highlands

Appendix D: Women on the Scottish Committee of the Communist Party, 1943–91

1943

Isa Alexander, Agnes Maxwell, Mrs Park (3 of 30 = 10%)

1944–46

Isa Alexander, Agnes Maxwell, Mrs Park (3 of 30 = 10%)

1946–47

Jenny Dand, Rhoda Fraser, Emily Swankie (3 of 30 = 10%)

1947–48

Rhoda Fraser, Marion Robertson, Emily Swankie (3 of 30 =10%)

1948–49

Rhoda Fraser, Marion Robertson, Emily Swankie (3 of 32 = 10%)

1949–50

Marion Robertson (1 of 31 = 3%)

1950–53

Rhoda Fraser, Anne Moffat, Agnes McLean, Jessie Taylor (4 of 36 = 17%)

1953–55

Rhoda Fraser, Anne McGowan, Agnes McLean, Marion Robertson, Jean Boath (5 of 39 = 13%)

1955–58

May Halfpenny, Marion Henery, Margaret Hunter, Agnes McLean (4 of 42 = 10%)

1958–60

Minnie Aitkin, May Halfpenny, Marion Henery, Margaret Hunter, Agnes McLean, Margaret Rose. (6 of 45 = 14%)

1960–62

Minnie Aitkin, May Halfpenny (?), Marion Henery, Margaret Hunter, Agnes McLean, Margaret Rose (6 of 45 = 16%)

1962–64

Minnie Aitkin, Hannah Fletcher, Marion Henery, Margaret Hunter*, Agnes McLean, Margaret Rose, Irene Swan (7 of 45 = 16%)

*Margaret Hunter resigned from the Scottish Committee and became National Women's Officer during this period.

1964–66

Honor Arundel, Cathy Brown, Marion Henery, Jane McKay, Agnes McLean, Margaret Rose, Irene Swan (7 of 45 =16%)

1966–68

Honor Arundel, Cathy Brown, Marion Henery, Agnes McLean, Margaret Rose, Mabs Skinner, Irene Swan (7 of 45 =16%)

1968–70

Mamie McConnell, Pat Milligan, Margaret Paris, Margaret Rose, Mabs Skinner, Irene Swan (6 of 43 = 14%)

1970–72

Pat Milligan, Margaret Paris, Mabs Skinner, Irene Swan, Helen Turner (5 of 45 = 11%)

1972–74

Pat Milligan, Irene Swan, Margaret Paris, Mabs Skinner (4of 45 =10%)

1974–76

Irene Swan, Marion Easedale, Mabs Skinner, Cathy Dobbie, June Tait (5 of 45 = 12%)

1976–78

Cathy Dobbie, Mary Harrison, Jane McKay, June Tait, Marion Easedale, Irene Swan, (6 of 45 = 13%)

1978–80

Ouaine Bain, Mary Harrison, Jane McKay, June Tait, Elinor Dick, Carol Downes, Pat Milligan, Mary McIntosh, Maureen Sanders (9 of 45 = 20%)

1980–82

Ouaine Bain, Carol Downes, Mary Harrison, Mary McIntosh, Pat Milligan, Maureen Sanders, (6 of 45 = 13%)

1982–84

Ouaine Bain*, Irene Brown, Irene Caleary, Katy Campbell*, Marion Easedale, Mary Harrison, Alice-Ann Jackson, Frances Lockhart, Pat Milligan, Morag Parnell, Anna Sardesai, Monica Tumelty. (12 of 45 = 26%)

*Ouaine Bain and Katy Campbell resigned from the Scottish Committee during this period.

1984–86

Irene Brown, Irene Caleary, Cath Cunningham, Marion Easedale, Ella Egan, Mary Harrison, Alice-Ann Jackson, Frances Lockhart, Grace McFall, Pat Milligan, Morag Parnell, Anna Sardesai, Yvonne Strachan, Monica Tumelty. (14 of 45 = 31%)

1986–88

Elspeth Cameron, Jackie Carruthers, Cath Cunningham, Marion Easedale, Ella Egan, Jackie Gulstead, Lorraine Hamilton, Mary Harrison, Alice-Ann Jackson, Gillian Keale, Frances Lockhart, Grace McFall, Pat Milligan, Jean Muir, Jo Nisbett, Moira Scobie. (16 of 45 = 36%)

1989–91

Irene Brown, Barbara Catt, Marion Easedale, Irene Elliot, Jackie Gulstead, Mary Harrison, Gillian Keele, Sylvia Latham, Jean Muir, Grace McFall, Jo Nisbett, Moira Scobbie, Yvonne Smith, Mhairi Stewart. (14 of 45 = 31%)

1991

Irene Brown, Barbara Catt, Edith Constable, Janice Cornwall, Mary Hamilton, Sylvia Latham, Jean Muir, Frieda Park, Helen Sanders, Mhairi Stewart, Isobel Tait, Louise Tierney, (12 of 45 = 27%)

Appendix E: World Youth Festivals

1st	1947	Prague, Czechoslovakia
2nd	1949	Budapest, Hungary
3rd	1951	East Berlin, German Democratic Republic
4th	1953	Bucharest, Romania
5th	1955	Warsaw, Poland
6th	1957	Moscow, Soviet Union
7th	1959	Vienna, Austria
8th	1962	Helsinki, Finland
9th	1968	Sofia, Bulgaria
10th	1973	East Berlin, German Democratic Republic
11th	1978	Havana, Cuba
12th	1985	Moscow, Soviet Union
13th	1989	Pyongyang, North Korea

Appendix F: Those who Visited the Socialist Countries

May Annan*
Ouaine Bain*
Cathy Brown*
Janey Buchan
Katy Campbell*
Jessie Clark*
Mary Cowan*
Mary Docherty*
Marion Easedale*
Ella Egan*
Susan Galloway
Frieda Park*
Mary Park*
Jenny Richardson*
Marion Robertson*
Irene Swan*
Marion Henery*
Rose Kerrigan*
Jean Mackay*
Pat Milligan*
Alice Milne*
Katherine Gallin*

*Indicates those who visited the Soviet Union.

Notes

Chapter 1

1. S. Reynolds, *Britannica's Typesetters: Women Compositors in Edinburgh* (Edinburgh 1989) p. 142.
2. On the literature of European CPs, see P. Anderson 'Communist Party history', in R. Samuel (ed.) *People's History and Socialist Theory* (London, 1981). p. 145.
3. J. Hinton, 'Coventry communism: a study of factory politics in the second World War', in *History Workshop Journal*, issue 10 (Autumn 1990) p. 92.
4. C. Farman, *The General Strike* (London, 1974) p. 54.
5. H. Dewar, *Communist Politics in Britain: The CPGB From its Origins to the Second World War* (London, 1976) p. 137.
6. H. Pelling, *The British Communist Party: A Historical Profile* (London, 1958)
7. K. Morgan, *Against Fascism and War: Ruptures and Continuities in British Communist Politics 1935–41* (Manchester, 1989) p. 8.
8. E. Burns, *An Introduction to Marxism* (London, 1937); M. Cornforth, *Dialectical Materialism: An Introduction*, vol. 1, *Materialism and the Dialectical Method*, vol. 2, *Historical Materialism*, vol. 3, *Theory of Knowledge* (London, 1952) new edition 1977.
9. A. Hutt, *The Post War History of the British Working Class* (London, 1937); T. A. Jackson, *Ireland Her Own* (London, 1946); A. L. Morton, *A People's History of England* (London, 1938).
10. J. Klugmann, *History of the Communist Party of Great Britain*, vol.1, *Formation and Early Years 1919–1924* (London, 1968)
11. N. Branson, *History of the Communist Party of Great Britain 1927–1941* (London, 1985).
12. N. Branson, *History of the Communist Party of Great Britain 1941–1951* (London, 1997).
13. See B. Darke, *The Communist Technique in Britain* (London, 1952); and D. Hyde, *I Believed: The Autobiography of a Former British Communist* (London, 1952).
14. K. Newton, *The Sociology of British Communism* (London, 1969).
15. Ibid., p. 9.
16. Ibid., p. 48.
17. Ibid., p. 6.
18. Ibid., p. 43.
19. Ibid., p. 9.
20. Ibid., pp. 100, 110.

21. Ibid., p. 107.
22. Ibid.; Dewar, *Communist Politics in Britain*, p. 15.
23. H. Pollitt, *Serving My Time: An Apprenticeship to Politics* (London, 1940).
24. W. Gallacher, *Revolt on the Clyde* (London, 1936).
25. W. Hannington *Unemployed Struggles 1919–1936* (London, 1937).
26. R. Stewart, *Breaking the Fetters* (London, 1967).
27. P. Piratin, *Our Flag Stays Red* (London, 1948, new edn 1978).
28. R. Croucher, *We Refuse to Starve in Silence (1920–46): A History of the National Unemployed Workers Movement* (London, 1987).
29. Ibid., p. 103.
30. Ibid., p. 149.
31. Ibid., p. 206.
32. Ibid., pp. 139–40.
33. H. Corr, 'Helen Crawfurd (1877–1954)', in W. Knox (ed.) *Scottish Labour Leaders 1918–1939* (Edinburgh, 1984) pp. 81–6.
34. Ibid.
35. M. Docherty, *A Miner's Lass* (Preston, 1992).
36. H. McShane with J. Smith, *No Mean Fighter* (London, 1978).
37. H. Crawfurd Anderson, 'Memoirs' n.d. Manuscript in Marx Memorial Library, copy in William Gallacher Memorial Library (henceforth WGML) Glasgow.
38. Ibid., p. 342.
39. M. Woodhouse and B. Pearce, *Essays in the History of Communism in Britain* (London, 1975).
40. S. Bornstein and A. Richardson, *Two Steps Back: Communists and the Wider Labour Movement 1935–1945: A Study in Relations Between Vanguard and Class* (London, 1982).
41. Morgan, *Against Fascism and War*, p. 6.
42. W. Thompson, *The Good Old Cause: British Communism 1920–1991* (London, 1992).
43. Ibid., pp. 171–217.
44. S. Bruley, *Leninism, Stalinism and the Women's Movement in Britain 1920–1939* (New York, 1986).
45. Ibid., p. 124.
46. Ibid., p. 262.
47. Ibid., p. 299.
48. C. M Gabbidon, 'Party Life: An Examination of the Branch Life of the CPGB Between the Wars', D.Phil. thesis, Sussex University, 1991.
49. Ibid., p. 7.
50. Ibid., Chapter 1, pp. 22, 25, also note 54, show the importance of the Socialist Sunday school to the party in Glasgow.
51. Ibid. p. 40.
52. Ibid. p. 80.
53. Morgan, *Against Fascism and War*, p. 9.
54. S. Nujam, 'A Radical Past: The Legacy of the Fife Miners', Ph.D. thesis, Edinburgh University, 1988.

55. Ibid., p. 5.
56. Ibid., p. 7.
57. Ibid., p. 59.
58. Ibid., p. 203.
59. S. Macintyre, *Little Moscows: Communism and Working Class Militancy in Inter-War Britain* (London, 1980).
60. Ibid., p. 35.
61. Ibid., pp. 55–6, 68, 74.
62. R. Price, *Labour in British Society* (London, 1986).
63. M. Savage, *The Dynamics of Working Class Politics: The Labour Movement in Preston, 1880–1940* (Cambridge, 1987).
64. Price, *Labour in British Society*, p. 3.
65. Ibid., p. 216.
66. Under Labour governments there were the Donovan Commission Report 1968 and Bullock Report 1977.
67. Price, *Labour in British Society*, p. 225.
68. Ibid. p. 240.
69. Savage, *The Dynamics of Working Class Politics*, p. 179.
70. Ibid., p. 193.
71. M. Savage, 'Urban Politics and the Rise of the Labour Party, 1919–39', in L. Jamieson and H. Corr (eds) *State, Private Life and Political Change* (Basingstoke, 1990) p. 209.
72. W. Knox, 'The Political and Workplace Culture of the Scottish Working-Class', in H. Corr and L. Jamieson (eds) *Politics of Everyday Life: Continuity and Change in Work and the Family*, (Basingstoke, 1990) pp. 162–85.
73. Ibid., p. 171.
74. Ibid., p. 180.
75. V. I Lenin, *What Is To Be Done?* (Moscow, 1902, reprint 1947).
76. A. Exell, 'Morris Motors in the 1930s', Part 1, *History Workshop Journal*, issue 6, Autumn 1978, pp. 52–78, Part 2, *History Workshop Journal*, issue 7, pp. 45–65, Part 3, 'Morris Motors in the 1940s', *History Workshop Journal*, issue 9, pp. 90–114.
77. Macintyre, *Little Moscows*, p. 148.
78. Ibid., p. 170.
79. Ibid., p. 145.
80. S. Macintyre, *A Proletarian Science: Marxism in Britain 1917–1933* (Cambridge, 1980) p. 23.
81. Ibid., p. 86.
82. R. McKibbin, *The Ideologies of Class and Social Relations in Britain 1880–1950* (Oxford, 1990) p. 7.
83. Ibid., p. 38.
84. Ibid., pp. 6, 7, 11, 26, 32, 38, 41.
85. P. Graves, *Labour Women: Women in British Working Class Politics 1918–1939* (Cambridge, 1994).
86. Ibid., p. 86.
87. Ibid., pp. 156–7.

88. Ibid., p. 63.
89. Ibid., p. 208.
90. Ibid., p. 204.
91. Ibid., p. 42.
92. Ibid.
93. Pelling, *The British Communist Party*, pp. 174–80.
94. Thompson, *The Good Old Cause*, pp. 187–96.
95. Morgan, *Against Fascism and War*.
96. J. Attfield and S. Williams (eds) *1939: The Communist Party of Great Britain and the War* (London, 1984).
97. F. King and G. Matthews (eds) *About Turn: The British Communist Party and the Second World War*. The Verbatim Record of the Central Committee Meetings of 25 September and 2–3 October 1939 (London, 1990).
98. A. Phillips, *Divided Loyalties: Dilemmas of Sex and Class* (London, 1987) p. 107.
99. G. Andrews, N. Fishman and K. Morgan (eds) *Opening the Books: Essays on the Social and Cultural History of the Communist Party* (London, 1995).
100. S. Bruley, 'Women and Communism: A Case Study of the Lancashire Weavers in the Depression', in G. Andrews, N. Fishman and K. Morgan (eds) *Opening the Books: Essays on the Social and Cultural History of the Communist Party* (London, 1995) pp. 64–82.
101. H. F. Srebrnik, *London Jews and British Communism 1935–45* (Ilford, 1995).
102. N. Fishman, *The British Communist Party and the Trade Unions 1933–45* (London, 1994).
103. M. Worley, 'The British Communist Party 1920–45', *The Historian*, no. 55, Autumn 1997, pp. 26–8. At the time the author was completing a thesis on the CPGB.
104. K. Morgan (ed.) 'Communism in Britain and the British Empire', *Science and Society*, vol. 61, no. 1, special issue, Spring 1997.
105. I. MacDougall, *Voices from the Spanish Civil War* (Edinburgh, 1986); *Voices from the Hunger Marches* (Edinburgh, 1990). His more recent oral works are *Hard work Ye Ken: Midlothian Women Farmworkers* (Edinburgh, 1993); *Hoggie's Angels: Tattie Howkers' Remember* (Edinburgh, 1995); and *Mungo Mackay and the Green Table* (Edinburgh, 1995).
106. J. McCrindle and S. Rowbotham (eds) *Dutiful Daughters: Women Talk about their Lives* (London, 1977).
107. P. Cohen, *Children of the Revolution: Communist Childhood in Cold War Britain* (London, 1997).
108. Ibid., pp. 32–42.

Chapter 2

1. Socialist precept no. 10, Socialist Precepts and Declaration card, National Council of British Socialist Sunday Schools, undated (post 1907), TD1206/2/1–3, Glasgow City Archive/Strathclyde Regional Archive (henceforth GCA/SRA).

2. F. Reid, 'Socialist Sunday Schools in Britain 1892–1939', *International Review of Social History*, vol. 11, 1966, pp. 23–4. 'The modern Socialist Sunday School movement is to be dated from this Glasgow inception.' I am grateful to W. Hamish Fraser for alerting me to this article.
3. Reid, 'Socialist Sunday Schools in Britain', p. 24.
4. W. Knox (ed.) *Scottish Labour Leaders 1918–1939: A Biographical Dictionary* (Edinburgh, 1984) p. 84.
5. T. Islwyn Nicholas, *Tom Anderson: Apostle of Revolution* (WGML, Glasgow, 1930) p. 2.
6. GCA/SRA TD591, Tom Anderson Album, p. 1.
7. GCA/SRA, TD1399/1, Essays and lectures given by Alfred Russell 1900–1922, at a meeting held on 13 January 1907, p. 27.
8. GCA/SRA, TD1399/1, Russell, pp. 183–92.
9. *The Young Socialist*, vol. 17, no. 1, January 1917, 'The New Needlework Classes' by L. Glasier Foster was to be a regular feature (p. 7).
10. Reid, 'Socialist Sunday Schools in Britain 1892–1939', p. 29.
11. Socialist Sunday Schools; Aims, Objects and Organisations, National Council of British Socialist Sunday Schools (henceforth NCBSSS) (undated) Basic principles unaltered since 1892, p. 6 (WGML, Glasgow).
12. In *The Young Socialist*, vol. 21, no.10, October 1921, p. 2. the editor mentions the Sunbeams for the first time and suggests that the name be adopted. Also interview with Edith Findlay 10 September 1995, p. 4.
13. Socialist Sunday Schools, NCBSSS, but an older undated edition p. 4 (WGML).
14. Rose Kerrigan, 9 July 1995, p. 3.
15. Edith Findlay, 10 September 1995, p. 4.
16. Marion Henery, 6 April 1994 and 17 November 1995, pp. 1, 3.
17. Glasgow and District Socialist Sunday Schools Union, Memorandum of Season's Arrangement's 1929–30, p. 18 (WGML).
18. Mary Docherty, 14 May 1994 and 14 March 1995, p. 1.
19. National Library of Scotland 1964, *The Revolution: Means the Abolition of the Capitalist State and the Inauguration of an Industrial Republic: A Magazine for Young Workers* (official organ of the Socialist School), see vol. 1, no. 3, p. 40.
20. Ibid., p. 47.
21. Mitchell Library Glasgow Room (henceforth MLGR) G3335.330924, *John MacLean* by Comrade Tom (Tom Anderson) Glasgow, 1930, 2nd edition 1938, p. 14.
22. M. Docherty, *A Miner's Lass*, p. 27.
23. Ibid.
24. S. Nujam, 'A Radical Past: The Legacy of the Fife Miners', Ph.D. thesis, Edinburgh University, 1988, p. 211.
25. Mary Docherty, 14 May 1994 and 14 March 1995, pp. 1–2.
26. Marion Henery, 6 April 1994 and 17 November 1995, p. 1.
27. Edith Findlay, 10 September 1995, p. 4.
28. J. Smith, 'Labour Tradition in Glasgow and Liverpool', *History Workshop Journal*, 17 (Spring 1984) p. 37.

29. W. Kendall, *The Revolutionary Movement in Britain 1900–1921* (London, 1969) pp. 68, 72.
30. It led Helen Crawfurd, to see Presbyterianism as more democratic than the 'English or Roman church', 'Autobiography' (WGML) p. 48.
31. 'Glasgow has hitched its wagon to a star, and is soaring so high as almost to defy competition' (*The Young Socialist*, vol. 14, no.1, January 1914) p. 7.
32. *The Young Socialist*, vol. 15, no.12, December 1915, p. 191.
33. GCA/SRA RU4/5/102, The EC of Rutherglen Socialist Sunday School, March 1916.
34. *The Young Socialist*, vol. 17, no. 2, February 1917, pp. 15–16.
35. *The Young Socialist*, vol. 17, no. 10, October 1917, p. 111.
36. 'ABC of Conscientious Objection', *The Young Socialist*, vol. 17, no. 12, December 1917, p. 135.
37. Rose Kerrigan, 9 July 1995, p. 5.
38. R. J Morris, 'The ILP, 1893–1932: Introduction', in Alan McKinlay and R. J. Morris (eds) *The ILP on Clydeside 1893–1932: From Foundation to Disintegration* (Manchester, 1991) p. 4.
39. A. McKinlay, 'Doubtful Wisdom and Uncertain Promise: Strategy, Ideology and Organisation, 1918–1922', in Alan McKinlay and R. J. Morris (eds) *The ILP on Clydeside 1893–1932: From Foundation to Disintegration* (Manchester, 1991) p. 129.
40. Rose Kerrigan, 9 July 1995, p. 5.
41. A. Kollantai, 'Working Women's Day and the Third International', in J. Riddell (ed.) *The Communist International in Lenin's Time: Founding of the Communist International: Proceedings and Documents of the First Congress: March 1919* (New York, 1987) p. 310.
42. H. Corr, 'Helen Crawfurd', p. 84.
43. *The Young Socialist*, vol. 17, no. 9, September 1917, p. 107.
44. H. Crawfurd, 'Autobiography', p. 191 (WGML).
45. Ibid., p. 191.
46. Ibid., pp. 84–5.
47. Marion Robertson, 19 April 1994, p. 18.
48. *Daily Worker*, 17 January 1933.
49. Effie O'Hare, 23 March 1994 and 20 March 1996, p. 9; see also pp. 12, 19, 44–5.
50. S. Damer, *Rent Strike! The Clydebank Rent Struggles of the 1920s* (Clydebank, 1982) p. 4.
51. J. Hyslop, Interview, 9 March 1983, Tape 0060–1, Side 1, Clydebank Public Library (CPL).
52. F. Hart, 'Sixty Exciting Years', unpublished autobiography, copy (CPL) p. 73.
53. *Evening Times*, 13, 14 and 15 March 1941.
54. W. Gallacher, *Revolt on the Clyde*, p. 189.
55. Interview with Rose Kerrigan by Catriona Burness, 15 July 1993, p. 4.
56. Rose Kerrigan, 9 July 1995, p. 9.
57. M. Hill, *Red Roses for Isabel: Highlights of the Life of Isabel Brown* (Preston, 1982) p. 10.

58. Hart, 'Sixty Exciting Years', p. 69.
59. Hill, *Red Roses for Isabel*, p. 27.
60. 'Isabel Brown in my estimation, if you have got to have a heroine at all, that is mine. She died when she was 81, she just got on fine with me' (Mabs Skinner, 15 April 1994, pp. 15–16).
61. Hill, *Red Roses for Isabel*, p. 90.
62. Scottish Committee Organisation Report for April 1949, WGML, p. 6.
63. Effie O'Hare, 20 March 1994 and 23 March 1994, p. 43.
64. The Young Communist International, *Between the Fourth and Fifth Congresses: 1924–1928* (CPGB, London, 1928) p. 147.
65. Ibid., p. 109.
66. Ibid., p. 151.
67. Marion Easdale, 23 March 1994, p. 1.
68. Ibid., p. 4.
69. Mary Park, 13 December 1994 and 13 November 1996, pp. 2–3.
70. Edith Findlay, 10 September 1995, p. 15.
71. Jim Service, 19 November 1998 and 3 February 1999.
72. Mary Park, 13 December 1994 and 13 November 1996, pp. 49–50.
73. See B. Cowe, 'The Making of a Clydeside Communist', *Marxism Today*, April 1973.
74. Rose Kerrigan, 9 July 1995, p. 2.
75. Rose Kerrigan, 9 July 1995, pp. 2–3.
76. Mary Cowan, 16 March 1994, pp. 1–2.
77. Ibid.
78. Isa Porte, 12 December 1996, p. 16.
79. Interview with Joe and Marion Henery, tape 7, side 2 (WGML).
80. J. McLean, 'The 1926 General Strike in Lanarkshire', *Our History Journal*, Spring 1976, p. 65.
81. Mary Docherty, 14 May 1994 and 14 March 1995, p. 4.
82. Ibid.
83. Ibid., and M. Docherty (ed.) *Auld Bob Selkirk: A Man in a Million* (Cowdenbeath, 1996) p. 108.
84. Isa Porte, 12 December 1996, p. 17.
85. R. Gallacher, 'The Vale of Leven 1914–1975: Changes in Working Class Organisation and Action', in T. Dickson (ed.) *Capital and Class in Scotland*, (Edinburgh, 1982) p. 194.
86. Effie O'Hare, 23 March 1994, p. 2.
87. Marion Easdale, 23 March 1994, p. 1.
88. Ibid., p. 2.
89. L. Kibblewhite and A. Rigby, *Fascism in Aberdeen: Street Politics in the 1930s* (Aberdeen, 1978) p. 30.
90. Ibid., p. 8.
91. Alice Milne, 10 July 1994, p. 3.
92. Ibid.
93. Kibblewhite and Rigby, *Fascism in Aberdeen*, p. 10.

94. See *Challenge*, vol. 1, no. 9, October 1935, p. 1; vol. 5, no. 3, 21 January 1939, p. 1; vol. 5, no. 5, 4 February 1939, p. 1; vol. 5, no. 31, 12 August 1939, p. 2.
95. *Advance*, vol. 1, no. 2, April 1938, p. 1.
96. Bob Horne, 15 September 1994, p. 13.
97. May Annan, 22 April 1994, p. 1.
98. They were especially prophetic for the people of Clydebank because of the bombardment and devastation they suffered in March 1941 after three nights of continuous bombing, which killed 534 people, injured hundreds and displaced thousands. It was the worst and most destructive bombing anywhere in Scotland during the Second World War.
99. Jim Service, 19 November 1998 and 3 February 1999.
100. *Scottish Marxist*, no. 16, Summer 1978.
101. *Communist Party of Great Britain Scottish District Congress*, July 1937, (WGML) p. 1.
102. Ibid., p. 4.
103. Ibid., p. 1.
104. Isobel Service, 26 November 1998 and 28 January 1999.
105. Jenny Richardson 31 March 1994 said 'there was a big picture of Keir Hardie so there was always that talk in the house' (p. 1).
106. (MLGR) G3335, GDSSSU northwest, 18 September 1941, in reply to a request from Glasgow Trades Council and Burgh Labour Party.
107. (MLGR), G3335, GDSSSU, Glasgow North West Monthly Delegate Meeting, 21 September 1941.
108. (MLGR) G3335. 19 October 1941 meeting.
109. (MLGR), G3335, GDSSSU, 4 January 1942 meeting.
110. (MLGR), G3335, GDSSSU management committee meeting, 12 November 1942.
111. (MLGR) G3335, GDSSSU, minutes from 5 June 1941, ILP Shettleston and 14 August 1941, Partick ILP both requesting speakers.
112. (MLGR), G3335, GDSSSU AGM, 12 April 1942 minutes.
113. (MLGR) G3335, GDSSSU delegate meeting, 14 April 1957 – they visited the Knightswood and Nitshill branches.
114. (MLGR), G3335, GDSSSU Minute Book Session starting 1950–53 College House and Lansdowne Crescent.
115. GDSSSU Minute Book Session starting 1950–53, p. 6.
116. (MLGR), G3335, GDSSSU meeting, 17 September 1950.
117. (MLGR), G3335, GDSSSU Management Committee, 14 December 1950, p. 36.
118. (MLGR), G3335, GDSSSU meeting, 20 May 1951, p. 80.
119. (MLGR), G3335, GDSSSU meeting, 23 August 1951, p. 89.
120. (MLGR), G3335, GDSSSU meeting, 20 January 1952, p. 117.
121. (MLGR), G3335, GDSSSU meeting, 16 February 1952, p. 125.
122. (MLGR), G3335, GDSSSU, 20 April 1952, p. 140.
123. (MLGR), G3335, GDSSSU Management Committee, 13 November 1952, p. 177.
124. (MLGR), G3335, GDSSSU Management Committee, 22 April 1954.

125. (MLGR), G3335, GDSSSU Management Committee, 12 April 1956.
126. (MLGR), G3335, GDSSSU Delegate meeting, 22 April 1956.
127. (MLGR), G3335, GDSSSU Management Committee meeting, 17 January 1957.
128. (MLGR), G3335, GDSSSU minutes October 1955–October 1958. Minutes of Delegate meeting, Sunday 15 December 1957. Visits from YCL Choir to Pollok, Springburn and Knightswood.
129. (MLGR), G3335, GDSSSU Management Committee, 17 October 1957.
130. (MLGR), G3335, GDSSSU Delegate meeting, 20 February 1957.
131. (MLGR), G3335, GDSSSU Delegate meeting, 16 September 1956.
132. (MLGR) G3335, GDSSSU, Robert Smillie Centenary Booklet, 8 June 1957.
133. GCA/SRA, TD1399/1, Essays and lectures given by Alfred Russell, p. 29.
134. (MLGR), G3335, GDSSSU Govanhill Socialist Sunday School Juvenile Roll Book 1940–55 session 1951–52.
135. Ibid.
136. Ibid.
137. *Young Socialist*, vol. 21, no.10, October 1921, the sub-editor remarks that having read in *Communist* about the YCL, it was only doing what the Socialist Sunday School already did (p. 12).
138. Reid, 'Socialist Sunday Schools in Britain 1892–1939', p. 39
139. Ibid., p. 43.
140. GCA/SRA, TD1399/2, essays and lectures by Alfred Russell, paper read at Glasgow educational meeting of the Socialist Sunday School, 25 January 1920.
141. GCA/SRA TD1399/2, lecture given on 'International Heroes' to Springburn Socialist Sunday School, 11 January 1920, Alfred Russell, pp. 198–9.
142. Ibid., lesson given on 'The Paris Commune' to Springburn on 14 and 21 March 1920, p. 207.

Chapter 3

1. May Annan, 22 April 1994.
2. Of the CPGB women interviewed, eight joined the YCL/CP before 1939. Nine joined between 1940 and 1950, five between 1951 and 1960, nine between 1961 and 1970 and two after 1971. The discrepancy is because one interviewee's membership lapsed for a period.
3. Willie Thompson, *The Good Old Cause: British Communism 1920–91* (London, 1992). See Appendix on Communist Party membership 1921–1991 for the complete British figures (p. 218).
4. *Twentieth National Congress: Resolutions and Proceedings*, 21, 22, 23 February 1948, CPGB (London, 1948) p. 16.
5. *Twenty-first Congress of the CPGB* (London, 1949) p. 16.
6. *Communist Party of Scotland Report*, January 1945–June 1946 and Congress Report (WGML) p. 12.
7. Ibid., p. 12.

8. I am referring to communist work in the factories during the war, which was not always as subservient to the needs of the Soviet Union as the Polit Bureau pronounced. Bob Horne, 15 September 1994, p. 18 and 18 October 1994, pp. 1–6 illustrates how there was less stress on industrial action after the Soviet Union was attacked than in the period before, but in Scotland it would have been suicide for CP members to have relinquished industrial gains that had just been won from 1939–41.
9. *Communist Party of Scotland Report*, p. 12 (as above).
10. *The British Road to Socialism* (London, CPGB, 1951) p. 12; also 1952 edition pp. 11, 15 and 16.
11. J. Gollan, *People's Democracy for Britain* (London, 1952) p. 7.
12. *Twenty Second National Congress of the Communist Party: Report of the Executive Committee Covering the Period November 1949 to December 1951* (London, 1951) pp. 5, 18.
13. J. Gollan, *Scotland Needs 150,000 Jobs: A Memorandum on Scotland's Reconversion Problem* (Glasgow, 1946) p. 29.
14. W. Lauchlan, *Scotland and the Crisis* (Glasgow, 1947) (WGML) states 'The mobilization of women for work in the textiles, clothing, engineering and other industries can be facilitated by operating the principle of Equal Pay for Equal Work' (p. 8).
15. *Scotland and its Future: Short Term Plan for Scotland Adopted by the Scottish Congress of the Communist Party* (Glasgow, 1947) (WGML) p. 6.
16. *The Socialist Road for Britain* (London, CPGB, 1949) pp 10, 27.
17. *Whither Scotland?* Pictorial published by the Scottish Committee of the Communist Party (Glasgow, 1945) p. 1
18. Ibid., pp. 10–13.
19. J. Gollan, *Scottish Prospect* (Glasgow, 1948).
20. Gollan, *Scotland Needs 150,000 Jobs*, p. 7.
21. Ibid.
22. Gollan, *Scottish Prospect*, p. 212.
23. *Daily Worker*, 16 December 1949.
24. *A Parliament for Scotland: The Communist View* (Glasgow, CPGB).
25. Aitken Ferguson, *Scotland* (Glasgow, 1938) published by the Scottish District Committee of the CPGB. Though briefer, this is a forerunner to Gollan's work a decade later.
26. Ibid., p. 3.
27. Ibid.
28. 'But they *shall* be free', Communist Party memorandum on Scotland's future. Scottish Committee of the CP to the Royal Commission, 1 January 1953 (WGML) p. 3.
29. Ibid., p. 3.
30. Ibid., p. 8.
31. W. Lauchlan, *A Future for Scotland and her People*, Report to the Scottish Congress of the Communist Party (Glasgow, 1953) (WGML) p. 17.
32. *Communist Policy to Meet the Crisis*, Report of the 21st National Congress of the CPGB, opening remarks by A. Horner (London 1949) p. 4.

33. *Twenty-third National Congress of the Communist Party*, Report of the Executive Committee covering the period January 1952 to December 1953, p. 5.
34. Alice Milne, 10 July 1994, p. 12.
35. Letter to Jack Gaster from R. McIlhone, 10 November 1949 (WGML).
36. *Daily Worker*, 25 May 1949. The deputation consisted of R. McIlhone, Harry McShane and Margaret Hunter.
37. Ban on Communist Party Meetings. R. McIlhone's statement to magistrates Committee 10 April 1951. The deputation consisted of R. McIlhone, H. McShane and M. Robertson (WGML) p. 1.
38. *Glasgow Herald*, 5 May 1949. Progressives won 55 seats, The Labour Party 56.
39. *Glasgow Herald*, 7 May 1949. This was Victor D. Warren, assistant regional manager of ICI.
40. *World News and Views*, vol. 30, no. 30, 29 July 1950, p. 358. McGovern is not mentioned here but in the *Glasgow Herald*, 8 July 1950.
41. Scottish Committee Organisation Report for April 1949 (WGML) p. 6.
42. May Annan, 22 April 1994, p. 4.
43. *Glasgow Herald*, 25 February 1950. The result was W. W. Hamilton (Labour) 23,576; P. W. Nil Fraser (Conservative) 10,131; W. Gallacher (Communist) 9363.
44. Agenda for the National Covenant Committee Meeting, 29 July 1950. (Bob Horne Collection) Also, see the *Daily Mail*, 31 July 1950.
45. *Organisation Report for June 1950* (Glasgow, 1950) (WGML) p. 1.
46. Ibid. 'Where our propagandists go right into the attack, the opposition is silenced.'
47. Ibid., p. 8.
48. *Glasgow Herald*, 2 August 1950.
49. W. Hamish Fraser, *Glasgow Trades Council*, Mitchell Library Glasgow Collection 331 880941445:FRA, pp. 14–15.
50. *Twenty-Second National Congress of the Communist Party: Report of the Executive Committee covering the period November 1949 to December 1951* (London, 1951) p. 6.
51. Ibid., pp. 4, 11.
52. H. Pollitt, *Britain Arise* (London, 1952) p. 13.
53. 'But I was more or less just an ordinary member and then women did more in the peace question, the Stockholm Appeal, we did a lot with that.' Isa Porte, 23 March 1994 and 12 December 1996, p. 2.
54. J. Gollan, *End the Bans* (London, 1956) p. 7.
55. *Draft Report to the Political Committee*, Scottish District CPGB, 1948 (WGML) p. 8.
56. Jenny Richardson, 31 March 1994, p. 7.
57. *Draft Report to Political Committee 1948* states 'the excellent response to May day with the Party surpassing itself in the size, bearing and colour of its contingents' (WGML) p. 7.
58. *Twentieth National Congress: Resolutions and Proceedings*, 21, 22, 23 February 1948, CPGB (London, 1948) p. 24.
59. *Twenty-first National Congress* (London, 1949) p. 20.

60. *Twentieth National Congress* (London, 1948) p. 56.
61. *Scottish Congress 1953: Report of the Scottish Committee covering the period January 1951–January 1953* (WGML) p. 15.
62. Ibid., p. 14.
63. Mary Park, 13 November 1996, p. 53.
64. Irene Swan, 23 September 1995, p. 6.
65. Isobel Service, 19 November 1998, p. 1.
66. Jim Service, 19 November 1998, p. 3.
67. Jenny Richardson, 31 March 1994, p. 3.
68. J. Service, 'The Party and YCL as a Cultural Force', *Britain's Cultural Heritage* (London, 1952) p. 57.
69. *Scottish Committee 1948 Congress*, Report of the Scottish Committee of the Communist Party covering the period October 1947–September 1948 (WGML) p. 8.
70. 'The BBC has become the open propagandist of the "Cold War", with progressives rigidly excluded from broadcasting', *Marxist Study Themes*, no. 9, *The British State* (London, CPGB, 1954) p. 21.
71. Jenny Richardson, 31 March 1994, p. 3.
72. *Twenty-second Congress: Report of the EC*, The National Cultural Committee held a conference on 'The American threat to British Culture' in April 1951, p. 7.
73. B. Simon, 'The British Universities', *Britain's Cultural Heritage* (London, 1952) p. 59.
74. *Scottish Congress 1953*, Report of the Scottish Committee covering the period January 1951–January 1953 (WGML) p. 15.
75. These were the Cooperative Festival, Glasgow Socialist Festival, Ayr Music Festival and the Glasgow Music Festival. Isobel Service, 19 November 1998, p. 27.
76. Isobel Service, 19 November 1998.
77. *Draft Report to the Political Committee*, Scottish District CPGB, 1948 (WGML) p. 3.
78. Effie O'Hare, 20 March 1996, p. 39.
79. May Annan, 22 April 1994, p. 3.
80. *Twenty-first Congress of the CPGB, 1949* (London, 1949) p. 6.
81. Alice Milne, 10 July 1994, p. 13.
82. Michael McGahey (1925–1999).
83. Isa Porte, 23 March 1994 and 12 December 1996, p. 9.
84. *How to Sell Literature* (London, CPGB, 1942) p. 3.
85. Ibid. *Marxist Study Themes*, no. 9, *The British State* (London, CPGB, 1954).
86. Cathy Brown, 29 May 1994, p. 5.
87. Marion Easedale, 23 March 1994, p. 6.
88. Mary Cowan, 16 March 1994, p. 6.
89. Marion Robertson, 19 April 1994 (additions 20 October 1995) p. 20.
90. J. Mahon, *Twenty-fifth National Congress*, report on Inner Party Democracy (p. 51).
91. Mary Docherty, 14 May 1994 and 14 March 1995, p. 12.
92. Scottish Congress Report: covering the period January 1945–June 1946 (Glasgow, 1946) (WGML) p. 19.

93. Scottish District Report, June 1951 (WGML) p. 23.
94. *Scottish Congress*, Report of the Scottish Committee covering the period April 1953–January 1955, Glasgow 1955 (WGML) p. 9.
95. Report of the Scottish Committee of the Communist Party covering the period from January 1945 to June 1946 (WGML) p. 19.
96. Alice Milne, 10 July 1994, pp. 19–20.
97. Jenny Richardson, 31 March 1994, p. 7.
98. Cathy Brown, 29 May 1994, p. 3.
99. Janey Buchan, 4 October 1994, p. 17.
100. Report of the work of the Scottish Committee of the Communist Party January–December 1944 (WGML) p. 12.
101. Ibid., p. 12.
102. Ibid., p. 13.
103. It would confirm its name as the advisory committee during this decade. Also see Chapter 4 specifically on this body.
104. Report of the work of the Scottish Committee of the Communist Party covering the period October 1946–August 1947, p. 14.
105. Ibid., p. 15.
106. Report of the Scottish Committee of the Communist Party covering the period October 1947–September 1948 (WGML), p. 11.
107. Ibid., p. 11.
108. Ibid., p. 12.
109. Jessie Clark, 4 April 1994, p. 8.
110. Mabs Skinner, 15 April 1994, p. 4.
111. May Annan, 22 April 1994, p. 6.
112. C. M. Gabbidon, 'Party Life: An Examination of the Branch Life of the CPGB Between the Wars', D.Phil. thesis, Sussex University, 1991, p. 56.
113. Marion Robertson, 19 April 1994 (additions 20 October 1995) p. 13.
114. Ibid., p. 14.
115. Marion Henery, 6 April 1994 and 17 November 1995.
116. Marion Henery, 6 April 1994 and 17 November 1995, p. 9.
117. Marion Easedale, 23 March 1994, p. 8.
118. Alice Milne, 10 July 1994, p. 18.
119. Katherine Gallin, 13 April 1994, pp. 6–7.
120. *Twenty-fifth National Congress of the Communist Party (Special Congress) April 1957*.
121. May Annan, 22 April 1994, p. 11.
122. *Twenty-fifth National Congress*, Report on inner party democracy by J. Mahon (p. 53).
123. *How to Organise Public Meetings* (London, CPGB, 1942) p. 3.
124. Ibid., p. 5.
125. J. R. Campbell, *Forty Fighting Years: The Communist Record* (London, 1960) p. 8.
126. K. Morgan, *Harry Pollitt: Lives of the Left* (Manchester, 1993) p. 6.
127. Janey Buchan, 4 October 1994, pp. 1–2.
128. Bob Horne interviews (15 April 1994–4 May 1995) mentions Campbell several times and how he was strongly influenced by him as a young activist.

129. W. Gallacher, *Relaxation: A Collection of Satirical Political Verse* with a Foreword by R. Palme Dutt (London, Daily Worker Bazaar Committee, 1950).
130. Ella Egan, 17 November 1996, pp. 1–2.
131. Isa Porte, 23 March 1994 and 12 December 1996, p. 13.
132. Marion Henery, 6 April 1994 and 17 November 1995, p. 34.
133. *Evening Citizen*, 19 August 1938.
134. M. Seton, 'About Paul Robeson', *Paul Robeson Souvenir Programme* (WGML).
135. Jenny Richardson, 31 March 1994, p. 22.
136. Marion Robertson, 19 April 1994. 'Cranston's used to have a restaurant and they had a wee room up the stair and I went doon with another woman and we went in and I'll never forget the size of his hands, he was such a big man and when he stood up, they were massive and I thought he was just wonderful' (p. 9).
137. *Twenty first Congress of the Communist Party 1949*, Report of the Executive Committee covering the period February 1948 to July 1949, p. 5.
138. *Glasgow Herald*, 2 May 1960v
139. James Hunter, 18 July 1995, pp. 1–2.
140. Irene Swan, 23 September 1995, p. 10.
141. James Hunter, 18 July 1995, pp. 2–3.
142. *Comment*, vol. 5, no. 11, 18 March 1967, p. 166.
143. Cathy Brown, 29 May 1994, p. 6.
144. Jessie Clark, 4 April 1994, p. 3.
145. Jessie Clark, 4 April 1994, p. 4.
146. Effie O'Hare, 20 March 1996, p. 36.
147. *Draft Report to the Political Committee 1948* (Glasgow, 1948) p. 12.
148. Report of the Executive Committee to the 26th National Congress of the Communist Party covering the period January 1956–December 1958, p. 12.
149. S. Bruley, *Leninism, Stalinism and the Women's Movement in Britain 1920–39* (New York, 1986) p. 2.
150. Ibid. p. 167.
151. E. Burns, 'Women's Fight for Liberation', *Communist Review*, November 1952, p. 344.
152. Pat Milligan, 15 March 1994 and 11 May 1994.

Chapter 4

1. *Scottish Communist Party Congress Report 21–22 September 1946* (Glasgow, 1946) p. 14 (WGML).
2. *Communist Party Organisation Report for April 1949: Report to Political Committee 1950*, p. 7 (WGML).
3. Mabs Skinner, 15 April 1994.
4. Mabs Skinner, 15 April 1994, pp. 1–2.
5. *Health for the People: Memorandum on Scotland's Health Services* published by the Scottish Committee of the Communist Party (after 1943) p. 7.
6. Ibid., p. 14.
7. Ibid., p. 24.

8. N. Branson, *History of the Communist Party of Great Britain 1941–51* (London, 1997) p. 44.
9. P. Bain, 'Is You Is Or Is You Ain't My Baby? Women's Pay and the Clydeside Strikes of 1943', *Scottish Labour History Society Journal*, no. 30, 1995, p. 52.
10. *Duffy Meets.* Radio Clyde interview, Agnes McLean with Sheila Duffy first broadcast on 4 April 1989.
11. *Glasgow Herald*, 13 April 1943.
12. J. Eaton and C. Gill, *The Trade Union Directory* (London, 1983) p. 85.
13. *Duffy Meets.* Radio Clyde interview, April 1989.
14. G. Braybon and P. Summerfield, *Out of the Cage: Women's Experiences in Two World Wars* (London, 1987) p. 176.
15. Ibid., p. 176.
16. *Duffy Meets.* Radio Clyde interview.
17. *Glasgow Herald*, 17 June 1941.
18. *Glasgow Herald*, 20 June 1941, p. 6.
19. Alice Milne, 10 July 1994, p. 15.
20. *Children First*, a discussion of Scottish schools issued by the Scottish committee of the Communist Party (Glasgow, 1956) p. 4.
21. Ibid., p. 10.
22. Ibid., p. 11.
23. Cathy Brown, 29 May 1994, p. 31.
24. *The Party's Work Amongst Women in Scotland*, Marion Henery Collection (henceforth MHC) (Glasgow, CP, 1956).
25. Jessie Clark, 4 April 1994, p. 6.
26. *Report of the Scottish Committee of the Communist Party covering the period from January 1945 to June 1946* (Glasgow, 1946) (WGML) p. 31. There was also a full-time woman organizer in Fife, Jenny Dand. Also, only 39 of the 235 delegates at the congress on 21–22 September 1946 were women and only one was a factory delegate; 26 were housewives (p. 16).
27. Isa Porte, 16 February 1994 and 12 December 1996, p. 1.
28. Mary Park, 13 December 1994 and 13 November 1996, p. 8.
29. May Annan, 22 April 1994, p. 18.
30. Isa Porte, 23 March 1994 and 12 December 1996.
31. *Communist Party Organisation Report for April 1949*, Report to the Political Committee 1950 (WGML) p. 7.
32. *Report of the Scottish Committee covering the period January 1951 to January 1953* (WGML) p. 12.
33. *Communist Review*, April 1951, p. 108.
34. *The Party's Work Amongst Women In Scotland* (MHC) p. 2.
35. May Annan, 22 April 1994, p. 15.
36. *Scottish Bulletin*, 2 February 1946.
37. Jenny Richardson, 31 March 1994, p. 10.
38. See 'Rhoda Fraser: The New DNB'. Thanks here to Audrey Canning who has unearthed and accumulated much information about Rhoda Fraser and many other women in the labour movement in Scotland.
39. *Scottish Congress Report 1948* (WGML) p. 11.

40. *Scotland Demands*, Scottish District Special, 1947.
41. Jenny Richardson, 31 March 1994, p. 10.
42. Marion Robertson, 19 April 1994, p. 22.
43. *World News and Views*, vol. 33, no. 47, November 1953, p. 561.
44. *The Party's Work amongst Women in Scotland* (MHC).
45. C. Thornton and W. Thompson, 'Scottish Communists, 1956–7', *Science and Society*, vol. 61, no. 1, Spring 1997, p. 89.
46. *World News and Views*, November 1953.
47. *Scottish District Report*, November 1953 (WGML) p. 17.
48. Ibid.
49. Ibid.
50. May Annan, 22 April 1994.
51. Marion Henery, 6 April 1994 and 17 November 1995, p. 10.
52. Marion Henery, author's notes from meeting, 10 November 1995.
53. Thornton and Thompson 'Scottish Communists, 1956–7', *Science and Society.*
54. Alice Milne, 10 July 1994, pp. 16–17.
55. Isa Porte, 16 February 1994 and 12 December 1996, p. 9.
56. Jessie Clark, 4 April 1994, p. 4.
57. *Scottish Bulletin*, 2 February 1946. 'It is interesting to note that Scotland is the only district to increase its January sales of *Woman Today* – these having leapt from 700 in October to 1100 in January.' However, sales were only 600 per issue by 1956. *Party Work Amongst Women in Scotland* (MHC) p. 4.
58. Marion Robertson, 19 April 1994, p. 23.
59. Ibid., p. 24.
60. Jessie Clark, 4 April 1994, p. 17.
61. Jenny Richardson, 31 March 1994, p. 7.
62. *Draft Report to Political Committee 1948* (WGML).
63. District Women Cadres School 26/7 June 1954, Kenilworth Hotel, Queen Street, Glasgow (MHC).
64. National Residential School for Women Cadres on 'The Road to Socialism', 3–10 November 1956, Copy of syllabus (MHC).
65. Letter from Rhoda Fraser, CP Women's Department of the Scottish District Committee to Area Organisers, Branch Secretaries and Secretaries of Women's Groups, November 1954 (MHC).
66. Ibid.
67. Ibid.
68. *World News*, vol. 2, no. 13, 26 March 1955, p. 254.
69. *World News*, vol. 3, no. 1, 7 January 1956, p. 14.
70. Ibid.
71. Alice Milne, 10 July 1994, p. 16.
72. The first one being at the Shelbourne Hotel, Edinburgh, 5–6 November 1955. Application form (MHC).
73. J. Cohen, Report of Scottish District Women's School, 8th–9th June 1963, Balloch 13th June 1963 (MHC) p. 2; also reproduced as 'A Women's School in Scotland', *Party Life*, vol. 1, no. 7, October–November 1963, pp. 8–9.
74. Ibid.

75. Ibid., p. 3.
76. 'Participation by the students in the groups and in general class discussion was very good indeed, very lively at times, but one got the impression that there had not been a great deal of preparatory reading of the recommended material.' Report of Ayr School (MHC).
77. Ibid. The breakdown, which was not always given, was housewives (12), clerical workers (4), industrial workers (6), services (2) and students (2).
78. There were six district women's residential schools in the 1960s: 1963, Balloch, 50 students, tutor Jack Cohen and Glasgow, 17 students, tutor Jim Hill; 1964, Glenshee, 14 students, tutor Margaret Hunter; 1966, Ayr, 20 students, tutor Finlay Hart; 1968, Ayr, 36 students, tutor James Klugmann; and 1969, Ayr, 26 students, tutor Joan Bellamy. Typewritten list (MHC).
79. The attendance from areas to the 1963 school in Balloch was Glasgow 25; Lanarkshire 5; Dunbartonshire and Renfrewshire 7; Edinburgh 2; Aberdeen 4; Fife 1; and West Lothian 5. For the Ayr school in 1968 Glasgow 19; Lanarkshire 3; Dunbartonshire 11; Stirlingshire 1; Edinburgh 2; and West Lothian 1. The slight discrepancy in numbers may be due to non-party people. List of schools (MHC).
80. E. Burns, *A Call to Co-operators* (London, CPGB, 1954) p. 8.
81. *Draft Report to Political Committee 1948* (WGML) p. 2.
82. *Scottish Co-operator*, 21 May 1949 (MHC).
83. *Scottish Co-operative Women's Guild: Rules of the Guild and the Branches and Standing Orders* (Glasgow, 1948).
84. Marion Robertson, 19 April 1994, p. 19.
85. Marion Henery, 6 April 1994 and 17 November 1995, pp. 29–30.
86. CP/CENT/PERS/3/03/ (CPA) Hand-written submission by Marion Henery dated 31 March 1955.
87. *The Party's Work Amongst Women in Scotland* (MHC) p. 3.
88. Marion Henery, 6 April 1994 and 17 November 1995, p. 29.
89. *Scottish Co-operator*, 21 May 1949.
90. *Report of the Scottish Congress, 26–27 March 1955.*
91. *57th Annual Congress of the Scottish Cooperative Women's Guild*, Dunoon Pavilion 19–20 May 1949 (MHC) pp. 1–2.
92. Burns, *A Call to Co-operators*, p. 6.
93. *Scottish Co-operative Women's Guild: Sixtieth Annual Report and Balance Sheet for the year ending march 1952.* SCWS Ltd. (MHC) p. 27.
94. *Scottish Co-operative Women's Guild: Sixty-first Annual Report and Balance Sheet for year ending March 1953* (MHC) p. 15.
95. Ibid., p. 18.
96. When educating children for instance, something that the Women's Co-operative Guild had always looked down on or ignored compared with the Socialist Sunday School.
97. *Scottish Co-operative Women's Guild: Sixty-first Annual Report* (MHC) p. 23.
98. *Scottish Co-operative Women's Guild: Sixtieth Annual Report* (MHC) p. 4.
99. Ibid., p. 10.
100. *Scottish Co-operative Women's Guild: Sixty-first Annual Report* (MHC) p. 3.

101. *Scottish Co-operative Women's Guild: Sixty-second Annual Report and Balance Sheet for Year Ending March 1954* (MHC); the fall was from 43,182 members in 1948 to 32,000 in 1954 (p. 20).
102. Ibid. p. 21.
103. Ibid., p. 23.
104. Ibid., p. 24.
105. (AJA) TD1206/1/4 (SRA/GCA) copy of the *Scottish Co-operator*, 22 January 1955, p. 7.
106. Ibid., 8 January 1955, p. 12.
107. Ibid.
108. Ibid., *Scottish Co-operator*, 19 November 1955, p. 21.
109. Marion Robertson, 19 April 1994, p. 18.
110. *The People will Triumph: Report of the Scottish Congress of the Communist Party*, 26 and 27 March 1955 (WGML) p. 4.
111. Ibid.
112. Ibid.
113. Marion Henery, 6 April 1994 and 17 November 1995, p. 31.
114. Burns, *A Call to Co-operators* (London 1954) p. 9.
115. Ibid., p. 13.
116. *Speakers Notes on the Independent Commission of Inquiry into the Co-operative Movement* (MHC) (London, 1958) p. 1.
117. Ibid., p. 2.
118. Ibid., p. 1.
119. D. Ainley, *Co-ops: The Way Ahead* (London, CPGB, 1962) p. 5.
120. Ibid., p. 11.
121. Ibid., p. 14.
122. *Report of the Scottish Committee of the Communist Party covering the Period April 1955 to January 1958* (WGML) (Glasgow, 1958) p. 11.
123. Ibid.
124. *Scottish Women's Bulletin*, no. 1, April 1964 (MHC) p. 1. The bulletin was mainly the work of Isa Porte.
125. Ibid.
126. Ibid., p. 4.
127. Women's Advisory Committee, Scottish Women's Conference, Sunday 8 October 1967 (MHC).
128. *Scottish Women's Bulletin*, no. 2, May 1964 (MHC) p. 3.
129. Ibid.
130. *Scottish Women's Bulletin*, no. 3, June 1964 (MHC) p. 4.
131. *Scottish Women's Advisory Committee: Detection and Prevention of Cervical Cancer, Campaign Notes April 24 1964* (MHC).
132. Ibid.
133. Letter from Marion Henery to the Department of Health for Scotland, 20 April 1964 (MHC).
134. *Scottish Women's Bulletin*, May 1964, p. 4.
135. Quoted in the *Scottish Women's Bulletin*, no. 4, September 1964 (MHC) p. 3.
136. Ibid.

137. Campaign Notes on the Cervical Cancer Issue (MHC) p. 2.
138. April 1964–March 1965, typewritten notes on the issue (one page) (MHC).
139. *Glasgow Herald*, 3 March 1965.
140. Letter from Marion Henery to Judith Hart, 17 March 1965 (MHC).
141. Letter from Scottish Office to Marion Henery, 4 June 1965 (MHC).
142. Ibid.
143. SWAC meeting, 4 April 1964 (MHC).
144. Ibid.
145. Katherine Gallin, 13 April 1994, pp. 8–9. The author had assumed the same before this interview. Another example of being corrected by oral testimony.
146. Scottish Women's Advisory Committee meeting, 9 April 1967 (MHC).
147. Letter to Scottish Office from women's deputation signed Mabs Skinner (Inverness), Margaret Rose (Aberdeen), Margaret McGill (Glasgow), Nan Wilson (Kirkintilloch), and Mary Healy (Greenock). (MHC) 29 June 1967.
148. *Scottish Women's Bulletin*, no. 4, September 1964 (MHC) p. 2.
149. *Comment*, vol. 3, no. 10, 6 March 1965, p. 155.
150. *Comment*, vol. 4, no. 10, 5 March 1966.
151. Letter from Margaret Hunter to Marion Henery, 30 January 1967.
152. Scottish Committee CPGB District Congress Report 1962 (WGML) p. 2.
153. Isobel Service, 26 November 1998 and 28 January 1999, p. 10.
154. *Comment*, vol. 4, no .42, 15 October 1966, p. 667.
155. Ibid.
156. *Comment*, vol. 6, no. 12, 23 March 1968, pp. 181–2.
157. Minutes of the Scottish Women's Advisory Committee, 12 November 1967 (MHC) p. 1.
158. Scottish Women's Conference Sunday (MHC) 8 October 1967, p. 1.
159. Minutes of the Scottish Women's Advisory Committee, 12 November 1967.
160. Pat Milligan took over from Marion Henery in 1968.
161. Pat Milligan, 15 March 1994 and 11 May 1994, p. 8.
162. Jean McCrindle, 28 June 1995, pp. 8–9.
163. *Comment*, vol. 6, no. 51, 21 December 1968, p. 818.
164. Minutes of the Scottish Women's Advisory Committee, 22 January 1968 (MHC) p. 1.
165. *Communist Review*, November 1952, p. 344.
166. 'Women in Capitalist Britain', CP Central Education Department November 1955 (WGML).
167. *Report of the Scottish Committee of the Communist Party covering the period January 1958–January 1960* (WGML) p. 5.
168. *World News*, vol. 5, no. 43, 25 October 1958, p. 633.
169. *Report of the Scottish Committee 1958–60.*
170. *World News*, vol. 2, no. 36, 3 September 1955, p. 690.
171. May Annan, 22 April 1994, p. 18.
172. Cathy Brown, 29 May 1994.

Chapter 5

1. Jean Mackay, 25 February 1994, p. 11.

2. R. Palme Dutt, *World Politics 1918–1936* (London, 1936) p. 275.
3. Mary Docherty, 14 May 1994 and 14 March 1995, pp. 27–8. This is in Cowdenbeath, Fife.
3. Mary Docherty, 14 May 1994 and 14 March 1995, p. 27.
4. Ibid., p. 28.
5. A. Brown (ed.) *The Soviet Union: A Biographical Dictionary* (London, 1990) pp. 54–5.
6. A. Nove, *An Economic History of the USSR* (London, 1969) 1982 edn p. 144.
7. R. Palme Dutt, *World Politics*, p. 275, admits there were 'great sacrifices'.
8. Marion Henery, 6 April 1994 and 17 November 1995, p. 16.
9. W. Hannington, *Unemployed Struggles 1918–36* (London, 1936) 1977 edn, p. 230.
10. Marion Henery, 6 April 1994 and 17 November 1995, p. 17.
11. F. Nutina, *The Soviet Law on Marriage* (New York, 1933) p. 4.
12. Nove, *An Economic History of the USSR*, p. 199.
13. Rose Kerrigan, 9 July 1995, p. 9.
14. See P. Sloan, *Russia Without Illusions*, with a Preface by B. Webb (Manchester, 1938) about her time there from 1931 (pp. 9–11).
15. *Our History Journal*, no. 12, January 1988, p. 21.
16. M. Pollitt, *Defeat of Trotskyism* (London, 1937) p. 7.
17. Pollitt, *Defeat of Trotskyism*, p. 20.
18. F. King and G. Matthews, *About Turn: The British Communist Party and the Outbreak of the Second World War*. The verbatim record of the Central Committee meetings of 25 September and 2–3 October 1939, with an Introduction by Monty Johnstone (London, 1990).
19. May Annan, 22 April 1994, p. 3.
20. Alice Milne, 10 July 1994, p. 6.
21. J. Attfield and S. Williams, *1939: The Communist Party of Great Britain and the War. Proceedings of a Conference held on 21 April 1979 organised by the Communist Party History Group* (London, 1984) p. 107.
22. Effie O'Hare, 23 March 1994 and 20 March 1996, p. 16.
23. W. Cowe, *Scotland and the War* (Glasgow, CPGB, 1940) (WGML).
24. W. Cowe, *Scotland for the Offensive: A Call for a Fighting Lead* (Glasgow, CPGB, 1941) (WGML).
25. Nove, *An Economic History of the USSR*, p. 271.
26. M. Henderson, *Dear Allies: A Story of Women in Monklands and Besieged Leningrad* (Monklands District Libraries, 1988) p. 18.
27. 'Aye, Minnie Aitken, ... she worked in industry and had no spare time because it was all devoted to the party.' Marion Henery, 6 April 1994 and 17 November 1995, p. 31.
28. Henderson, *Dear Allies*, p. 31.
29. *Glasgow Herald*, 6 February 1943.
30. Henderson, *Dear Allies*, p. 120.
31. Alice Milne, 10 July 1994, p. 10.
32. I. Deutscher, *Stalin* (Oxford, 1949) 1986 edn, p. 534.
33. Ibid., p. 558.

34. Marion Robertson, 19 April 1994, p. 35.
35. G. Wigoder (ed.) *Dictionary of Jewish Biography* (Tel Aviv, 1990) p. 391.
36. *Glasgow Herald*, 21 July 1950.
37. Wigoder (ed.) *Dictionary of Jewish Biography*.
38. *Festival of Youth: Budapest 1949* (London, 1949) p. 3 (WGML).
39. Ibid., p. 17.
40. Ibid., p. 15.
41. *Glasgow Herald*, 1 August 1951.
42. *Glasgow Herald*, 6 May 1949.
43. Jenny Richardson, 31 March 1994, p. 4.
44. *The Journey to Berlin: Report of a Commission of Inquiry into certain events at Brussels, the Channel Ports, Innsbruck and Saalfelden in August 1951*, National Council for Civil Liberties (London, 1952) p. 3 (WGML).
45. Jenny Richardson, 31 March 1994, p. 4.
46. Ibid., p. 5.
47. *The Innsbruck Story* (London, British Youth Festival Preparatory Committee, 1951) p. 6. Bob Horne Collection (henceforth BHC).
48. Jenny Richardson, 31 March 1994, p. 5.
49. *Glasgow Herald*, 9 August 1951.
50. Jenny Richardson, 31 March 1994, p. 6.
51. *Glasgow Herald*, 22 August 1951.
52. *The Innsbruck Story*, p. 3.
53. Ibid., p. 24.
54. *The Guardian*, 17 August 1951.
55. Isobel Service, 26 November 1998 and 28 January 1999, p. 28.
56. Derek Aldcroft, *The European Economy 1918–1980* (London, 1978) p. 162.
57. Mary Park, 13 December 1994 and 13 November 1996, pp. 30–1.
58. W. Gallacher, *The Tyrants' Might is Passing* (London, 1954) p. 81.
59. *World News and Views*, vol. 2, no. 36, 3 September 1955 p. 693.
60. Janey Buchan, 4 October 1994 and 21 January 1997, p. 21.
61. Jim Service, 26 November 1998 and 26 January 1999, mentions the building programmes much in evidence (p. 14).
62. *World News and Views*, vol. 2, no. 52, 31 December 1955, p. 961.
63. *World News and Views*, vol. 3, no. 11, 17 March 1956, p. 164.
64. N. S. Khrushchev, *Report of the Central Committee: 20th Congress of the Communist Party of the Soviet Union February 1956* (London, 1956) p. 78. The YCL had 'more than 18 million' members (p. 87).
65. Ibid., p. 80.
66. Ibid., pp. 85–6. Here he also briefly mentions the lack of women in leading posts.
67. *Glasgow Herald*, 16 May 1956.
68. A. Pries, 'Khrushchev's Secret Speech: Confusion of Tongues', *Journal of Contemporary Society*, vol. 6, no. 1, March 1990, p. 82.
69. Marion Easedale, 23 March 1994, p. 18.
70. *World News and Views*, vol. 30, no. 30, 29 July 1950, p. 354.
71. Ibid.

72. Harry Pollitt, *In Memory of Joseph Stalin and Klement Gottwald* (London, 1953) pp. 3–13. A pure eulogy to Stalin.
73. Mary Park, 13 December 1994 and 13 November 1996, pp. 26–7.
74. Rose Kerrigan, 9 July 1995, p. 2.
75. Janey Buchan, 4 October 1994 and 21 January 1997, p. 24.
76. *Resolutions of the World Peace Council* (Paris, 1951) (BHC) p. 3.
77. Brown (ed.) *The Soviet Union: A Biographical Dictionary*, pp. 88–9.
78. H. F. Srebrnik, *London Jews and British Communism 1935–1945* (Ilford, 1995) pp. 94–5.
79. G. Wigoder (ed.) 'Solomon Mikhoels (1890–1948)', *Dictionary of Jewish Biography*, pp. 349–50.
80. *The Reasoner*, no. 1, July 1956, p. 25. I am grateful to Willie Thompson for providing copies.
81. Bob Horne, who was at the meeting, thought this was Rhoda Fraser.
82. Janey Buchan, 4 October 1994 and 21 January 1997, p. 24.
83. *The New Reasoner* was published from 1957 to 1959 by people who left the CP in 1957 and had published *The Reasoner* from July to November 1956 while in the CP.
84. Jean McCrindle, 28 June 1995, p. 12.
85. *The Reasoner*, no. 1, July 1956, p. 9.
86. *World News and Views*, vol. 2, no. 36, 3 September 1955, p. 694.
87. *World News and Views*, vol. 2, no. 35, 27 August 1955, p. 676.
88. *World News and Views*, vol. 3, no. 17, 28 April 1956, p. 268.
89. Cathy Brown, 29 May 1994, p. 19.
90. *The Reasoner*, no. 1, July 1956, p. 5.
91. *World News and Views*, vol. 3, no. 47, 24 November 1956, pp. 748–9.
92. *World News and Views*, vol. 29, no. 5, 29 January 1949, p. 50.
93. The Rev. S. G. Evans, *The Trial of Cardinal Mindzenty: An Eye Witness Account* (Birmingham, 1949) p. 6.
94. *World News and Views*, no. 46, p. 730.
95. Jenny Richardson, 31 March 1994, p. 14.
96. *Daily Worker*, 17 November 1956.
97. *The Observer*, 25 November 1956.
98. C. Coutts, *Eye Witness in Hungary* (London, 1957) p. 17.
99. *The Counter-Revolutionary Conspiracy of Imre Nagy and his Accomplices* (Budapest, 1958).
100. G. Kallai, *The Counter-Revolution in Hungary in the Light of Marxism–Leninism* (Budapest, 1956) (WGML) p. 23.
101. Isobel Service, 26 November 1998 and 28 January 1999, p. 8.
102. W. Thompson, *The Good Old Cause: British Communism 1920–91* (London, 1992) p. 105.
103. Jack Ashton, 18 November 1996, p. 6.
104. See D. Renton, 'Why I left the Communist Party', *The Newsletter*, vol. 1, no. 1, 10 May 1957.
105. Jack Ashton, 18 November 1996, p. 7.

106. C. Thornton and W. Thompson, 'Scottish Communists, 1956–7', *Science and Society*, vol. 61, no. 1, Spring 1997, p. 86.
107. Ella Egan, 17 October 1996 and 17 November 1996, p. 28.
108. S. Howe, 'Anti-Colonialism in British politics: The Left and the End of Empire 1939–64', D.Phil. thesis, Oxford University, 1984, p. 271.
109. *The Reasoner*, November 1956, p. 2.
110. Jean McCrindle, 28 June 1995, p. 18.
111. Jessie Clark, 4 April 1994, p. 10.
112. Marion Robertson, 19 April 1994, p. 39.
113. *World News and Views*, vol. 6, no. 43, 24 October 1959.
114. Jean McCrindle, 28 June 1995, p. 23.
115. W. Thompson, 'The New Left in Scotland', in I. MacDougall (ed.) *Essays in Scottish Labour History: A Tribute to W. H. Marwick* (Edinburgh, 1978) p. 217.
116. *Report of the Executive Committee to the 26th National Congress of the Communist Party covering the period January 1956–December 1958*, p. 4.
117. May Annan, 22 April 1994, p. 33.
118. Alice Milne, 10 July 1994, pp. 23–4.
119. Cathy Brown, 29 May 1994, p. 19.
120. Nove, *An Economic History of the USSR*, p. 353.
121. Effie O'Hare, 23 March 1994 and 20 March 1996, p. 22.
122. May Annan, 22 April 1994.
123. A. Brown (ed.) *The Soviet Union: A Biographical Dictionary*, pp. 384–5.
124. Katherine Gallin, 13 April 1994, pp. 18–19.
125. May Annan, 22 April 1994, p. 34.
126. Ouaine Bain, 27 June 1994 and 17 August 1994, p. 40.
127. Anna Sardesai, 28 August 1994, p. 9.
128. J. Franklin, *The Cuban Revolution and the United States: A Chronological History* (Melbourne, 1992) p. 57.
129. Ella Egan, 17 October 1996 and 17 November 1996, p. 29.
130. Isa Porte, 12 December 1996, p. 19.
131. Ouaine Bain, 27 June 1994 and 17 August 1994, p. 41.
132. M. Johnstone, 'The CPGB, the Comintern and the War 1939–41: Filling in the Blank Spots', in K. Morgan (ed.) *Science and Society*, vol. 61, no. 1, p. 33.
133. D. Johnson, 'A Party Women's Delegation to the USSR', *Party Life*, vol. 1, no. 7, October–November 1963, pp. 4–6, gives a descriptive account of the same visit by a party delegation of women including May Annan.
134. *The Reasoner*, no. 1, p. 9.
135. S. Parsons, '1956: What happened inside the CPGB', *The Communist Party and 1956*, Our History Pamphlet no. 88 (London, 1993) pp. 33–5.
136. Slightly underestimated in K. Hudson, '1956 and the Communist Party', *The Communist Party and 1956*, p. 23.
137. *Report to the Executive Committee on Inner Party Democracy*, December 1956 (London, 1956) pp. 38–44.
138. Ibid., p. 7.
139. Ibid., p. iv.
140. Ibid., p. 27.

141. Jack Ashton, 18 November 1996, on a visit to Hungary was rebuked by the Minister of Culture. 'I was expounding my views on these events, the October and November events … and he just looked at me across this gathering and he said "Comrade, can I make a point with you? Do you know who was at fault in these events?" "Our Party" meaning the Hungarian Workers' Party … "We were at fault." In other words the Party was the main factor in the events that led to whether you want to call it a counter-revolution or whatever you want to do. "No, we were at fault." So that was a salutary lesson for me' (p. 6).
142. *36 Million Communists Say…: Statements and Appeal of the World's Communist Parties, Moscow, November 1960* (London, 1960) p. 3.

Chapter 6

1. Ouaine Bain, 27 June 1994 and 17 August 1994, p. 7.
2. J. Gollan, *Britain's Future* (London, 1963) p. 15.
3. *Report of the Scottish Committee of the Communist Party covering the Period June 1964 to June 1966* (Glasgow, 1966) p. 4.
4. Gollan, *Britain's Future*, p. 17.
5. *Twenty-Seventh Congress Report* (London, 1961) p. 43.
6. B. Wainwright, *Close all US Bases* (London, 1958) p. 4.
7. Willie Thompson, 13 June 1994.
8. Marion Easedale, 23 March 1994 and 17 November 1996, p. 23.
9. Isa Porte, 16 February 1994 and 12 December 1996, p. 5.
10. May Annan, 22 April 1994, p. 38.
11. Mary Park, 13 December 1994 and 14 November 1996, p. 55.
12. Kathryn Chalmers, 22 March 1994.
13. *Daily Record*, 4 March 1961.
14. Alan McKinlay, 'Doubtful Wisdom and Uncertain Promise', pp. 132–3.
15. Kathryn Chalmers, 22 March 1994, p. 1.
16. Barbara Thorpe, 31 August 1995 and 14 September 1995, p. 2.
17. Maureen Sanders, 25 March 1994, p. 2.
18. *Report of the Executive Committee of the Communist Party of Great Britain From January 1961 to December 1962* (London, 1962) p. 14.
19. *Report of the Scottish Committee of the Communist Party Covering the Period January 1962 to January 1964* (Glasgow, 1964) p. 6.
20. Ibid. *Report of the Scottish Committee of the Communist Party* adult membership increased as follows: 1962 (6451); 1963 (7079); 1964 (7661).
21. *Twenty-seventh Congress of the Communist Party*. F. Stanley, *The Communist Party and Young People* (London, 1961) pp. 3–4.
22. Noreen Thompson, 28 June 1994, p. 2.
23 Jean Mackay, 25 February 1994, p. 5.
24. Noreen Thompson, 28 June 1994, p. 3.
25. *Glasgow Herald*, 26 October 1962.
26. Katy Campbell, 28 March 1994 and 11 February 1997, p. 31.

27. *Glasgow Herald*, 3 October 1962. The increase in unemployed school leavers was 23 per cent up on the 1961 figure.
28. *Glasgow Herald*, 21 September 1962.
29. *Twenty-Ninth Communist Party Congress Report*, p. 16.
30. Christine Sloan, 24 March 1994 and 26 April 1994, p. 3.
31. Ouaine Bain, 27 June 1994 and 17 August 1994, p. 7.
32. Katy Campbell, 28 March 1994 and 11 February 1997, p. 36.
33. Willie Thompson, 13 June 1994, p. 3.
34. Willie Thompson, 13 June 1994, p. 9.
35. Katy Campbell, 28 March 1994 and 11 February 1997, p. 5.
36. This was at the Whitsun weekend of 23 May to 3 June 1967 at The Trend '67 international youth festival run by the YCL.
37. Ouaine Bain, 27 June 1994 and 17 August 1994, p. 4.
38. *Challenge*, April 1967.
39. Noreen Thompson, 28 June 1994, pp. 4–5.
40. *Challenge* (new series) May 1969.
41 Ouaine Bain, 27 June 1994 and 17 August 1994, pp. 7–8.
42. *Scottish Bulletin*, 22 January 1969 (Willie Thompson Collection, henceforth WTC).
43. Anna Sardesai, 27 August 1994, p. 5.
44. *Scottish Marxist*, no. 1, summer, June 1972, p. 64.
45. Cathy Brown, 29 May 1994, p. 5.
46. John Foster, 23 November 1994, pp. 2–3 suggests there was a noticeable deficiency in branch organization at this time which had developed from the constitutional separation of industrial and area branches in the 1940s.
47. Anna Sardesai, 27 August 1994, p. 8.
48. Irene Swan, 23 September 1995 and 28 October 1995, p. 36.
49. *Challenge* (old series) September 1966.
50. *Challenge* (new series: the month is not always apparent) no. 4, March 1968.
51. *Report of the Scottish Committee of the Communist Party covering the Period June 1964 to June 1966*, p. 1.
52. Alice Milne, 10 July 1994, p. 28.
53. Scottish Committee meeting, 22 December 1968, hand-written notes (WTC).
54. *Challenge*, April 1967.
55. Christine Sloan, 24 March 1994.
56. *Challenge*, no.17, January 1970.
57. Ibid.
58. Anna Sardesai, 27 August 1994, p. 30.
59. *Challenge* (new series) no. 5, April 1968.
60. Isa Porte, 16 February 1994 and 12 December 1996, p. 6.
61. *Cogito* (YCL theoretical journal) supplement no. 4, Frieda Park Collection, (henceforth FPC) 1968, p. 1.
62. These were the USSR, Poland, GDR, Hungary and Bulgaria.
63. Ouaine Bain, 27 June 1994 and 17 August 1994, p. 7.
64. *Cogito*, supplement no. 5, October 1968, pp. 1–9.
65. Ibid.

66. *Cogito*, no. 4, p. 5.
67. Ibid .
68. Cathy Brown, 29 May 1994, p. 9.
69. Marion Henery, 6 April 1994 and 17 November 1995, p. 18.
70. *Report of the Scottish Committee of the Communist Party Covering the Period July 1966 to July 1968*, p. 4.
71. Ibid.
72. Katy Campbell, 28 March 1994 and 11 February 1997, p. 19.
73. Pat Milligan, 15 March 1994 and 11 May 1994, p. 14.
74. CPGB Press and Publicity Department, 20 August 1969, *Information Notes on The International Communist Conference* (WTC).
75. *Cogito*, no.7, p. 1.
76. Ibid.
77. Twenty-eighth Congress Report, p. 47.
78. Ibid.
79. *Report of the Scottish Committee of the Communist Party July 1966 to July 1968*, p. 2.
80. *Scottish Marxist*, no. 13, Spring 1977, p. 35.
81. *Report made by J. Reid, Scottish Secretary, at the Scottish Congress 9–10th November, 1968* (WTA) p. 4.
82. Marion Robertson, 19 April 1994 and 20 October 1995, p. 43.
83. *People Before Profits: Communist Party General Election Manifesto* (London, 1970) p. 6.
84. *Comment*, vol. 7, no. 19, 10 May 1969.
85. *Facts about Women in Britain Today*, Central Education Department and Women's Department, Democratic Left Scotland Archive (henceforth DLSA) (CPGB) June 1970, p. 1.
86. Ibid.
87. Ibid., p. 2.
88. *Report of the Scottish Committee of the Communist Party covering the Period July 1968 to July 1970* (WGML), p. 3.
89. Ibid., p. 5.
90. A. Murray, *UCS: The Fight for the Right to Work* (London, 1971) p. 3.
91. Ibid., *Report of the Scottish Committee of the Communist Party*, p. 1.
92. Irene Swan, 23 September 1995 and 28 October 1995, p. 16.
93. Murray, UCS: The Fight for the Right to Work, p. 6.
94. Christine Sloan, 24 March 1994 and 26 April 1994, p. 7.
95. W. Thompson and F. Hart, *The UCS Work-In*, with a Foreword by J. Reid (London, 1972) p. 53.
96. Ella Egan, 17 October 1996 and 7 November 1996, p. 34.
97. May Annan, 22 April 1994, pp. 19–20.
98. Jean Mackay, 25 February 1994.
99 Jean Mackay, 25 February 1994.
100. Irene Swan, 23 September 1995 and 28 October 1995, p. 17.
101. *Evening Citizen*, 9 February 1973.
102. *Glasgow Herald*, 22 February 1973.
103. *Glasgow Herald*, 7 March 1973.

104. *Daily Record*, 7 March 1973.
105. May Annan, 22 April 1994, pp. 21–2.
106. Jack Ashton, 18 December 1996, p. 17.
107. *Scottish Congress Report 1972 Discussion Statement* (Glasgow 1972) (WGML) p. 3.
108. *Challenge*, no. 4, February 1972.
109. *Comanaiche*, monthly report of the Scottish YCL, no. 1, November 1972, a short-lived publication. The title is Gaelic for 'the Communicator' (FPC) p. 2.
110. Ibid., p. 3.
111. Ibid., p. 6.
112. *Comanaiche*, no. 2, December 1972 (FPC) p. 7.
113. Ibid., p. 4.
114. *Labour Monthly*, vol. 54, no. 5, May 1972, p. 211.
115. Irene Swan, 23 September 1995 and 28 October 1995, p. 65.
116. *Labour Monthly*, May 1972, p. 212.
117. *Labour Monthly*, vol. 55, no. 1, January 1973, p. 35.
118. Barbara Thorpe, 31 August 1995 and 14 September 1995, p. 20.
119. *Challenge*, no. 31, February 1976.
120. Ouaine Bain, 27 June 1994 and 17 August 1994, p. 44.
121. Noreen Thompson, 28 June 1994, p. 20.
122. *Scottish Marxist*, no. 5, November 1975, states that the Chilean Defence Committee was launched on 13 September 1975 in Glasgow, p. 3.
123. *Labour Monthly*, vol. 58, no. 1, January 1976, p. 21.
124. Irene Swan, 23 September 1995 and 28 October 1995, p. 63.
125. *Tolpuddle*, no. 1, 1971, p. 6.
126. Ibid., p. 7.
127. *Tolpuddle*, no. 2, 1971, p. 3.
128. Ibid., p. 4.
129. J. Franklin, *The Cuban Revolution and the United States: A Chronological History* (Melbourne, 1992) p. 101.
130. Irene Swan, 23 September 1995 and 28 October 1995, p. 25.
131. Isobel Service, 26 November 1998 and 26 January 1999.
132. Barbara Thorpe, 31 August 1995 and 14 September 1995, p. 6.
133. *Report of the Executive Committee of the Communist Party January 1969 to December 1969*, p. 12.
134. *Party Life*, vol. 1, no. 2, December 1962, p. 8.
135. *Communist Review*, November 1952. 'The further advance of the women's movement in Britain must depend upon the organized strength of the working people and their determination to move forward along the road to socialism. It cannot be a separate movement, nor have a different direction' (p. 348).
136. Maureen Sanders, 25 March 1994, p. 4.
137. Women's Liberation: CP Women's Conference, 3 October 1970 (MHC).
138. *Challenge*, 26 March 1971.
139. *'Women in Society' Draft of Report to Congress* (DLSA) 26 October 1971.
140. *The Communist Party: Thirty-second National Congress Amendments submitted by branches and District Committees November 1971* (London, 1971) (DLSA) pp. 41–52.

141. *Marxism and the Family*: Selected contributions from a discussion in *Marxism Today* (London, 1974) p. 9.
142. Ouaine Bain, 27 June 1994 and 17 August 1994, pp. 4–5.
143. Ouaine Bain, 27 June 1994 and 17 August 1994, p. 26.
144. *Report of the Scottish Committee of the Communist Party July 1968-July 1970* p. 3.
145. *Scottish Congress 1974: Resolutions from Branches* (WGML). On SWAC these were Pollokshields, Kelvin, Paisley, Glenrothes and East Kilbride branches pp. 2–3.
146. Ibid., Pollokshields resolution – 'that this is a result of viewing the development of women comrades as a small, separate problem facing the party, when in fact it is a major problem of obvious political and social importance' (p. 2).
147. *Report of the Scottish Committee of the Communist Party Covering the Period August 1974 to September 1976* (p. 6).
148. Ibid.
149. Ouaine Bain, 27 June 1994 and 17 August 1994, p. 27.
150. The NAC was founded in 1975. See Phillips, *Divided Loyalties*, p. 7.
151. Katherine Gallin, 13 April 1994.
152. Katy Campbell 23 March 1994 and 11 February 1997, p. 7
153. G. N. Serebrennikov, *The Position of Women in the USSR* (London, 1937) pp. 252–6 explains the high values on women working and as mothers and the reason for prohibiting abortion.
154. Ouaine Bain, 27 June 1994 and 17 August 1994, p. 26.
155. Anna Sardesai, 27 August 1994, p. 16.
156. R. Small, *Women: The Road to Equality and Socialism* (London, 1972) p. 17.
157. *Scottish Marxist*, no. 9, Summer 1975, pp. 23–6.
158. Anna Sardesai, 27 August 1994, p. 17.
159. *Scottish Marxist*, no. 10, Winter 1975, p. 42.
160. Frieda Park, 7 November 1994, p. 9.
161. *Morning Star*, 1 May 1975.
162. Mary Cowan, 16 March 1994, p. 23.
163. Ibid., p. 30.
164. *Scottish Congress 1968*, Composite Resolution no. 3, Young Communist League (WTC).
165. John Foster, 23 November 1994.
166. CPGB, *Weekly Letter*, no.41 – the figure for London was 5998, Lancashire 3997. However, it was reported the number of cards issued for the end of 1968 was only 4430 with an aim for 5330. EC minutes, 17 November 1968 (WTC).
167. B. Matthews, *Democracy and the Fight for Socialism* (London, 1976) p. 7.
168. Ibid., p. 8.
169. *Challenge*, no. 32, March/April 1976.
170. *Challenge*, no. 36, August/September 1976.
171. *Report of the Scottish Committeeof the Communist Party: Covering the Period August 1972–1974*, p. 3.
172. *Report of the Scottish Committee, 1974–76*, p. 3.

173. *Report of the Scottish Committee of the of the Communist Party, 1972–74*, p. 5.
174. *Report of the Scottish Committee of the Communist Party: Covering the Period August 1974–September 1976*, p. 3.
175. *Comment*, vol. 14, no. 4, 21 February 1976, pp. 55–7.
176. *Comment*, vol. 10, no. 3, 29 January 1972.
177. *Scottish Marxist*, no. 11, Spring 1976, p. 11.
178. Katy Campbell 28 March 1994 and 11 February 1997, p. 24.

Chaper 7

1. Pat Milligan, 15 March 1994 and 11 May 1994, p. 36.
2. *Report of the Work of the Scottish Committee October 1976–August 1978.* In this period between which the new draft of *The British Road to Socialism* was debated, party membership had fallen from 6580 in 1976 to 5660 in 1978, a fall of 920 (DLSA) p. 5.
3. John Foster 23 November 1994 p. 8.
4. *Glasgow: A Call to Action. Communist Party Policies* (Glasgow 1977) p. 2.
5. Ibid., p. 6.
6. Ibid., p. 10.
7. In 1975 there had been mass arrests including many party members protesting outside a meeting of the National Front in Kingston Halls, Glasgow.
8. J. Gollan, *Socialist Democracy: Some Problems* (London, 1976).
9. *The British Road to Socialism: Programme of the Communist Party* (London, 1978) p. 45.
10. *The British Road to Socialism: Communist Party Programme* (London 1968) p. 28. This edition puts less stress on the programme's anti-monopoly alliance of the 1950s.
11. *The British Road to Socialism* (London, 1978) pp. 46–7.
12. Ibid., pp. 25–6.
13. Pat Milligan, 15 March 1994 and 11 May 1994, p. 28.
14. Frieda Park, 11 November 1994, p. 38.
15. Noreen Thompson, 28 June 1994, p. 21.
16. *Report of the Work of the Scottish Committee October 1976–August 1978.* 'Almost every branch held meetings on *The British Road to Socialism.*'
17. John Foster, 23 November 1994, p. 10.
18. Douglas Chalmers, 5 December 1996.
19. Noreen Thompson, 28 June 1994, p. 7.
20. One of the interviewees joined a few years later for a brief period. Cathy Brown, 29 May 1994, p. 25.
21. Douglas Chalmers, 5 December 1996. 'I went down in 1977 and I was *absolutely shocked* at the divisions in the party' (p. 2).
22. *A Characteristic of the Differences in the Glasgow Communist Party: A Basis for Discussion.* Ian McKay, 25 July 1977, p. 1. Mckay obviously fears the end of the 'strong concept of party unity and adherence to majority decisions, which has always been a strong feature of the Party in Glasgow'.

23. Ibid., p. 2.
24. Ibid., p. 8.
25. Ibid., p. 11.
26. Ouaine Bain, 17 August 1994, p. 15.
27. Ibid., p. 19.
28. *Report of Commission on Inner-party Democracy: with Alternative Proposals: Comments of the Executive Committee* (London, 1979) There were 68 submissions (p. 6).
29. CP/CENT/ORG/9/2 Communist Party Archive (henceforth CPA). At the meeting of the Scottish committee of the CP on 10 August 1979 it was decided to circulate branches and ask for submissions.
30. Douglas Chalmers, 5 December 1996.
31. Ouaine Bain, 17 August 1994, p. 25.
32. Barbara Thorpe, 31 August 1995 and 14 September 1995, p. 22.
33. Marion Easedale, 23 March 1994 and 17 December 1996, p. 23.
34. CP/CENT/ORG/9/2 (CPA) Minutes of the SWAC, 1 September 1979, p. 1.
35. *Introduction to Feminism: A Communist Party Education Pack* (London, 1982) p. 59.
36. Ibid., p. 63.
37. Maureen Sanders, 25 March 1994, p. 10.
38. Ibid., pp. 19–20.
39. CP/CENT/ORG/9/2 (CPA) Minutes of the SWAC, 26 January 1980, p. 2.
40. Katy Campbell, 23 March 1994 and 11 February 1997, p. 8.
41. *Report of the Work of the Scottish Committee of the Communist Party November 1978–1979*, p. 5.
42. *A Discussion Document on Gay Rights*, Glasgow CP committee (Glasgow, 1978) p. 1.
43. Ibid., p. 7.
44. *Challenge*, March/April 1976.
45. *Guidelines For Men.* Drawn up by the National Women's Advisory, June 1986.
46. Ouaine Bain, 17 August 1994, p. 31.
47. CP/CENT/ORG/9/1 (CPA) CP Glasgow committee, 6 September 1977. Letter from M. Sanders and I. McKay to branches and leading women comrades.
48. Glasgow CP Women's Advisory, *A Discussion Document on Child Care* (Glasgow, 1978) p. 3.
49. Ibid., p. 5.
50. Ibid., p. 8.
51. Ibid., pp. 8–9.
52. CP/CENT/ORG/9/2 (CPA), document compiled by Noreen Thompson and Caroline Green. Minutes of Glasgow Women's Advisory Committee, 27 September 1978.
53. *Women's Right to Work*, day conference, 8 November 1980, leaflet/form (DLSA).
54. CP/CENT/ORG/9/2 (CPA) Minutes of Glasgow Women's Advisory Committee, 27 September 1978, mentions a 'Reclaim the Night' march a few days after a week highlighting rape.
55. Anna Sardesai, 28 April 1994, p. 33.

56. Frieda Park, 11 November 1994, p. 18.
57. *Report of the Work of the Scottish Committee of the Communist Party*, November 1980–October 1982 (DLSA) p. 5.
58. At the 37th Congress in November 1981 the composite resolution on Women (Document no. 59) pointed to the problems women faced generally because of Tory policies and also the need to address the gender imbalance in the party.
59. *What Future for Glasgow?* Glasgow committee CP (Glasgow, 1980) p. 2.
60. The CP in Scotland distributed 50,000 leaflets on the war, the most of any leaflet. *Report of the Work of the Scottish Committee*, November 1980–October 1982, p. 2.
61. Ouaine Bain, 17 August 1994, p. 38.
62. D. Priscott, *The Roots of Thatcherism* (London, 1986) p. 4.
63. Ibid., p. 5.
64. *Report of the Work of the Scottish Committee of the Communist Party November 1978–1979*, p. 2.
65. *Introduction to Feminism*, p. 27.
66. Ibid., p. 28.
67. Pat Milligan, 15 March 1994 and 11 May 1994, p. 33.
68. Marion Easedale, 23 March 1994 and 17 December 1996, pp. 23–4.
69. Susan Galloway, 11 October 1995 and 1 November 1995, p. 21.
70. Irene Swan, 28 October 1995, p. 48.
71. Ibid., p. 26.
72. Susan Galloway, 11 October 1995 and 1 November 1995, pp. 19–20.
73. Marion Easedale, 23 March 1994 and 17 December 1996, p. 25.
74. Douglas Chalmers, 5 December 1996. 'Oh definitely, I mean I was the *Morning Star* organizer in Dundee when I was in the YCL so I was really involved in the *Morning Star*. I grafted at it and my brother was the assistant editor so I was involved right up [to] the nines' (p. 14).
75. Jessie Clark, 4 April 1994, p. 23.
76. *Straight Left*, March 1979, first issue. This group had previously organized around the theoretical magazine *Communist*.
77. Isa Porte, 23 March 1994 and 12 December 1996, p. 22.
78. This was the son of Mary Park and brother of Frieda Park. The person responsible was a party member who was suspended for three months and charged by the police.
79. Cathy Brown, 29 May 1994, p. 26.
80. Douglas Chalmers, 5 December 1996.
81. Katy Campbell, 23 March 1994 and 11 February 1997, p. 27.
82. Christine Sloan, 24 March 1994 and 26 April 1994, p. 34.
83. Susan Galloway, 11 October 1995 and 1 November 1995. 'In Partick branch the branch members were expelled from the party around that time because they were continuing to support the *Star*' (p. 17).
84. The Communist Campaign Group formed and held meetings in Scotland, it attracted those expelled, those who had left and those not recarded. The strategy was to wait and see if there was any change in the CPGB before

setting up a new party. *Morning Star*, 17 February 1986; John Foster, 23 November 1994, p. 18.

85. Douglas Chalmers, 5 December 1996, p. 23.
86. John Foster, 23 November 1994. 'And you can see the intense embarrassment; these people [who] were supposed to be liberals were going through this bloody charade of total administrative control and terrifying people with authoritarian methods and these were the people who were claiming that they were the liberals and writing up in *Marxism Today* they were leading Britain towards the new liberal democratic socialism or some kind of nonsense and they were the most bureaucratic authoritarians' (p. 18).
87. *Report of the Work of the Scottish Committee 1984–6*, there were now 90 branches in 14 areas: 72 local branches and 18 workplace branches (including two student branches) p. 5.
88. Barbara Thorpe, 31 August 1995 and 14 September 1995, p. 24.
89. *Report of the Work of the Scottish Committee 1984–6*, p. 4.
90. Kathryn Chalmers, 22 March 1994.
91. Susan Galloway, 11 October 1995 and 1 November 1995, p. 12.
92. *Report of the Work of the Scottish Committee of the Communist Party 1982–4* (DLSA) p. 3.
93. Ibid., p. 2.
94. S. Corrigan, C. Cunningham and M. Thorburn, 'Fife Women Stand Firm', in V. Seddon (ed.) *The Cutting Edge: Women and the Pit Strike* (London, 1986) p. 32.
95. Ella Egan, 17 October 1996 and 7 November 1996, pp. 15–16.
96. Ella Egan, 17 October 1996 and 7 November 1996, p. 17.
97. B. Campbell, 'Proletarian Patriarchs and the Real Radicals', in V. Seddon (ed.) *The Cutting Edge*, pp. 249–82.
98. *Focus*, 28 March 1985, letter from Sophia Young of Glasgow.
99. Cathy Brown, 29 May 1994, p. 29.
100. Corrigan et al., 'Fife Women Stand Firm', p. 40.
101. Ella Egan, 17 October 1996 and 7 November 1996, p. 18.
102. CP/CENT/WOM/5/2, National Women's Advisory, 23 September 1985, analysis of meeting of women against pit closures held on 20 September 1985, p. 2.
103. Ibid.
104. Ibid .
105. Ella Egan, 17 October 1996 and 7 November 1996, p. 18.
106. Irene Swan, 28 October 1995, p. 45.
107. Anna Sardesai, 28 April 1994, p. 31.
108. Pat Milligan, 15 March 1994 and 11 May 1994, p. 18.
109. Ibid., pp. 16–17.
110. Pat Milligan, 15 March 1994 and 11 May 1994. 'Yes, posted it to Gerry and Gerry phoned and said "we can't have that" and I said "well why not? That's how it was" and Gerry said "Well, the comrade from the Romanian embassy – it's a courtesy, we normally send something to him." I don't know exactly what I said but the essence of it was I was saying "well courtesies are all very well but

that is actually how I found that Congress and I was the only member of our executive there but every word that is down there is absolutely true" and Gerry said "oh well, it's about diplomacy and would you mind very much" because Gerry's a very, very nice lad – "toning it down a wee bit?". I can't remember, I think I did another two drafts but as far as I'm aware that never saw the light of day that report of mine' (p. 18).

111. Christine Sloan, 24 March 1994 and 26 April 1994, p. 28.
112. Marion Easedale, 23 March 1994 and 17 December 1996, pp. 19–20.
113. Christine Sloan, 24 March 1994 and 26 April 1994, p. 27.
114. Mary Park, 13 December 1994 and 13 November 1996.
115. Jean Mackay, 25 February 1994, p. 13.
116. Frieda Park, 11 November 1994, p. 31.
117. Marion Easedale, 23 March 1994 and 17 December 1996, pp. 26–7.
118. *A Manifesto for the New Times* (London, 1989) p. 5.
119. Jenny Richardson, 31 March 1994, p. 19.
120. Ibid., pp. 19–20.
121. Douglas Chalmers, 5 December 1996. 'And I was absolutely flabbergasted. It was to discuss the new constitution and we had people there some of my colleagues hadn't seen for quite a few years, had sort of dropped out although veterans of the movement you might say, suddenly appeared back at the meeting which I thought "Oh that's good" because I do welcome their point of view and it's nice to have that generational spread. And then the obvious fundamental ideological differences that came out shocked me' (p. 32).
122. Frieda Park, 11 November 1994, p. 54.
123. Marion Easedale, 23 March 1994 and 17 December 1996, p. 33.

Chapter 8

1. Barbara Thorpe, 31 August 1995 and 14 September 1995, p. 34.
2. Katy Campbell, 25 March 1994 and 11 February 1997, p. 29.
3. Barbara Thorpe, 31 August 1995 and 14 September 1995, p. 31.
4. Katherine Gallin, 13 April 1994, p. 20.
5. Susan Galloway, 11 October 1995 and 1 November 1995, p. 29.
6. Maureen Sanders, 25 March 1994, pp. 18–19.
7. *Focus*, 18 July 1985.
8. Marion Easedale, 23 March 1994 and 17 November 1996, p. 22.
9. J. Foster and C. Woolfson, *The Politics of the UCS Work In* (London, 1986).
10. Anna Sardesai, 27 August 1994, p. 39.
11. Irene Swan, 23 September 1995 and 28 October 1995, p. 49.
12. CP/CENT/PERS/3/06, Submission by Margaret Hunter, 21 February 1955, p. 1.
13. Jessie Clark, 4 April 1994, p. 6.

Bibliography

Archives

Interviews by author for thesis – transcript copies of some of the following interviews to be stored at the Scottish Oral History Centre at University of Strathclyde, Glasgow SOHCA/O1O:

Annan, May
Ashton, Jack
Bain, Ouaine
Brown, Cathy
Buchan, Janey
Campbell, Katy
Chalmers, Douglas
Chalmers, Kathryn
Clark, Jessie
Cowan, Mary
Docherty, Mary
Easedale, Marion
Egan, Ella
Findlay, Edith
Foster, John
Gallin, Katherine
Galloway, Susan
Henery, Marion
Horne, Bob
Hunter, Jimmy
Kerrigan, Rose
McCrindle, Jean
Mackay, Jean
Milligan, Pat
Milne, Alice
O'Hare, Effie
Park, Frieda
Park, Mary
Porte, Isa
Richardson, Jenny
Robertson, Marion
Sanders, Maureen
Sardesai, Anna
Service, Isobel
Service, Jim
Skinner, M.
Sloan, Christine
Swan, Irene
Thompson, Noreen
Thompson, Willie
Thorpe, Barbara

Audio

Duffy Meets – Radio Clyde interview Agnes McLean with Sheila Duffy first broadcast 4 April 1989

Old Reds – BBC Radio Four Programme on the CPGB first broadcast 10 August 1995

Clydebank Public Library- Reading Room

Hart, F., unpublished autobiography

Hyslop, J. Interview, 9 March 1983, Tape 0060–1, photographs as ARP warden

Communist Party Archive: National Museum of Labour History, Manchester

CP/CENT/PERS/3/03/ – Written Submission by Margaret Hunter

CP/CENT/ORG/9/2 – Scottish Committee Minutes

CP/CENT/ORG/9/2 – Minutes of the Scottish Women's Advisory Committee

CP/CENT/ORG/9/1 – Glasgow Committee Minutes

CP/CENT/WOM/5/2 – National Women's Advisory Committee

Communist Party of Great Britain (CPGB)

36 Million Communists Say…: Statements and Appeal of the World's Communist Parties, Moscow, November 1960 (London, 1960)
A Characteristic of the Differences in the Glasgow Communist Party: A Basis for Discussion (Glasgow, 1977)
A Discussion Document on Gay Rights, Glasgow CP committee (Glasgow, 1978)
A Manifesto for the New Times (London, 1989)
A Parliament for Scotland: The Communist View (Glasgow, n.d.)
Communist Policy to meet the Crisis; Report of the 21st National Congress of the CPGB, opening remarks by Arthur Horner (London, 1949)
Facts about Women in Britain Today, Central Education Department and Women's Department, Democratic Left Scotland Archive (henceforth DLSA) (CPGB) June 1970
Festival of Youth: Budapest 1949 (London, 1949)
Glasgow Committee CP, *What Future for Glasgow?* (Glasgow, 1980)
Glasgow CP Women's Advisory, *A Discussion Document on Child Care* (Glasgow, 1978)
Glasgow: A Call to Action. Communist Party Policies (Glasgow, 1977)
How to Organise Public Meetings (London, 1942)
How to Sell Literature (London, 1942)
Introduction to Feminism: A Communist Party Education Pack (London, 1982)
Marxism and the Family. Selected contributions from a discussion in *Marxism Today* (London, 1974)
Marxist Study Themes, no. 9, *The British State* (London, 1954)
National Women's Advisory, *Guidelines For Men* (London, 1986)
People Before Profits: Communist Party General Election Manifesto (London, 1970)
Report of Commission on Inner-Party Democracy: With Alternative Proposals Comments of the Executive Committee (London, 1979)
Report to the Executive Committee on Inner Party Democracy, December 1956 (London, 1956)
Resolutions of the World Peace Council (Paris, 1951) (BHC)
Scotland and its Future: Short Term Plan for Scotland Adopted by the Scottish Congress of the Communist Party (Glasgow, 1947)
Scottish Committee, *Whither Scotland?* (Glasgow, 1945)
Scottish Congress Reports
Scottish District Reports
The British Road to Socialism (London, 1951)
The British Road to Socialism: Communist Party Programme (London, 1968)
The British Road to Socialism: Programme of the Communist Party (London, 1978)
The Counter-Revolutionary Conspiracy of Imre Nagy and his Accomplices (Budapest, 1958) pamphlet with a photo and document section at the back
The Innsbruck Story (London, British Youth Festival Preparatory Committee, 1951) (BHC)
The Journey to Berlin: Report of a Commission of Inquiry into certain events at Brussels, the Channel Ports, Innsbruck and Saalfelden in August 1951, National Council for Civil Liberties (London, 1952)

The Socialist Road for Britain (London, 1949)
World News and Views
Young Communist International, *Between the Fifth and Sixth Congresses: 1924–1928* (London, 1928)

Democratic Left, Scotland. Collection held by Dr Willie Thompson (WTC)

Scottish Bulletin
Scottish Committee meetings – handwritten notes of Dr W. Thompson
Weekly Letter

Glasgow City Archive (formerly Strathclyde Regional Archive)

RU4/5/102 – The Executive Committee of Rutherglen Socialist Sunday School
TD591, Tom Anderson Collection
TD1399/2, Essays and lectures given by Alfred Russell

Mitchell Library (Glasgow) – Glasgow Room (MLGR)

College Socialist Sunday School Management Committee and Delegate Committee meeting minutes
Daily Record
Evening Citizen
Govanhill School Roll Book 1940–1955
Guardian
Hamish Fraser, W. *Glasgow Trades Council*, 331 880941445:FRA
John MacLean by Comrade Tom [Tom Anderson] G3335.330924

Newspapers and journals

Challenge
Changes
Cogito
Comainche
Comment
Communist
Communist Campaign Review
Co-operator
Daily Worker/Morning Star
Edinburgh Evening Times
Focus
Forward
Glasgow Herald
IRIS
Labour Monthly
Link
Marxism Today
Oral History Journal
Our History Journal
Party Life
Reasoner, The
Scottish Marxist
Seven Days
Seven Days
Straight Left
Tolpuddle
Woman Today
Women in Action
World Marxist Review
World News and Views
Young Socialist

Personal collections – letters, minutes of meetings, magazines, recordings, leaflets, photographs

Ouaine Bain
Marion Easedale
Ella Egan
Marion Henery
Bob Horne
Effie O'Hare
Eric Park
Frieda Park
Mary Park
Billy Quin
Marion Robertson
Christine Sloan

Willie Thompson Barbara Thorpe

William Gallacher Memorial Library (WGML)

'But they *shall* be free', Communist Party memorandum on Scotland's future. Scottish Committee of the CP to the Royal Commission, 1 January 1953
Crawfurd, H. 'Autobiography' (unpublished)
Kallai G. *The Counter-Revolution in Hungary in the Light of Marxism–Leninism* (Budapest, 1956)
Paul Robeson Souvenir Programme
Scottish Committee Organisation Report for April 1949

Secondary Works: Books, Articles, Chapter in Books, Theses

Ainley, D., *Co-ops: The Way Ahead* (London, 1962)
Aldcroft, Derek, *The European Economy 1918–1980* (London, 1978)
Anderson, P., 'Communist Party history', in Raphael Samuel (ed.) *People's History and Socialist Theory* (London, 1981)
Andrews, G., N. Fishman and K. Morgan, *Opening the Books: Essays on the Social and Cultural History of the British Communist Party* (London, 1995)
Attfield, J. and S. Williams, *1939: The Communist Party of Great Britain and the War. Proceedings of a Conference Held on 21 April 1979. Organised by the Communist Party History Group* (London, 1984)
Bain, P. 'Is you is or is you ain't my baby? Women's pay and the Clydeside strikes of 1943', *Scottish Labour History Society Journal*, no. 30, pp. 35–60
Bornstein, S. and A. Richardson, *Two Steps Back: Communists and the Wider Labour Movement 1935–1945: A Study in Relations Between Vanguard and Class* (London, 1982)
Branson, N. *History of the Communist Party of Great Britain 1927–1941* (London, 1985).
History of the Communist Party of Great Britain 1941–1951 (London, 1997)
Braybon, G. and P. Summerfield, *Out of the Cage: Women's Experiences in Two World Wars* (London, 1987)
Brown, A. (ed.) *The Soviet Union: A Biographical Dictionary* (London, 1990)
Bruley, S. *Leninism, Stalinism and the Women's Movement in Britain 1920–1939* (New York, 1986)
Bruley, S. 'Women and communism: a case study of the Lancashire weavers in the depression', in G. Andrews, N. Fishman and K. Morgan (eds) *Opening the Books: Essays on the Social and Cultural History of the Communist Party* (London, 1995) pp. 64–82
Burns, E. *An Introduction to Marxism* (London, 1937)
'Women's Fight for Liberation', *Communist Review*, November 1952
A Call to Co-operators (London, 1954)
Campbell, B. 'Proletarian patriarchs and the real radicals', in V. Seddon (ed.) *The Cutting Edge*, pp. 249–82
Campbell, J. R. *Forty Fighting Years: The Communist Record* (London, 1960)

Cohen, P. *Children of the Revolution: Communist Childhood in Cold War Britain* (London, 1997)

Cornforth, M., *Dialectical Materialism: An Introduction* (3 vols, London, 1952, new edition 1977) vol. 1, *Materialism and the Dialectical Method*, vol. 2, *Historical Materialism*, vol. 3, *Theory of Knowledge*

Corr, H. 'Helen Crawfurd (1877–1954)', in W. Knox (ed.) *Scottish Labour Leaders 1918–1939* (Edinburgh, 1984) pp. 81–6.

Corrigan, S., C. Cunningham and M. Thorburn, 'Fife women stand firm', in V. Seddon (ed.) *The Cutting Edge: Women and the Pit Strike* (London, 1986) pp. 30–49

Coutts, C. *Eye Witness in Hungary* (London, 1957)

Cowe, B. 'The making of a Clydeside communist', *Marxism Today*, April 1973

Cowe, W. *Scotland and the War* (Glasgow, 1940)

Scotland for the Offensive: A Call for a Fighting Lead (Glasgow, 1941)

Croucher, R. *We Refuse to Starve in Silence (1920–46): A History of the National Unemployed Workers Movement* (London, 1987)

Damer, S. *Rent Strike! The Clydebank Rent Struggles of the 1920s* (Clydebank, 1982)

Darke, B. *The Communist Technique in Britain* (London, 1952)

de Beauvior, S. *The Second Sex* (London, 1953)

Deutscher, I. *Stalin* (Oxford, 1949) 1966 edn

Dewar, H. *Communist Politics in Britain: The CPGB from its Origins to the Second World War* (London, 1976)

Docherty, M. *A Miner's Lass* (Preston, 1992)

(ed.) *Auld Bob Selkirk: A Man in a Million* (Cowdenbeath, 1996)

Dutt, R. Palme, *World Politics 1918–1936* (London, 1936)

Eaton, J. and C. Gill, *The Trade Union Directory* (London, 1983)

Evans, The Revd S. G. *The Trial of Cardinal Mindzenty: An Eye Witness Account* (Birmingham, 1949)

Exell, A. 'Morris Motors in the 1930s', Part 1, *History Workshop Journal*, issue 6, Autumn 1978, pp. 52–78, Part 2, *History Workshop Journal*, issue 7, pp. 45–65, Part 3, 'Morris Motors in the 1940s', *History Workshop Journal*, issue 9, pp. 90–114

Farman, C. *The General Strike* (London, 1974)

Ferguson, A. *Scotland* (Glasgow, 1938)

Fishman, N. *The British Communist Party and the Trade Unions 1933–45* (London, 1994)

Foster, J. and C. Woolfson, *The Politics of the UCS Work In* (London, 1986)

Franklin, J. *The Cuban Revolution and the United States: A Chronological History* (Melbourne, 1992)

Frieden, B. *The Feminist Mystique* (New York, 1963)

Gabbidon, C. M. 'Party life: an examination of the branch life of the CPGB between the wars', D.Phil. thesis, Sussex University, 1991

Gallacher, R. 'The Vale of Leven 1914–1975: changes in working class organisation and action', in T. Dickson (ed.) *Capital and Class in Scotland* (Edinburgh, 1982) pp. 186–211

Gallacher, W. *The Case for Communism* (London, 1948)

Relaxation: A Collection of Satirical Political Verse with a Foreword by R. Palme Dutt (London, Daily Worker Bazaar Committee, 1950)
The Tyrants' Might is Passing (London, 1954)
Revolt on the Clyde (London, 1977)

Gollan, J. *Scotland Needs 150,000 Jobs: A Memorandum on Scotland's Reconversion Problem* (Glasgow, 1946)
Scottish Prospect (Glasgow, 1948)
People's Democracy for Britain (London, 1952)
End the Bans (London, 1956)
Britain's Future (London, 1963)
Socialist Democracy: Some Problems (London, 1976)

Graves, P. *Labour Women: Women in British Working Class Politics 1918–1939* (Cambridge, 1994)

Hannington, W. *Unemployed Struggles 1919–1936* (London, 1936, reprint 1977)

Henderson, M. *Dear Allies: A Story of Women in Monklands and Besieged Leningrad* (Monklands District Libraries, 1988)

Hill, M. *Red Roses for Isabel: Highlights of the Life of Isabel Brown* (Preston, 1982)

Hinton, J. 'Coventry communism: a study of factory politics in the Second World War', *History Workshop Journal*, Autumn (1980)

Hinton, J. and R. Hyman, *Trade Unions and Revolution: The Industrial Politics of the Early British Communist Party* (London, 1975)

Howe, S. 'Anti-colonialism in British politics: the left and the end of empire 1939–1964', D.Phil. thesis, Oxford University, 1984

Hudson, K. '1956 and the Communist Party', *The Communist Party and 1956*, Our History Pamphlet no. 88 (London, 1993) pp. 1–23

Hutt, A. *The Post War History of the British Working Class* (London, 1937)

Hyde, D. *I Believed: The Autobiography of a Former British Communist* (London, 1952)

Islwyn Nicholas, T. *Tom Anderson: Apostle of Revolution* (Glasgow, 1930)

Jackson, T. A. *Ireland Her Own* (London, 1946)

Johnson, D. 'A Party Women's Delegation to the USSR', *Party Life*, vol. 1, no. 7, October–November 1963, pp. 4–6

Johnstone, M. 'The CPGB, the Comintern and the war 1939–41: filling in the blank spots', in K. Morgan (ed.) *Science and Society*, vol. 61, no. 1

Kendall, W. *The Revolutionary Movement in Britain 1900–1921* (London, 1969)

Khrushchev, N. S. *Report of the Central Committee: 20th Congress of the Communist Party of the Soviet Union February 1956* (London, 1956)

Kibblewhite, L. and A. Rigby, *Fascism in Aberdeen: Street Politics in the 1930s* (Aberdeen, 1978)

King, F. and G. Matthews (eds) *About Turn: The British Communist Party and the Second World War*. The verbatim record of the Central Committee meetings of 25 September and 2–3 October 1939 (London, 1990)

Klugmann, J. *History of the Communist Party of Great Britain*, vol. 1, *Formation and Early Years 1919–1924* (London, 1968)

Knox, W. 'Introduction: a social and political analysis of Scottish labour leadership between the two world wars', in W. Knox (ed.) *Scottish Labour Leaders 1918–1939* (Edinburgh, 1984)

Knox, W. *Scottish Labour Leaders 1918–1939* (Edinburgh, 1984)

Knox, W. 'The political and workplace culture of the Scottish working-class', in H. Corr and L. Jamieson (eds) *Politics of Everyday Life: Continuity and Change in Work and the Family* (Basingstoke, 1990) pp. 162–85

Kollantai, A. 'Working Women's Day and the Third International', in J. Riddell (ed.) *The Communist International in Lenin's Time: Founding of the Communist International: Proceedings and Documents of the First Congress: March 1919* (New York, 1987)

Lauchlan, W. *Scotland and the Crisis* (Glasgow, 1947)

A Future for Scotland and her People, Report to the Scottish Congress of the Communist Party (Glasgow, 1953)

Lenin, V. I. *What is to be Done?* (Moscow, 1902, reprint 1947)

McCrindle, J. and S. Rowbotham (eds) *Dutiful Daughters: Women Talk about their Lives* (London, 1977)

MacDougall, I. *Mungo Mackay and the Green Table* (Edinburgh, 1995)

Voices from the Spanish Civil War (Edinburgh, 1986)

Voices from the Hunger Marches (2 vols, Edinburgh, 1990 and 1991)

Hard Work Ye Ken: Midlothian Women Farmworkers (Edinburgh, 1993)

Hoggie's Angels: Tattie Howkers' Remember (Edinburgh, 1995)

Macintyre, S. *A Proletarian Science: Marxism in Britain 1917–1933* (Cambridge, 1980)

Little Moscows: Communism and Working Class Militancy in Inter-War Britain (London, 1980)

McKibbin, R. *The Ideologies of Class and Social Relations in Britain 1880–1950* (Oxford, 1990)

McKinlay, A. 'Doubtful wisdom and uncertain promise: strategy, ideology and organisation, 1918–1922', in Alan McKinlay and R. J. Morris (eds) *The ILP on Clydeside 1893–1932: From Foundation to Disintegration* (Manchester, 1991) pp. 123–53

McLean, J. 'The 1926 general strike in Lanarkshire', *Our History Journal*, Spring 1976

MacLeod, A. *The Death of Uncle Joe* (Suffolk, 1997)

McShane, H. with J. Smith, *No Mean Fighter* (London, 1978)

Matthews, B. *Democracy and the Fight for Socialism* (London, 1976)

Morgan, K. *Against Fascism and War: Ruptures and Continuities in British Communist Politics 1935–41* (Manchester, 1989)

Harry Pollitt: Lives of the Left (Manchester, 1993)

(ed.) 'Communism in Britain and the British Empire', *Science and Society*, vol. 61, no. 1, special issue, Spring 1997

Morris, R. J. 'The ILP, 1893–1932: introduction', in Alan McKinlay and R. J. Morris (eds) *The ILP on Clydeside: From Foundation to Disintegration* (Manchester, 1991) pp.1–19

Morton, A. L. *A People's History of England* (London, 1938)

Murray, A. *UCS: The Fight for the Right to Work* (London, 1971)

Nassibian, A. 'Attitudes on Clydeside towards the Russian Revolution 1917–1924', M.Litt., University of Strathclyde, 1977

Newton, K. *The Sociology of British Communism* (London, 1969)

Nove, A. *An Economic History of the USSR* (London, 1969)

Nujam, S. 'A radical past: the legacy of the Fife miners', Ph.D. thesis, Edinburgh University, 1988

Nutina, F. *The Soviet Law on Marriage* (New York, 1933)

Parsons, S. '1956: what happened inside the CPGB', *The Communist Party and 1956*, Our History Pamphlet no. 88 (London, 1993) pp. 24–38

Pelling, H. *The British Communist Party: A Historical Profile* (London, 1958)

Phillips, A. *Divided Loyalties: Dilemmas of Sex and Class* (London, 1987)

Piratin, P. *Our Flag Stays Red* (London, 1948, new edn 1978)

Pollitt, H. *Defeat of Trotskyism* (London, 1937)

Serving My Time: An Apprenticeship to Politics (London, 1940)

Britain Arise (London, 1952)

In Memory of Joseph Stalin and Klement Gottwald (London, 1953)

Price, R. *Labour in British Society* (London, 1986)

Pries, A., 'Khrushshev's secret speech: confusion of tongues', *Journal of Contemporary Society*, vol. 6, no. 1, March 1990

Priscott, D. *The Roots of Thatcherism* (London, 1986)

Reid, F. 'Socialist Sunday Schools in Britain 1892–1939', *International Review of Social History*, vol. 11, 1966, pp. 23–4

Renton, D. 'Why I left the Communist Party', *The Newsletter*, vol. 1, no. 1, 10 May 1957

Reynolds, S. *Britannica's Typesetters: Women Compositors in Edinburgh* (Edinburgh, 1989)

Salt, C. and Wilson, M. *We are of One Blood: Memories of the First 60 Years of the Woodcraft Folk 1925–1985* (London, 1985)

Savage, M. *The Dynamics of Working Class Politics: The Labour Movement in Preston, 1880–1940* (Cambridge, 1987)

'Urban politics and the rise of the Labour Party, 1919–39', in L. Jamieson and H. Corr (eds) *State, Private Life and Political Change* (Basingstoke, 1990) p. 209

Serebrennikov, G. N. *The Position of Women in the USSR* (London, 1937)

Service, J. 'The party and YCL as a cultural force', *Britain's Cultural Heritage*, (London, 1952) pp. 57–8

Simon, B. 'The British universities', *Britain's Cultural Heritage* (London, 1952) pp. 33–8

Sloan, P. *Russia Without Illusions*, with a Preface by Beatrice Webb (Manchester, 1938)

Small, R. *Women: The Road to Equality and Socialism* (London, 1972)

Smith, J. 'Labour tradition in Glasgow and Liverpool', *History Workshop Journal*, 17 (Spring 1984) pp. 32–56

Srebrnik, H. F. *London Jews and British Communism 1935–45* (Ilford, 1995)

Stanley, F. *The Communist Party and Young People* (London, 1961)

Stewart, R. *Breaking the Fetters* (London, 1967)

Thompson, W. 'The New Left in Scotland', in I. MacDougall (ed.) *Essays in Scottish Labour History: A Tribute to W. H. Marwick* (Edinburgh, 1978)

Thompson, W. and F. Hart, *The UCS Work-In*, with a foreword by Jimmy Reid (London, 1972)

Thompson, W. *The Good Old Cause: British Communism 1920–1991* (London, 1992)

Thornton, C and W. Thompson, 'Scottish communists, 1956–7', *Science and Society*, vol. 61, no.1, Spring 1997, pp. 68–93

Wainwright, B. *Close all US Bases* (London, 1958)

Wigoder, G. (ed.) *Dictionary of Jewish Biography* (Tel Aviv, 1990)

Wood, I. 'John Wheatley 1869–1930', in W. Knox (ed.) *Scottish Labour Leaders 1918–1939* (Edinburgh, 1984)

Woodhouse, M. and B. Pearce, *Essays in the History of Communism in Britain* (London, 1975)

Worley, M. 'The British Communist Party 1920–45', *The Historian*, no. 55, Autumn 1997, pp. 26–8

Index